Professional & Administrative Career Exam

The Arco Self-Tutor for High Test Scores

PROFESSIONAL AND ADMINISTRATIVE CAREER EXAMINATION

BY
David R. Turner, M.S. in Ed.

arco 219 Park Avenue South
New York, N.Y. 10003

Second Edition (B-3689)
Second Printing, 1978

COPYRIGHT © 1978 by
Arco Publishing Company, Inc.

All rights reserved. No part of this
book may be reproduced in any form,
by any means, without permission in
writing from the publisher.

Published by ARCO PUBLISHING COMPANY, INC.
219 Park Avenue South, New York, N.Y. 10003

Library of Congress Catalog Card Number 75-16559
ISBN 0-668-03812-8 (Library Edition)
ISBN 0-668-03653-2 (Paper Edition)

Printed in the United States of America

CONTENTS

HOW TO USE THIS INDEX
Slightly bend the right-hand edge of the book. This will expose the corresponding Parts which match the index, below.

PART

WHAT THIS BOOK WILL DO FOR YOU 7

How this book was prepared; what went into these pages to make them worth your while. How to use them profitably for yourself in preparing for your test. The essentials of successful study.

PART ONE
APPLYING AND STUDYING FOR YOUR EXAM

OFFICIAL ANNOUNCEMENT 11

Some important preparatory information to help you put your best foot forward.

APPLYING FOR FEDERAL JOBS 15

Keeping posted. Federal job information centers. Where to apply.

ALL ABOUT THE EXAM 29

Facts that foreshadow the test. The kinds of questions you may be asked. How you will be scored.

TECHNIQUES OF STUDY AND TEST-TAKING 45

Although there's no substitute for "knowing your stuff," these nineteen tips could raise your score substantially. The chapter tells you how to use this book to greatest advantage, and how to conduct yourself cleverly on the exam itself.

PART TWO
A SAMPLE EXAM FOR PRACTICE

FIRST SAMPLE EXAMINATION 51

The first big step in your journey. Quite similar to the Exam you'll actually take, this one is a professionally constructed yardstick for measuring your beginning knowledge and ability. Score yourself objectively and plan further study to concentrate on eliminating your weaknesses.

UNDERSTANDING AND USING WRITTEN LANGUAGE 55
    Read and Deduce
    Synonyms

DERIVING GENERAL PRINCIPLES FROM PARTICULAR DATA 60
    Letter Series
    Abstract Reasoning

DERIVING CONCLUSIONS FROM GIVEN DATA 64
    Read and Infer
    Logical Sequence

QUANTITATIVE ABILITY 74

CHART AND TABLE INTERPRETATION 80

DERIVING CONCLUSIONS FROM INCOMPLETE
DATA PLUS GENERAL KNOWLEDGE 84

...continued on next page

CONTENTS continued

PART 1 2 3 4

PART THREE
PRACTICE WITH SUBJECTS ON WHICH YOU ARE LIKELY TO BE TESTED

TOP SCORES ON READING TESTS 97
How to increase your reading speed. Cues and clues to improve your reading comprehension. Analysis of reading test questions. Success steps to better scores.

TOP SCORES ON VOCABULARY TESTS 119
Six valuable steps in building your word power. Also, two charts of prefixes and suffixes, with sample words, show how a knowledge of etymology can help increase your vocabulary. **Synonyms Practice.**

ABSTRACT REASONING 131
Symbols test your ability to see relationships.

LETTER SERIES 140
This challenging type of question tests your ability to see the relationship between elements of a series. Step-by-step analysis of sample questions teaches how to determine the rule that binds the elements together. Test-type quizzes give practice in selecting the answer that follows the rule.

NUMERICAL RELATIONS 149
A chance to tackle those basic problems from which most examination questions are derived. Includes Profit and Loss, Addition of Fractions, Interest, Assessment, Cubic Volume, Literal Problems, Rate, Time and Distance, Time and Work, Proportions, and Mixture Problems. Simple, straightforward, step-by-step explanations. Sample questions with explanatory answers.

PART FOUR
FINAL EXAM AND ADVICE

FINAL SAMPLE EXAMINATION 181
An examination specially constructed to give you a comprehensive and authoritative view of the actual test. An opportunity to employ all you've learned. A situation that closely simulates the real thing.

UNDERSTANDING AND USING WRITTEN LANGUAGE 185
DERIVING GENERAL PRINCIPLES FROM PARTICULAR DATA 190
DERIVING CONCLUSIONS FROM GIVEN DATA 194
QUANTITATIVE ABILITY 203
CHART AND TABLE INTERPRETATION 207
DERIVING CONCLUSIONS FROM INCOMPLETE
DATA PLUS GENERAL KNOWLEDGE 213

ARCO BOOKS 223
You'll want to consult this list of Arco publications to order other invaluable career books related to your field. The list also suggests job opportunities and promotions that you might want to go after with an Arco self-tutor.

Professional & Administrative Career Exam

WHAT THIS BOOK WILL DO FOR YOU

Even though this course of study has been carefully planned to help you get in shape by the day your test comes, you'll have to do a little planning on your own to be successful. And you'll also need a few pointers proven effective for many other good students.

If you want to take an exam but are reluctant for fear that you've been away from school too long, or for fear that your skills are a bit rusty, don't sell yourself short. You'll get the greatest help from this book by understanding how it has been organized, and by using it accordingly. Study carefully this concise, readable treatment of what is required by your exam, and your way will be clear. You will progress directly to your goal. You will not be led off into blind alleys and useless digressions.

We believe that you can improve your exam scores measureably with the help of this "self-tutor." It's a carefully thought-out homestudy course which you can readily review in less than twenty hours. It's a digest which you might have been able to assemble after many hundred hours of laborious digging. Since you'll have quite enough to do without that, consider yourself fortunate that we have done it for you.

To prepare for a test you must motivate yourself . . . get into the right frame of mind for learning from your "self-tutor." You'll have to urge yourself to learn. That's the only way people ever learn. Your efforts to score high will be greatly aided because you'll have to do this job on your own . . . perhaps without a teacher. Psychologists have demonstrated that studies undertaken for a clear goal (which you initiate yourself and actively pursue) are the most successful. You, yourself, want to pass this test. That's why you bought this book and embarked on this program. Nobody forced you to do it, and there may be nobody to lead you through the course. Your self-activity is going to be the key to your success in the forthcoming weeks.

Used correctly, your "self-tutor" will show you what to expect and will give you a speedy brush-up on the major problems crucial to your exam. Even if your study time is very limited, you will:

- gain familiarity with your examination;
- improve your general test-taking skill;

- improve your skill in analyzing and answering questions involving reasoning, judgment, comparison, and evaluation;
- improve your speed and skill in reading and understanding what you read—an important ability in learning, and an important component of most tests.

This book will pinpoint your study by presenting the types of questions you will get on the actual exam. You'll score higher even if you only familiarize yourself with these types.

This book will help you find your weaknesses and find them fast. Once you know where you're weak, you can get right to work (before the exam), and concentrate on those soft spots. This is the kind of selective study which yields maximum results for every hour spent.

This book will give you the *feel* of the exam. Many of our practice questions are taken from previous exams. Since previous exams are not always available for inspection by the public, our sample test questions are quite important for you. The day you take your exam you'll see how closely the book conforms.

This book will give you confidence *now*, while you are preparing for the exam. It will build your self-confidence as you proceed. It will beat those dreaded before-test jitters that have hurt so many other test-takers.

This book stresses the modern, multiple-choice type of question because that's the kind you'll undoubtedly get on your exam. In answering these questions you will add to your knowledge by learning the correct answers, naturally. However, you will not be satisfied with merely the correct choice for each question. You will want to find out why the other choices are incorrect. This will jog your memory . . . help you remember much you thought you had forgotten. You'll be preparing and enriching yourself for the exam to come.

Of course, the great advantage in all this lies in narrowing your study to just those fields in which you're most likely to be quizzed. Answer enough questions in those fields and the chances are very good that you'll meet a few of them again on the actual test. After all, the number of questions an examiner can draw upon in these fields is rather limited. Examiners frequently employ the same questions on different tests for this very reason.

By creating the "climate" of your test, this book should give you a fairly accurate picture of what's involved, and should put you in the right frame of mind for passing high.

Arco Publishing Company has been involved with trends and methods in testing ever since the firm was founded in 1937. We have *specialized* in books that prepare people for exams. Based on this experience it is our modest boast that you probably have in your hands the best book that could be prepared to help *you* score high. Now, if you'll take a little advice on using it properly, we can assure you that you will do well.

Professional & Administrative Career Exam

PART ONE

Applying and Studying For Your Exam

GENERAL SCHEDULE — BASIC PER ANNUM RATES

PAY RATES OF THE GENERAL SCHEDULE (5 U.S.C. 5332)

AS ADJUSTED BY EXECUTIVE ORDER FALL 1977

Grade	1	2	3	4	5	6	7	8	9	10	Within-Grade Increase
GS-1	$6,219	$6,426	$6,633	$6,840	$7,047	$7,254	$7,461	$7,668	$7,875	$8,082	$207
GS-2	7,035	7,270	7,505	7,740	7,975	8,210	8,445	8,680	8,915	9,150	235
GS-3	7,930	8,194.	8,458	8,722	8,986	9,250	9,514	9,778	10,042	10,306	264
GS-4	8,902	9,199	9,496	9,793	10,090	10,387	10,684	10,981	11,278	11,575	297
GS-5	9,959	10,291	10,623	10,955	11,287	11,619	11,951	12,283	12,615	12,947	332
GS-6	11,101	11,471	11,841	12,211	12,581	12,951	13,321	13,691	14,061	14,431	370
GS-7	12,336	12,747	13,158	13,569	13,980	14,391	14,802	15,213	15,624	16,035	411
GS-8	13,662	14,117	14,572	15,027	15,482	15,937	16,392	16,847	17,302	17,757	455
GS-9	15,090	15,593	16,096	16,599	17,102	17,605	18,108	18,611	19,114	19,617	503
GS-10	16,618	17,172	17,726	18,280	18,834	19,388	19,942	20,496	21,050	21,604	554
GS-11	18,258	18,867	19,476	20,085	20,694	21,303	21,912	22,521	23,130	23,739	609
GS-12	21,883	22,612	23,341	24,070	24,799	25,528	26,257	26,986	27,715	28,444	729
GS-13	26,022	26,889	27,756	28,623	29,490	30,357	31,224	32,091	32,958	33,825	867
GS-14	30,750	31,775	32,800	33,825	34,850	35,875	36,900	37,925	38,950	39,975	1,025
GS-15	36,171	37,377	38,583	39,789	40,995	42,201	43,407	44,613	45,819	47,025	1,206
GS-16	42,423	43,837	42,251	46,665	48,079*	49,493*	50,907*	52,321*	53,735*		1,414
GS-17	49,696*	51,353*	53,010*	54,667*	56,324*						1,657
GS-18	58,245*										

* The rate of basic pay for employees at these rates is limited by section 5308 of title 5 of the United States Code to the rate for level V of the Executive Schedule (currently $47,500).

Professional & Administrative Career Exam

AN OFFICIAL ANNOUNCEMENT

Here's a fairly good example of the kind of official statements issued to describe your test and your job. Read it all rather carefully because there are clues here as to the kind of test you'll be taking and how you have to prepare yourself. In writing this book we have examined quite a number of these announcements and have guided ourselves accordingly. We urge that you read and understand all such statements that are issued to you, personally. They will undoubtedly contain facts that foreshadow your test.

PROFESSIONAL AND ADMINISTRATIVE CAREER EXAMINATION

The Federal Government needs persons with potential for advancement into responsible administrative and professional jobs. If you have a college degree or equivalent experience, this examination offers you the opportunity to compete for a wide variety of jobs in Federal agencies across the country. About 85 percent of these positions are filled outside the Washington, D.C. area. Most positions are filled at grade GS-5 and do not require specialized education or experience.

TO QUALIFY

To be eligible for employment consideration under this examination you must meet the experience and/or education requirements outlined below and score sufficiently high on those parts of the written test battery which are most related to the type of job being filled.

Experience and Education Requirements

1. For grade GS-5 positions:
   A bachelor's degree; or 3 years of responsible experience; or an equivalent combination of education and experience.

2. For grade GS-7 positions—One of these:
   a. A bachelor's degree plus one year of graduate study; or an LL.B. or J.D. degree from a recognized law school; or 4 years of responsible experience; or an equivalent combination of education and experience.
   b. A bachelor's degree, an earned rating of 90 or above in the written test, and either a 2.9 grade-point average on a 4.0 scale in all undergraduate courses, or rank in the upper third of your class, or membership in a national honorary scholastic society (other than freshman societies) recognized by the Association of College Honor Societies.

Written Test Requirements

All applicants must take a battery of written tests designed to measure abilities required for the various kinds of jobs covered by this examination. The written test battery requires approximately 4½ hours.

BASIS OF RATING

Ratings will be based upon your scores on the written tests and an evaluation of your experience and education. Six basic ratings will be assigned, one for each pattern of tested abilities appropriate for a particular group of jobs to be filled. You *must* achieve a rating of 70 or above for any one of these six ability patterns to be considered for jobs requiring those abilities.

Extra credit will be given in each of the basic ratings to applicants who present evidence of outstanding scholarship, as defined under "General Information."

Test results: You will receive your rating about 4 to 6 weeks after you take the written test.

GENERAL INFORMATION

Equal Employment Opportunity. You will receive consideration without regard to race, religion, color, national origin, sex, politics, or age.

Responsible Experience. In this announcement, responsible experience is experience in a professional, administrative, or other field which provides evidence of an ability to learn and perform at the required level the duties of positions filled through this examination. Routine clerical experience or experience in the trades and crafts is not qualifying.

Equivalent Combination. One academic year of full time undergraduate study (30 semester hours credit or 45 quarter hours credit) is equivalent to 9 months of responsible experience. A bachelor's degree equals three years of experience.

Outstanding Scholarship. To obtain credit under this provision, applicants must have a 3.50 grade-point average on a 4.0 scale for all undergraduate courses completed toward a baccalaureate degree; or must stand in the upper 10 percent of their graduating class of the college or university attended, or a major subdivision of the university, such as the College of Business Administration, or the College of Liberal Arts. Class standing or grade-point average must be based on all courses which have been completed at the time of selection. This provision applies to applicants who have graduated within the last 2 years, or who are currently seniors. Candidates claiming outstanding scholarship will be required to furnish proof of their scholastic achievement at time of selection.

Quality Graduates. Applicants with a 2.90 or higher grade-point average on a 4.0 scale, or who rank in the upper third of their class, or have membership in a national honorary scholastic society (other than freshman societies) recognized by The Association of College Honor Societies will be eligible for grade GS-7 for those job patterns in which they receive test scores of 90 or higher. All candidates qualifying for Grade GS-7 on this basis will be required to furnish proof of their scholastic achievement at the time of selection.

Positions at GS-9 and Above. Applicants with advanced degrees (master's or higher) or more experience than is required to qualify under this examination may also wish to file under the Mid-level Positions Announcement, which covers most of the same occupations at grades GS-9 through GS-12. Information is available at any U.S. Civil Service Commission Office.

Nonaccredited Schools. Successful completion of college study in nonaccredited institutions will be accepted to the extent that (1) the courses are accepted for advanced credit at an accredited institution; or (2) the institution is approved by a State education agency or a State university; or (3) the school is listed in the most recent edition of the Education Directory (Higher Education), published by the U.S. Office of Education.

Students. Applications will be accepted from students who expect to complete, within nine months, courses which would permit them to meet the requirements of this examination.

Consideration for Employment. Eligible candidates will be referred to Federal agencies for consideration in the order of their ratings under the ability pattern appropriate for the positions to be filled, with the highest standing eligibles referred first. For some positions requiring special skills, only persons possessing the necessary qualifications will be referred.

Salary. Federal salary levels are comparable to those for equivalent jobs in the private sector, and are reviewed and adjusted at regular intervals to maintain comparability. Current salary rates can be obtained at Federal Job Information Centers.

For additional information about Federal employment, see Civil Service Commission Pamphlet BRE-37 "Working for the U.S.A."

JOBS FILLED THROUGH THIS EXAMINATION

Most positions filled through this examination do not require education or experience in a specific field. Training for the specific duties of the position is provided by the employing agency. Over 90 percent of the jobs are in the occupational categories listed below.* All offer good opportunities for promotion and preparation for other positions, depending upon the quality and effectiveness of your performance. Where appropriate, major employers of each occupation are noted.

A. Regulation/Compliance

The Federal Government has responsibility for activities such as taxation, immigration, importing/exporting, and regulation of various industries and businesses to insure their adherence to terms of laws affecting their operations.

Customs Inspectors (Department of Treasury) work at major points of entry to inspect cargo, baggage, and mail entering or leaving the United States. Their activities involve continual contact with the traveling public, import/export firms, and employees of shipping companies.

Revenue Officers (Department of Treasury) arrange settlement of tax obligations owed to the Government by individual taxpayers and business concerns.

Immigration Inspectors (Department of Justice) interview persons seeking to enter the United States and examine their documents to determine the terms under which they are eligible to enter. This work is performed primarily at major air terminals and ports.

*Positions described here are grouped by broad subject matter category rather than by the "ability patterns" described above.

Import Specialists (Department of Treasury) appraise and examine merchandise and analyze import entry documents to determine the applicability of tariff schedules and restrictions.

Financial Institution Examiners audit banks and savings and loan associations to determine their compliance with regulations of the Federal Deposit Insurance Corporation and the Federal Home Loan Bank Board.

Tax Technicians (Department of Treasury) examine tax returns for inaccuracies, determine which provisions of law are applicable in each situation, and meet with taxpayers to acquire information concerning settlement of the case. *Preferred Qualifications:* College-level education which has included 6 semester hours in accounting; or appropriate experience.

B. Administration/Management Support

Effective functioning of an organization's programs requires the contribution of people working in a wide range of activities. Persons in this field provide the coordination, support, and advice in specialized areas that together make an agency's overall work possible.

Computer Specialists develop systems and programs utilizing automated data processing equipment. Persons hired for this occupation receive extensive training in the field of computer programming and systems analysis.

Personnel Specialists deal with the manpower needs of their organization. Among the many activities in this field are recruiting and assigning employees, planning and administering training programs, analyzing manpower needs, and formulating personnel management polices and programs.

Management Analysts study the way an organization operates and seek ways to increase its effectiveness and efficiency. They advise management on setting up and improving patterns of work assignments, organizational structure, and management techniques.

Contract and Procurement Specialists negotiate and regulate contracts between Government and the private sector of the economy for supplies and services.

Supply Specialists are concerned with managing the materials used by the government. Their activities include development of supply requirements, maintenance of property accounts, and distribution of material.

Budget Specialists study the needs and priorities of their agency and advise management on allocation and use of its resources.

Administrative Specialists coordinate work in two or more of the specialties listed above. Agencies ordinarily conduct specialized training programs to prepare employees for administrative work.

C. Claims and Benefits Examining

The Federal Government operates a number of pension, insurance, disability, and other benefit services. Persons employed in this field receive and review claims applications, determine claimants' eligibility, and authorize settlement.

Social Insurance Claims Examiners work on retirement, unemployment compensation, medicare/medicaid, and old-age insurance claims filed under programs administered by the Department of Health, Education and Welfare.

Civil Service Claims Examiners perform claims work under the benefit program for retired Federal employees.

Veterans Claims Examiners process claims for education/training benefits, retirement, disability, and special benefits for veterans.

Passport and Visa Examiners review applications for passports and visas from U.S. and foreign citizens travelling abroad and authorize issuance of travel documents.

D. Investigations/Law Enforcement

Federal duties in this field involve investigations of persons, activities, or records in connection with possible violations of laws or regulations.

Special Agents with the Department of Justice's Drug Enforcement Agency conduct investigations of criminal activity concerning violations of Federal drug laws. The investigations may involve surveillance, participation in raids, interviewing witnesses, interrogating suspects, searching for evidence, seizures of contraband and equipment, making arrests and inspecting records and documents. Strict physical standards must be met. Persons selected may be stationed anywhere in the United States or locations overseas, after completing an intensive training program.

Criminal Investigators gather information concerning violation of Federal statutes to build a case for Government prosecution of suspected criminals. Positions in this field may require strict physical standards and proficiency with firearms.

General Investigators perform non-criminal type investigations such as examination of private industry files to insure compliance with wage and hour laws, and background and security checks of applicants for Federal employment.

E. Social Services

The Federal Government operates or sponsors programs which extend various services and benefits to citizens. Persons working in this field are involved in providing these services to the public or in studying programs the Government sponsors.

Social Insurance Representatives are the primary contact between the Social Security Administration and the people it serves. They counsel persons concerning the benefits they are eligible to receive, and personally process particularly complicated or urgent claims.

Educational Specialists do research and planning for educational, recreational, and rehabilitative training programs in hospitals, agencies, and military installations. *Special requirements:* A bachelor's degree with a major in education or a subject field appropriate for the position.

Contact Representatives (Veterans Administration) extend the VA's service programs to the public. They counsel veterans on their entitlement to benefits, help applicants file their claims, and give personal attention to urgent cases.

F. Other Positions

Writers and Editors work primarily in public relations functions. They are responsible for preparing news releases, articles for periodicals, pamphlets and other informational materials on Federal activities.

Economists analyze and evaluate data and prepare reports which include recommendations on various phases of major economic problems. Work may also include compiling and interpreting statistical information on economic conditions or problems. *Special requirements:* A bachelor's degree with at least 21 semester hours (32 quarter hours) in economics and 3 semester hours (5 quarter hours) in statistics, accounting, or calculus.

EMPLOYMENT OUTLOOK

Lists of eligible candidates are maintained by each of the Civil Service Commission offices shown on page 16. Each makes referrals to Federal agencies within a defined geographical area. When you take the written test you will be asked to indicate where you wish to be considered for employment. Remember, in making your choices, that you must pay your own expenses in moving to your first duty location. Within any given area your employment opportunities will be best if you are available for most or all occupations.

For the past several years employment opportunities have been best in the New York and Chicago regions. Opportunities are most limited in the Boston, Denver, and St. Louis regions. Competition is very heavy for positions in Washington, D.C.

Professional & Administrative Career Exam

APPLYING FOR FEDERAL JOBS

The Federal Government, the largest employer in the United States, had about three million civilian workers early this year. Federal employees are engaged in occupations representing nearly every kind of job in private employment, as well as some unique to the Federal Government such as postal clerk, border patrolman, immigration inspector, foreign service officer, and Internal Revenue agent. Practically all Federal employees work for the departments and agencies that make up the executive branch of the government. The others are employed in the legislative and judicial branches. In this chapter we will discuss the kind of job you might get; how to hear about it, apply for it, and secure it. We will also give you a concise rundown on working conditions and benefits.

The majority of Federal jobs in the United States are covered by the civil service merit system. The Civil Service law provides for competitive examinations and mandates the selection of new employees from among those who make the highest scores. Responsibility for administering this merit system is entrusted to the U.S. Civil Service Commission.

The Commission, headquartered in Washington, D.C., maintains 65 local area offices in centers of population throughout the country. There is at least one such office in every state. These area offices announce and conduct examinations; evaluate applicants' work experience, training and aptitude; maintain the "eligible" lists for government employment; and refer qualified candidates to Federal agencies seeking new employees. Each area office also maintains a FEDERAL JOB INFORMATION CENTER — your best one-stop information source on Federal employment opportunities.

KEEPING POSTED

Your Federal Job Information Center provides information about:

— All current job opportunities in any part of the United States.

— Specific vacancies in shortage categories

— Opportunities for overseas employment

— Employment advisory service
— Job requirements and qualifications
— Application and examination procedures.

These centers are specially equipped to answer all inquiries about Federal employment opportunities. If you have any questions, write, visit, or phone your local Job Information Center. Or contact the Area Manager, U.S. Civil Service Commission, at your nearest area office.

The following also have civil service information: State Employment Service Offices, national and State headquarters of veterans' organizations, placement officials at colleges, and personnel officers in Government agencies.

Two New York newspapers, the *Civil Service Leader* and the *Chief*, run extensive listings of federal job openings in the state and metropolitan area, as well as some abroad. Check to see if similar publications serve your state. The government itself uses newspapers and sometimes the radio for recruitment.

As a special service to disabled veterans, the Civil Service Commission maintains a file of those who are interested in specific kinds of jobs. A ten-point veteran may write to the Commission in Washington, D.C., and ask that his name be placed in this file.

S1875

UNITED STATES CIVIL SERVICE REGIONS

Atlanta Area Office
U.S. Civil Service Commission
Federal Office Building
275 Peachtree Street, N.E.
Atlanta, Georgia 30303

Geographical Area Covered.
Alabama; Florida; Georgia; Kentucky (except Boyd, Henderson, Boone, Campbell, and Kenton Counties); Mississippi; North Carolina; South Carolina: Tennessee; Crittenden County, Arkansas; Floyd and Clark Counties, Indiana.

Boston Area Office
U.S. Civil Service Commission
John W. McCormack Post Office and Courthouse
Boston, Massachusetts 02109

Connecticut; Maine; Massachusetts; New Hampshire; Rhode Island; Vermont.

Chicago Area Office
U.S. Civil Service Commission
Steger Building, 18th Floor
28 E. Jackson Boulevard
Chicago, Illinois 60604

Illinois (except Madison and St. Clair Counties); Indiana (except Clark and Floyd Counties); Scott County, Iowa; Michigan; Minnesota (except Clay County); Ohio (except Belmont, Jefferson and Lawrence Counties); Wisconsin; Henderson, Boone, Campbell, and Kenton Counties, Kentucky.

Dallas Area Office
U.S. Civil Service Commission
1100 Commerce Street, 6th Floor
Dallas, Texas 75202

Arkansas (except Crittenden County); Louisiana; New Mexico; Oklahoma; Texas.

Denver Area Office
U.S. Civil Service Commission
U.S. Post Office Building
18th and Stout Streets
Denver, Colorado 80202

Colorado; Montana; North Dakota; South Dakota; Utah; Wyoming; Clay County, Minnesota.

Honolulu Area Office
U.S. Civil Service Commission
1000 Bishop Street
Honolulu, Hawaii 96813

Hawaii; Guam; Pacific Ocean Area.

New York Area Office
U.S. Civil Service Commission
26 Federal Plaza
New York, New York 10007

New York; New Jersey (except Camden County).

Philadelphia Area Office
U.S. Civil Service Commission
William J. Green, Jr. Federal Building
600 Arch Street
Philadelphia, Pennsylvania 19106

Delaware; Maryland (except Prince Georges, Charles, and Montgomery Counties); Pennsylvania; Virginia (except Arlington, Fairfax, Loudoun, Stafford, Prince William and King George Counties); West Virginia; Belmont, Jefferson and Lawrence Counties, Ohio; Boyd County, Kentucky; Camden County, New Jersey.

San Francisco Area Office
U.S. Civil Service Commission
P.O. Box 36122
450 Golden Gate Avenue
San Francisco, California 94102

Arizona; California; Nevada.

San Juan Area Office
U.S. Civil Service Commission
PAN AM Building
255 Ponce De Leon Avenue
Hato Rey, Puerto Rico 00917

Puerto Rico; Virgin Islands.

Seattle Area Office
U.S. Civil Service Commission
Federal Office Building
1st Avenue and Madison Street
Seattle, Washington 98104

Alaska; Idaho; Oregon; Washington.

St. Louis Area Office
U.S. Civil Service Commission
1520 Market Street
St. Louis, Missouri 63103

Iowa (except Scott County); Kansas; Missouri; Nebraska; Madison and St. Clair Counties, Illinois.

Washington, D.C. Area Office
U.S. Civil Service Commission
1900 E Street, N.W.
Washington, D.C. 20415

Washington Metropolitan Area (District of Columbia, Charles, Montgomery, and Prince Georges Counties, Maryland; Arlington, Fairfax, Loudoun, Stafford, Prince William, and King George Counties, Virginia; overseas areas except Pacific Ocean Area).

Professional & Administrative Career Exam

THE FEDERAL JOB ANNOUNCEMENT

When a position is open and a civil service examination is to be given for it, a job announcement is drawn up. This is generally from two to six printed pages in length and contains just about everything an applicant should know. The announcement begins with the job title and salary. A typical announcement then describes the work, the location of the position, the education and experience requirements, the kind of examination to be given, the system of rating. It may also have something to say about veteran preference and the age limit. It tells which application form is to be filled out, where to get the form, and where and when to file it. Study the job announcement carefully. It will answer many of your questions and help you decide whether you like the position and are qualified for it.

MEETING THE REQUIREMENTS

Before you apply, read the announcement carefully. It gives information about the jobs to be filled and what qualifications you must have to fill one of them.

If the announcement says that only persons who have 1 year of experience along certain lines will qualify and you don't have that experience, don't apply. If the announcement says that the jobs to be filled are all in a certain locality and you don't want to work in that locality, don't file. Many disappointed applicants would have been saved time and trouble if they had only read the announcement carefully.

Credit will be given for unpaid experience or volunteer work such as in community, cultural, social service and professional association activities, on the same basis as for paid experience, that is, it must be of the type and level acceptable under the announcement. Therefore, you may, if you wish, report such experience in one or more of the experience blocks at the end of your personal qualifications statement, if you feel that it represents qualifying experience for the positions for which you are applying. To receive proper credit, you must show the actual time, such as the number of hours a week, spent in such activities.

QUALITY OF EXPERIENCE

For most positions, in order to qualify *on experience* for any grade above the entrance level, an applicant must have either 6 months or 1 year of experience at a level comparable in difficulty and responsibility to that of the next lower grade level in the Federal Service. In some instances for positions at GS-11 and below, experience may have been obtained at two levels below that of the job to be filled.

Depending on the type of position, the next lower level may be either one or two grades lower. If you were applying for a position as a Stenographer (single grade interval position), at grade GS-5, you should have at least 1 year of experience doing work equivalent to that done by a Stenographer at the GS-4 level. If you were applying for a two-grade interval position, however, such as Computer Specialist GS-7, you would need at least 1 year of experience equivalent to that of a GS-5 Computer Specialist in Federal Service, or 6 months equivalent to the GS-6 level. Where necessary, the announcement will provide more specific information about the level of experience needed to qualify.

S1875

THE DUTIES

The words *Optional Fields* — sometimes just the word *Options* — may appear on the front page of the announcement. You then have a choice to apply for that particular position in which you are especially interested. This is because the duties of various positions are quite different even though they bear the same broad title. A public relations *clerk,* for example, does different work from a payroll *clerk,* although they are considered broadly in the same general area.

Not every announcement has options. But whether or not it has them, the precise duties are described in detail, usually under the heading: *Description of Work.* Make sure that these duties come within the range of your experience and ability.

SOME THINGS TO WATCH FOR

In addition to educational and experience requirements, there will be some general requirements you will have to meet.

Age: "How old are you?" There is no maximum age limit. However, persons over 70 are only given temporary appointments, which can be renewed. They are not covered under the retirement system, since retirement is mandatory at 70. The usual minimum age limit is 18, but high school graduates may apply at 16 for many jobs.

If you are 16 or 17 and are out of school but not a high school graduate, you may be hired only (1) if you have successfully completed a formal training program preparing you for work (for example, training provided under the Manpower Development and Training Act, in the Job Corps, in the Neighborhood Youth Corps, and in similar Government or private programs), or (2) if you have been out of school for at least 3 months, not counting the summer vacation, and if school authorities sign a form agreeing with your preference for work instead of additional schooling. The form will be given you by the agency that wants to hire you.

REMEMBER, JOB OPPORTUNITIES ARE BEST FOR THOSE WHO GRADUATE. IF YOU CAN, YOU SHOULD COMPLETE YOUR EDUCATION BEFORE YOU APPLY FOR FULL-TIME WORK.

If you are in high school, you may be hired for work during vacation periods if you are 16. (For jobs filled under the Summer Employment Examination, however, you must be 18 if still in high school.) You may also be hired for part-time work during the school year if you are 16 and meet all the following conditions:

(1) Your work schedule is set up through agreement with your school,
(2) Your school certifies that you can maintain good standing while working, and
(3) You remain enrolled in high school.

Some announcements may set a different minimum age limit. Be sure to check the announcement carefully before applying.

Physical requirements. What is your physical condition? You must be physically able to perform the duties of the position, and must be emotionally and mentally stable. This does not mean that a handicap will disqualify an applicant so long as he can do the work efficiently without being a hazard to himself or to others.

For most positions, appointees must have good distant vision in one eye and be able to read without strain printed material the size of typewritten characters. They may use glasses to meet these requirements.

Persons appointed are usually required to be able to hear the conversational voice. They may use a hearing aid to meet this requirement. Blind persons and deaf persons may apply and be examined for positions with duties they can perform.

An amputation of an arm, hand, leg, or foot does not in itself bar a person from Federal employment. Here again the test is whether the person can do the duties of the position satisfactorily and without hazard to himself or others.

The Federal Government is the world's largest employer of handicapped people and has a strong program aimed at their employment. It recognizes that, in almost every kind of work, there are some positions suitable for the blind, the deaf, and others with serious impairments. If reading is necessary to perform duties, the blind person is permitted to provide a reader at no expense to the Government.

Of course, there are some positions — such as border patrolman, firefighter, and criminal investigator — that can be filled only by people in topnotch physical condition. Whenever this is the case, the physical requirements are described in detail in the announcements.

ABOUT THE TEST

The announcement also tells you about the kind of test you will be given. Several kinds of examinations are given by the Civil Service Commission. At the very beginning the job announcement states whether this is an assembled or unassembled examination. In the former, applicants assemble to take their test—usually a written one. The announcement always tells you the kind of examination you must take, and often sample questions are attached. The tests used in each examination are designed to measure the ability of the applicant to perform the duties of the position for which the examination is given. The amount of time required to take the test, and the method of rating—a scale of 100, with 70 as the passing grade—are also mentioned in the announcement.

CLOSING DATE

When an examination is announced, qualifications statements are accepted as long as the announcement is "open." In some instances, the closing date for acceptance of statements is stated in the announcement. In other instances, the closing date is not stated in the announcement; instead, public notice of the closing date is given later.

You must apply before the closing date. However, if you cannot apply on time because of military service, you may apply after the closing date, but not later than 120 days after honorable discharge. If you're working outside the United States for a government agency or for an international organization (such as the United Nations), you may also file late under certain conditions.

Persons who have been granted "10-point veteran preference" by the Civil Service Commission may also apply after the closing date.

If you think that you are entitled to apply after the closing date, write to the office that issued the announcement and describe the circumstances. That office will let you know whether your qualifications statement can be accepted.

One further fact: It is not necessary to pay anyone for helping you obtain a civil service position with the United States Government. No such intervention is possible.

FOR FURTHER DETAILS: More detailed information about every aspect of Federal employment can be found in Arco's "Complete guide to U.S. Civil Service Jobs." See the last chapter, which deals with other helpful Arco Books.

Professional & Administrative Career Exam

THE APPLICATION FORM

After you study the job announcement and decide that you want the position, you will fill out and send in your application. Many prospective employees have foundered on the application because of slipshod, erroneous, incomplete, untruthful, or misleading answers. Do give the application the serious attention it must have. This chapter will explain how to answer the most important questions that regularly appear on civil service applications.

FILLING OUT THE APPLICATION FORMS

If you are satisfied that you meet the requirements listed in the announcement, the next step is to fill out the application forms. At first you may have to fill out only a small card, but sooner or later you will have to fill out a 2- or a 4-page personal qualifications statement. It is very important to do this carefully.

Answer every question in the statement. If you don't, the area office must write to you for the missing information. This will take time and delay action on your qualifications statement. You will ordinarily be given only one opportunity to send in this information. If you don't reply promptly, your statement will be canceled.

For many positions, written tests are not required, and civil service examiners rate applicants on their training and experience. Tell the whole story. You can't get credit for experience and training which you don't claim on your statement.

Follow the instructions in the announcement as to when and where to send your statement. Be sure to send it to the right office before the closing date.

WHAT TO EXPECT ON THE APPLICATION FORM

There are many different application forms. While there are minor differences in the questions asked, and the order in which they're presented, by and large this is what you can expect.

Name of examination, or kind of position applied for. This information appears in large type at the top of job announcements. All you have to do is to copy it fully.

Optional subject (if mentioned in announcement) — Many examination announcements have options, that is, a choice of the kind of work you want to do. To answer this question you write the specific option of the job you are applying for, again copying it from the announcement form.

AGE AND PLACE OF BIRTH

Your place of birth.
Your date of birth (month, day, year.)
Your Social Security Number.
The United States Government makes no distinction between people born abroad and those born in the United States in selecting workers for government positions.

THE "OMNIBUS" QUERY

We now reach the "omnibus" query. This consists of six parts and deals with specific information concerning certain preferences of yours about salary, length and location of employment. The information you provide in response to this question will enable the government to offer you a wider or narrower range of jobs and provide civil

S1875

service authorities with an idea of your feelings about a short-term job if one should come up.

An important part of this question asks you *what is the lowest entrance salary you will accept?*

EXPERIENCE

The "experience" item: This section consists of a series of blocks which you must fill in with the details of the positions you have held. The details which the Commission wants include: dates of employment, place of employment, name and address of employer, kind of business or organization (for example, dress manufacturing, wholesale grocer, service station, insurance agency), the number and kind of employees you supervised if you were in a supervisory position, the name and title of your immediate supervisor, the exact title of your position, the salary you earned when you started and your final salary, a description of your work. The government also wants to know your reason for desiring to change employment and the reasons for leaving your former positions.

If you were in the Armed Forces, list your military or merchant marine service and describe your major duty assignments.

HAVE YOU ANY SPECIAL APTITUDES?

Special Qualifications and Skills: This section is included so that you may cite any special qualifications not covered elsewhere in the application blank. It asks for a list of any special skills you possess, machines and equipment you can use, such as operation of shortwave radio, multilith, comptometer, keypunch, turret lathe, scientific or professional devices. Here, too, is a space in which you can list your typing and shorthand speed.

THE LAW AND FEDERAL EMPLOYMENT

LOYALTY QUERIES

The government asks two questions involving loyalty.

Are you now, or within the last ten years have you been, a member of the Communist Party, U.S.A., or any subdivision of the Communist Party, U.S.A.?

Are you now, or within the last ten years have you been, a member of an organization that to your present knowledge advocates the overthrow of the constitutional form of government of the U.S.A. by force or violence or other unlawful means?

If your answer to either question is "Yes," then you must list the name of the organization(s), the dates of your membership(s), and your understanding of the aims and purposes of the organization at the time of your membership.

DISABILITIES

Do you have, or have you had, heart disease, epilepsy, tuberculosis, or diabetes? Have you had a nervous breakdown? The government needs to know this to insure that you are not placed in a position which might impair your health, or which might be a hazard to you or others.

FOR FURTHER DETAILS: More detailed information about every aspect of Federal employment can be found in Arco's "Complete guide to U.S. Civil Service Jobs." See the last chapter, which deals with other helpful Arco Books.

Professional & Administrative Career Exam

YOU BECOME AN "ELIGIBLE"

People who are found to meet the requirements in the announcement are called "eligibles." Their names are put on a "list of eligibles." An eligible's chances of getting a job depend on how high he stands on this list and how fast agencies are filling jobs from the list.

Federal agencies can fill jobs in several ways—for instance, by promoting an employee already within the agency or by hiring an employee from another Federal agency who wants to change jobs. But when a job is to be filled from a list of eligibles, the agency asks the Civil Service examiners for the names of people on the list of eligibles for that job.

When the examiners receive this request, they send to the agency the names of the three people highest on the list. Or, if the job to be filled has specialized requirements, the examiners send the agency, from the general list, the names of the top three persons who meet those requirements. An applicant who has said he would not accept appointment in the place where the job is located is, of course, not considered.

The appointing officer makes a choice from among the three people whose names were sent to him. If that person accepts the appointment, the names of the other persons are put back on the list so that they may be considered for future openings.

That is the rule in hiring from all kinds of eligible lists, whether they are for typist, carpenter, chemist, or something else. For every vacancy, the appointing officer has his choice of any one of the top three eligibles on the list. This explains why the person whose name is on top of the list sometimes does not get an appointment when some of the persons lower on the list do. If the appointing officer chooses the No. 2 or No. 3 eligible, the No. 1 eligible doesn't get a job at once, but stays on the list until he is appointed or the list is terminated.

DRAFT STATUS

You may be considered for Federal employment regardless of your military service status, even though you may be subject to active duty in the near future. Reemployment rights with the Government are assured, and you will be eligible for any salary increases effective during your absence on active military duty.

VETERANS GET PREFERENCE

If you are a veteran, you may be eligible for additional benefits in getting a Government job and also in keeping it after you are hired. For example, "veteran preference" will add extra points to your passing score.

Disabled veterans or their wives, widows of certain veterans, and widowed or divorced mothers of some veterans who died in service or who were totally and permanently disabled get 10 extra points. Most other honorably discharged veterans get 5 points, depending upon length or dates of service.

KINDS OF APPOINTMENTS

If you are offered a job, the letter or telegram will show what kind of appointment is involved. Most appointments are either temporary, term, career-conditional, or career. You should know what these mean.

S1875

A *temporary* appointment does not ordinarily last more than 1 year. A temporary worker can't be promoted and can't transfer to another job. He is not under the retirement system. Persons over 70 can be given only temporary appointments, but they can be renewed.

A *term* appointment is made for work on a specific project that will last more than 1 year but less than 4 years. A term employee can be promoted or reassigned to other positions within the project for which he was hired. He is not under the retirement system.

If you accept a temporary or term appointment, your name will stay on the list of eligibles from which you were appointed. This means that you will remain eligible for permanent jobs that are normally filled by career-conditional or career appointments.

A *career-conditional* appointment leads after 3 years' service to a career appointment. For the first year, the employee serves a probationary period. During this time, he must demonstrate that he can do a satisfactory job and may be dismissed if he fails to do so. A career-conditional employee has promotion and transfer privileges. After a career-conditional employee completes his probation, he cannot be removed except for cause. However, in reduction-in-force (layoff) actions, career-conditional employees are dismissed ahead of career employees.

A *career* employee also serves a probationary period, as described above, and has promotion and transfer privileges. After he completes his probation, however, he is in the last group to be affected in layoffs.

WHY YOU MAY BE BARRED

Applicants may be denied examinations and eligibles may be denied appointments for any of the following reasons:

1. Dismissal from employment for delinquency or misconduct.

2. Physical or mental unfitness for the position.

3. Criminal, infamous, dishonest, immoral, or notoriously disgraceful conduct.

4. Intentional false statements, deception, or fraud.

5. Refusal to furnish testimony which the Commission may require.

6. Drunkenness.

7. Reasonable doubt as to loyalty to the Government of the United States.

8. Any legal or other disqualification.

An old conviction for civil or criminal offense will not of itself bar an applicant from U. S. government employment. Ordinarily a person who has been convicted of a felony must wait two years after release before his application will be considered. Exceptions can be made by the Civil Service Commission, which also decides whether or not to accept applications from persons who have been convicted of misdemeanors or who are under suspended sentence or on probation.

Professional & Administrative Career Exam

OTHER REQUIREMENTS

When you are being considered for a job, and again when you are appointed, you will learn about certain requirements you must meet—over and above the requirement that you be able to do the work. You will be informed of certain rules which, as a Federal employee, you will be expected to observe.

RESIDENCE REQUIREMENTS

Appointments to some positions in Washington, D.C., are apportioned by law among the States and territories. Persons being considered for these positions may be required to send in proof that they meet a 1-year residence requirement. This proof will be requested, when necessary, by the agency that is considering you for appointment.

MEMBERS OF FAMILY

Unless you are entitled to veteran preference, you may not be appointed (except temporarily) if two or more members of your family who live under the same roof have permanent Federal jobs. The agency that is considering you for appointment will ask you for this information.

AFFIDAVITS

You will be asked to swear (or affirm) to certain statements. If you swear to or affirm statements that are not true, you may be dismissed as a result. All prospective employees must swear (or affirm) that they will support and defend the Constitution of the United States.

You may also be asked to swear (or affirm) that you did not pay, or offer to pay, any money or anything of value to get your appointment.

FINGERPRINTS

Your fingerprints will be taken, either when you report for duty or when the investigation is begun.

The fingerprints will be sent to the Federal Bureau of Investigation for checking against their records. If you were ever convicted (for anything other than a minor traffic violation), and you did not admit the conviction on your qualifications statement, you may be dismissed, or if you are an applicant you may be denied appointment.

INVESTIGATION

In connection with your appointment, an investigation will be made to determine whether you are reliable, trustworthy, of good conduct and character, and of complete and unswerving loyalty to the United States. If your appointment is to a sensitive position (a position of trust in which you may have access to classified information), a determination will also be made as to whether your employment in the Government service would be clearly consistent with the interests of the national security.

REPORTING FOR DUTY

If you must travel in order to report for duty, you ordinarily pay your own way. The Government pays these travel expenses for only a few hard-to-fill positions.

PHYSICAL EXAMINATION

If necessary, you will be given a physical examination by a medical officer before appointment. If he finds that you are not physically qualified for the position, you cannot be appointed.

Professional & Administrative Career Exam

WORKING FOR THE U.S.

Working for the government is different from working in private industry. You can't always give orders and expect them to be carried out pronto; you're likely to bump into a regulation. You can't be too active politically; if you are, you'll be slapped down. There is a complicated system of judging and reporting on your work — a system that may affect your earning power. It's pretty easy to get fired. And with what seems sickening frequency, some Congressman sounds off against "inefficient bureaucrats" — meaning you. On the other hand, if you work authorized overtime, you get paid for it, your vacation and sick-leave time is generous, chances for promotions and pay increases are frequent, and the government often gives valuable training on the job. If you make government service a career, you'll retire with a substantial annuity.

SALARY AND WORKING CONDITIONS

After selecting its employees on the basis of merit, the Government pays them, and promotes them, on the same basis.

Employees are paid according to the principle of "equal pay for equal work." When jobs in the higher grades become vacant, or new ones are set up, the general practice is to fill them by promoting employees in lower grades who are qualified to perform the more difficult duties.

You will want to know more about these matters, and about other features of Federal employment. As you learn about them, you will find that the Government, the largest employer in the United States, is also a progressive employer.

PAY

In general, the Government pays good salaries. Its policy is that salaries of Government employees should be comparable to those paid by private employers for work of the same level of difficulty and responsibility.

Government salaries are reviewed frequently and changes made, or recommended to Congress, as needed. This means that persons choosing careers in Government may expect, over the years, pay realistically geared to the economy.

The Government has several pay plans. For most trades positions, wages are set from time to time to bring them into line with prevailing wages paid in the same locality by private industry.

A few Federal agencies and a few classes of employees have still other pay plans. The Tennessee Valley Authority, the Postal Service, the Foreign Service (Department of State), and physicians, dentists, and nurses in the Department of Medicine and Surgery of the Veterans Administration are examples.

Other employees (45 percent) are paid under the General Schedule (GS), which applies to most white-collar employees and to protective and custodial employees such as guards and messengers. Positions are graded by number according to how difficult the work is, starting with grade GS-1 and going up to grade GS-18.

Each grade has a set salary range; thus the grade of a position sets the pay. Hard-to-fill positions frequently have a higher salary range than other positions in the same grade. In all cases, salaries are listed in the announcement or in a separate supplement.

Hiring usually is done at the first rate of a grade. Employees who perform their work at an acceptable level of competence receive within-grade increases at intervals. They may qualify for these increases every year for 3 years; then the increases occur less frequently until the top rate of the grade is reached. Employees may be awarded additional within-grade increases for exceptionally meritorious work, but not above the top of the grade.

You will be interested in knowing how jobs get to be in one grade or another. Position classifiers study the duties of the jobs. They find out how difficult the duties are, how much responsibility the person holding the job has, and what knowledge of experience or skill goes into performing the duties. Then they put the jobs in appropriate grades under standards set by the Civil Service Commission.

HOURS OF WORK

The usual Government workweek is 40 hours. Most Government employees work 8 hours, 5 days a week, Monday through Friday, but in some cases the nature of the work may call for a different workweek.

As in any other business, employees sometimes have to work overtime. If you are required to work overtime while a Government employee, you will either be paid for overtime or given time off to make up for the extra time you worked.

ADVANCEMENT

Many of the men and women in top jobs in the Government began their careers "at the bottom of the ladder." They did their jobs well, and prepared for the job ahead. They learned more and more about the work of their agencies. As they became more useful on the job, they were promoted to one more important position after another.

Most agencies fill vacancies, whenever possible, by promoting their own employees. Promotion programs in every agency are designed to make sure that promotions go to the employees who are among the best qualified to fill higher positions. How fast employees are promoted depends upon openings in the higher grades, and upon their ability and industry.

Federal employees receive on-the-job training. They may also participate in individualized career development programs and receive job-related training in their own agency, in other agencies, or outside the Government (for example, in industrial plants and universities).

It is not always necessary to move to a new job in order to advance in grade. Sometimes an employee's work assignments change a great deal in the ordinary course of business. His job "grows." When that happens it is time for a position classifier to study the job again. If he finds that the job should be put in a higher grade because of the increased difficulty or responsibility of the duties, the change is made.

TRANSFERS

Transferring to other civil service jobs for which an employee is qualified is another way of getting a better job.

Agencies consider the qualifications of an employee for promotion as higher grade positions become vacant. However, for transfer to positions in other agencies, an employee would have to "find his own job," by such means as interviews with officials in those agencies. If he can find a vacant position in another agency, and if the hiring officer is impressed with his qualifications, arrangements may be made to transfer him.

Occasionally, the Job Information Center may be able to assist Federal employees in locating vacancies.

EFFICIENCY COUNTS

At intervals, employees are rated on their job performance. In most agencies, the ratings are "Outstanding," "Satisfactory," and "Unsatisfactory."

Employees with "Outstanding" ratings receive extra credit for retention in layoffs.

An employee whose rating is "Unsatisfactory" must be dismissed or assigned to another position with duties which he can be expected to learn to do satisfactorily.

INCENTIVE AWARDS

Government agencies encourage their employees to suggest better ways, or simpler ways, or more economical ways, of doing their jobs. They may give a cash award to an employee for a suggestion or invention that results in money savings or improved service. They may also reward outstanding job performance or other acts that are particularly meritorious and deserving of recognition.

VACATION AND SICK LEAVE

Most Federal employees earn annual leave, for vacation and other purposes, according to the number of years (civilian plus creditable military service) they have been in the Federal service. They earn it at the rate of 13 days a year for the first 3 years and 20 days a year for the next 12 years. After 15 years, they earn 26 days of annual leave each year.

Sick leave is earned at the rate of 13 days a year. You can use this leave for illnesses serious enough to keep you away from your work, and for appointments with a doctor, dentists, or optician. Sick leave that is not used can be saved for future use. It is one of the best forms of insurance an employee and his family can have in case of extended periods of illness.

New Year's Day, Washington's Birthday, Memorial Day, Independence Day, Columbus Day, Veterans' Day, Thanksgiving and Christmas are some of the holidays granted Federal employees. Most are celebrated on Mondays, in accordance with the new Monday Holiday Law.

INJURY COMPENSATION

The Government provides liberal compensation benefits, including medical care, for employees who suffer injuries in the performance of official duty. Death benefits are also provided if an employee dies as a result of such injuries.

GROUP LIFE INSURANCE

As a Federal employee, you may have low-cost term life insurance without taking a physical examination. Two kinds of insurance are provided—life insurance and accidental death and dismemberment insurance.

This low cost insurance is available to employees in amounts that usually exceed one's annual base pay by $2,000. The Government pays one-third of the premium cost and the employee, through payroll deductions, pays the remainder. The minimum amount of each kind of protection is $10,000. In addition, an employee may purchase an extra $10,000 of optional insurance; for this he pays full premium, also through payroll deductions.

HEALTH BENEFITS

The Government sponsors a voluntary health insurance program for Federal employees. The program offers a variety of plans to meet individual needs, including basic coverage and major medical protection against costly illnesses. The Government contributes part of the cost of premiums and the employee pays the balance through payroll deductions.

RETIREMENT

Seven percent of a career or career-conditional employee's salary goes into a retirement fund. This seven percent comes out of every paycheck. This money is withheld as the employee's share of the cost of providing him or his survivors with an income after he has completed his working career.

If you leave the Government before you complete 5 years of service, the money you put into the retirement fund can be returned to you. If you leave after completing 5 years of service, you have a choice of having your money returned or leaving it in the fund. If you leave it in the fund, you will get an annuity starting when you are age 62.

The Government has a liberal retirement system. For example, after working for 30 years, you may retire at age 55 and get a life-time annual income equal to 56¼% of the highest average salary you earned during any three consecutive years of your working career. Also, an employee who becomes disabled after at least five years of Government service may retire on an annuity at any age.

LAYOFFS

In Government, layoffs are called *reductions in force*, and may be caused by a cut in appropriations, a decrease in work, or some similar reason.

In a reduction in force, the four things which determine whether an employee goes or stays are: Type of appointment (career, career-conditional, temporary); whether he has veteran preference for this purpose (20-year retired veterans generally do not); seniority (how long an employee has worked for the Government); and job performance.

UNEMPLOYMENT COMPENSATION

Federal employees who are separated in layoffs or whose appointments are terminated are entitled to unemployment compensation similar to that provided for employees in private industry. They are covered by the unemployment insurance system under conditions set by the State in which they worked.

SEVERANCE PAY

Federal employees who are involuntarily separated without cause, and who are not entitled to an immediate retirement annuity, may be eligible for severance pay. This pay is based on years of service and years of age over 40, and may not exceed 1 year's basic compensation.

EMPLOYEE ORGANIZATIONS

There are a number of unions and other employee organizations in the Federal Government. Some of them are for special groups, such as postal employees. Others have general membership among Government employees. Their main objective is to improve the working conditions of Federal employees.

Federal employees are free to join or to refrain from joining such organizations.

GETTING ADDITIONAL INFORMATION

Information about Federal civil service job announcements can be obtained from any Federal Job Information Center. The Civil Service Commission also invites you to call and talk with their information specialists before writing a letter or filling out an application. They can save you time and effort by answering questions, mailing announcements, applications and pamphlets.

Physically handicapped, mentally restored, and rehabilitated offender applicants should direct their inquiries to the Selective Placement Specialist. Job information and assistance for the mentally retarded may be obtained from a local office of the State Vocational Rehabilitation Agency.

Professional & Administrative Career Exam

ALL ABOUT THE EXAM

If you want a preview of your exam, look these questions over carefully. We did ... as we compiled them from official announcements and various other sources. A good part of this book is based on these prophetic questions. Practice and study material is geared closely to them. The time and effort you devote to the different parts of this book should be determined by the facility with which you answer the following questions.

THE WRITTEN TEST

The written test makes it possible for an applicant to be considered for several different occupations through a single examination by measuring a number of abilities common to these occupations. Scores in each area of ability will be weighted according to job requirements. The test includes measures of the ability to understand and use written language; the ability to derive general principles from particular data; the ability to analyze data and derive conclusions; the ability to understand, interpret and solve problems presented in quantitative terms; the ability to derive conclusions from incomplete data supplemented by general knowledge; and the ability to discover the logical sequence of a series of events.

TAKING THE TEST

Competitors should give themselves every fair advantage in preparing for and taking the written test by following the practices and techniques suggested below:
1. Since the test is not a knowledge test such as the ones given in school, studying for the examination the night before will not be helpful. A good night's rest is a better idea.
2. The sample questions included in this pamphlet should be studied carefully. Also, the instructions included in each section of the actual test should be read as carefully as time will allow. A reasonable amount of time is allotted for this purpose in the examination room.
3. Each competitor should bring two medium No. 2 pencils already sharpened. Also, although the examiner will periodically indicate the time, it may be advisable to bring a watch as an aid in keeping track of the time during the examination.
4. Competitors should take into consideration possible difficulties in finding a parking place or in locating the examination room. Extra time should be allowed to avoid running the risk of arriving too late to be admitted to the examination.
5. Competitors must have all required forms completely filled out or they will not be admitted to the examination.

Following the above recommendations should help competitors to be relaxed and ready to concentrate fully on the test material.

Time limits

A definite time limit has been set for each part of the test. These time limits are ample but will not be enough if competitors waste their time on questions for which they do not know the answer. Before each part the examiner will announce the number of questions in that part and the length of time allowed. When the time is announced competitors should check their watches or the room clock, if there is one, so that they know when the time will be up. While competitors are taking the test they should occasionally check the time. The examiner will mention the time 10 minutes before it is up. After this reminder competitors should finish the questions in that section and try to allow a few minutes for making final decisions and checking their answers before the time is up.

How to mark the answer sheet

Competitors will be instructed to select the best choice of the suggested alternative answers for each question and to record this choice on a separate answer sheet. The question numbers on the answer sheet run across the page. Each answer must be shown by completely darkening the space corresponding to the letter that is the same as the letter of the correct answer. To avoid inaccurate scoring, the mark MUST be kept within the space and marks that have to be erased should be completely erased. Only one answer should be marked for each question since the scoring machine scores double answers as errors. All answers must be marked on the answer sheet; answers in the test booklet do not count. On the other hand, any figuring that needs to be done in answering a question should be done in the test booklet, NOT on the answer sheet.

How to answer the questions
If competitors first answer the questions that they know, they will not risk having time called before they have answered those questions for which they know the answers. When the answer is known after the first careful reading of a question, that answer should be marked on the answer sheet and the competitor should proceed to the next question without pausing. When a question appears especially difficult and is left until later, care should be taken that the corresponding number on the answer sheet is left unmarked.

Guessing
In this test the examiner will tell the competitors, "It will be to your advantage to answer every question you can since your score will be the number of questions you answer correctly." This statement means that guessing is not penalized and that the score is the actual number of right answers. It is advisable therefore to make an intelligent guess about the answer to a difficult question.

Additional suggestions
Oral directions by the examiner and written directions in the test booklet are given to help the competitor and should be followed closely. When the examiner is giving directions before the test, competitors should feel free to call for an explanation if they need one. They should not risk making mistakes because the directions are not clear to them. Those competitors who have taken certain courses in education and psychology may have been warned by their instructors to avoid using words such as "none," "always," "every" and "all" in making test questions for prospective students. It is often difficult to write an answer in such terms and a consensus exists that the correct answer usually contains words like "mostly," "may be," "often" and other indefinite expressions. The wrong choices are popularly supposed to be tipped off by "always," "every," etc. **This is not the case** in Civil Service examinations. If a choice seems good it should not be ruled out simply because it contains a word that is not "supposed" to be in a correct answer.

The written test consists of several sections which measure the abilities that are considered essential in carrying out the duties of the jobs filled through this examination. Since certain sections of the test apply more to some occupations than to others, part scores on the written test will be weighted and combined under different weighting patterns to obtain six basic ratings, each representing the combination of abilities appropriate for certain occupations.

Official Sample Questions That Forecast the Test

A look at the following questions is the easiest, quickest, most important help you can get from this book. These predictive questions give you foresight by providing an "overview" with which to direct your study. They are actual samples of the question types you may expect on your test.

Before you're finished with this book you'll get plenty of practice with the best methods of answering each of these question types. However, you're going to do a little work yourself. You're going to plan your study to make sure that each available hour is used most effectively. You're going to concentrate where it will do you the most good. And you'll take it easy where you have no trouble.

In other words, discover what you're going to face on the test and make plans to pace yourself accordingly.

Understanding and Using Written Language

This part of the exam tests both reading comprehension and word knowledge. The reading test consists of brief paragraphs followed by one or more questions. In each case, the correct answer is either a restatement of the main concept of the passage, or a conclusion inherent in its content. The vocabulary questions require making fine distinctions in meaning among closely related words.

TEST I. READ AND DEDUCE

Many Federal jobs require the ability to analyze, understand and interpret written material of varying levels of complexity and to retain the content for at least a limited period of time. Question-type I is primarily designed to test these comprehension and retention abilities. The following questions therefore require competitors to understand a given paragraph and to select an answer based on their comprehension of the conceptual content of the paragraph. The right answer is either (1) a repetition, formulated in different terminology, of the main concept or concepts found in the paragraph, or (2) a conclusion whose inherence in the content of the paragraph is such that it is equivalent to a restatement.

1. Through advertising, manufacturers exercise a high degree of control over consumers' desires. However, the manufacturer assumes enormous risks in attempting to predict what consumers will want and in producing goods in quantity and distributing them in advance of final selection by the consumers.

   The paragraph best supports the statement that manufacturers
   A) can eliminate the risk of overproduction by advertising
   B) completely control buyers' needs and desires
   C) must depend upon the final consumers for the success of their undertakings
   D) distribute goods directly to the consumers
   E) can predict with great accuracy the success of any product they put on the market

The conclusion derived by the correct alternative, C, is inherent in the content of the paragraph; although it acknowledges that advertising plays an important role in determining consumers' desires, it affirms that final selection rests with the consumers and that manufacturers therefore take *enormous* risks in attempting to predict final selection. Alternative B contradicts the opening sentence of the paragraph which refers only to a "high degree of control." Alternatives A and E likewise affirm the opposite of what the paragraph postulates, i.e., that the manufacturer's predictions entail enormous risks. Alternative D is almost irrelevant to the paragraph since distribution techniques have not been considered.

2. The function of business is to increase the wealth of the country and the value and happiness of life. It does this by supplying the material needs of men and women. When the nation's business is successfully carried on, it renders public service of the highest value.

   The paragraph best supports the statement that
   A) all businesses which render public service are successful
   B) human happiness is enhanced only by the increase of material wants
   C) the value of life is increased only by the increase of wealth
   D) the material needs of men and women are supplied by well-conducted business
   E) business is the only field of activity which increases happiness

31

The correct alternative, D, restates the main idea in the original paragraph that business increases the value and happiness of life by supplying the material needs of men and women. Alternative A derives its conclusion incorrectly, i.e., the proposition that all successful businesses render public service, cannot be logically reversed to "all businesses which render public service are successful." Alternatives B and C assume an equation between happiness and wealth which is not supported by the content of the paragraph. Alternative E likewise equates happiness with business endeavors or their products, which the content of the paragraph does not warrant.

3. Honest people in one nation find it difficult to understand the viewpoints of honest people in another. Foreign ministries and their ministers exist for the purpose of explaining the viewpoints of one nation in terms understood by the ministries of another. Some of their most important work lies in this direction.

   The paragraph best supports the statement that
   A) people of different nations may not consider matters in the same light
   B) it is unusual for many people to share similar ideas
   C) suspicion prevents understanding between nations
   D) the chief work of foreign ministries is to guide relations between nations united by a common cause
   E) the people of one nation must sympathize with the viewpoints of the people of other nations

The conclusion derived by the correct alternative, A, is inherent in the content of the paragraph; if honest people in one nation find it difficult to understand the viewpoints of honest people in another, it is because they often see matters in different lights. Alternatives B, C and D find little or no support in the paragraph: B is concerned with "many people" whereas the paragraph refers to people of different nations; C *assumes* that nations are suspicious of each other and that suspicion prevents understanding; D contradicts the main idea expressed by the paragraph since foreign ministries should work towards mutual understanding between nations having discrepant viewpoints whether or not they have a common cause. Alternative E sets forth an ethical command which to an extent stems from the content of the paragraph but which is not completely warranted by it as is the conclusion of alternative A.

4. Education should not stop when the individual has been prepared to make a livelihood and to live in modern society. Living would be mere existence were there no appreciation and enjoyment of the riches of art, literature and science.

   The paragraph best supports the statement that true education
   A) is focused on the routine problems of life
   B) prepares one for a full enjoyment of life
   C) deals chiefly with art, literature and science
   D) is not possible for one who does not enjoy scientific literature
   E) disregards practical ends

The correct alternative, B, restates the main idea presented in the paragraph that living is mere existence for those individuals who lack the enjoyment of art, literature and science. Alternative A directly contradicts this main idea, and alternatives C and E also contradict the paragraph which acknowledges that education should prepare the individual to make a livelihood although it shouldn't stop there. Alternative D goes beyond the paragraph in that it affirms that each individual *must* enjoy scientific literature whereas the original statement simply suggests that life in general would be limited if the riches of science, art and literature were not available for appreciation and enjoyment.

TEST II. SYNONYMS

Many Federal jobs require the use of clear and succinct verbal and written expression. Basic vocabulary limitations impede the precise correspondence of words and concepts and thus hinder effective language communication. Accordingly, the following questions present a key word and five suggested answers. The competitor's task is to find the suggested answer that is closest in meaning to the key word. The wrong alternatives may have a more or less valid connection with the key word. In some cases, therefore, the right choice differs from a wrong choice only in the degree to which its meaning comes close to that of the key word.

1. *Subsume* means most nearly
   A) understate
   B) absorb
   C) include
   D) belong
   E) cover

To *subsume* means to include within a larger class or order (alternative C). Alternative A is unrelated in meaning. Alternatives D and E are somewhat related since an element included in a group or class can be said to belong to it and to be covered by it. To a degree, likewise, it may be said that an element included in a group or class is absorbed (alternative B) by the group or class, although strictly speaking, a subsumed element partially preserves its individual identity whereas an absorbed element does not.

2. *Notorious* means most nearly
   A) condemned
   B) unpleasant
   C) vexatious
   D) pretentious
   E) well-known

Notorious means being or constituting something commonly known. Thus alternative E is almost synonymous in meaning. Alternatives B, C and D are unrelated in meaning, since a notorious individual may or may not be unpleasant, vexatious or pretentious. Alternative A hinges on a secondary nuance of the word notorious: being widely and unfavorably known. However, being unfavorably well-known does not necessarily imply being condemned.

3. *Novices* means most nearly
   A) volunteers
   B) experts
   C) trainers
   D) beginners
   E) amateurs

Novice designates one who has no training or experience in a specific field or activity and is hence a beginner (alternative D). An expert (alternative B) is therefore the exact opposite. A trainer (alternative C) may or may not be an expert but must certainly have a certain amount of knowledge. Volunteers (alternative A) are in most cases not novices since they usually volunteer for something they are knowledgeable in. An amateur (alternative E) is one who engages in a particular pursuit, study or science as a pastime rather than as a profession. Thus an amateur may be a novice in the initial stages of formal training, but more often than not will be an expert who has acquired expertise in a particular field through the consistent pursuit of a pastime or pleasure.

4. To *succumb* means most nearly
   A) to aid
   B) to oppose
   C) to yield
   D) to check
   E) to be discouraged

To *succumb* is to cease to resist or contend before a superior or overpowering force or desire, hence to yield (alternative C). Alternative B expresses the stage prior to succumbing. Alternative A is not related except perhaps accidentally—an individual who succumbs may involuntarily serve the purpose of the overpowering force. Alternative D is unrelated in meaning, and alternative E is related only vaguely in the sense that the succumbing party may be susceptible to discouragement.

Deriving General Principles from Particular Data

This is a test of your ability to formulate and test hypotheses. The data presented may be a series of letters or a group of symbols. You must determine the relationship or analogy that exists among the letters or symbols given, and then predict what the next alternative will be.

TEST III. LETTER SERIES

The ability to discover the underlying relations or analogies existing among specific data is important in many Federal jobs where solving problems involves the formation and testing of hypotheses. The questions in this section test this ability. Each question consists of a series of letters arranged in a definite pattern. The competitor must discover what the pattern is and decide which alternative gives the next letter in the series.

1. b c d b c e b c f b c g

   A) b B) c C) h D) i E) e

   The answer is A. The sequence maintains two letters (b c) in the same order while the third letter is in consecutive alphabetical order (d e f g). The pattern b c g has been completed and the next letter should begin the pattern b c h.

2. b c c c d e e e f g g g h i i

   A) g B) h C) i D) j E) f

   The answer is C. The pattern consists of letters written in alphabetical order with every second letter repeated three times. Since the last letter in the sequence, the i, is only repeated twice, it should be repeated a third time.

3. b n c d n e f g n h i j k

   A) n B) l C) m D) i E) j

   The answer is A. The sequence consists of a fixed letter (n) placed after consecutive letter periods. These periods acquire an additional letter each time and begin with the letter which alphabetically follows the last letter in the preceding period, i.e., *bn cdn efgn hijk*. The letter n must therefore be placed after the last period.

4. b c d b e f g e h i j h k l m

   A) k B) h C) l D) n E) o

   The answer is A. The series is an alphabetical progression of four-letter sequences where each fourth letter repeats the first letter of each sequence: *bcdb efge hijh klmk*.

TEST IV. ABSTRACT REASONING

As in the previous section the questions in this section measure the ability to discover the underlying relations or analogies existing among specific data. Each question consists of two sets of symbols where a common characteristic exists among the symbols in each set and where an analogy is maintained between the two sets of symbols. The competitor must discover which alternative gives the symbol that simultaneously preserves the characteristic common to the symbols in the second set and the analogy with the symbols in the first set.

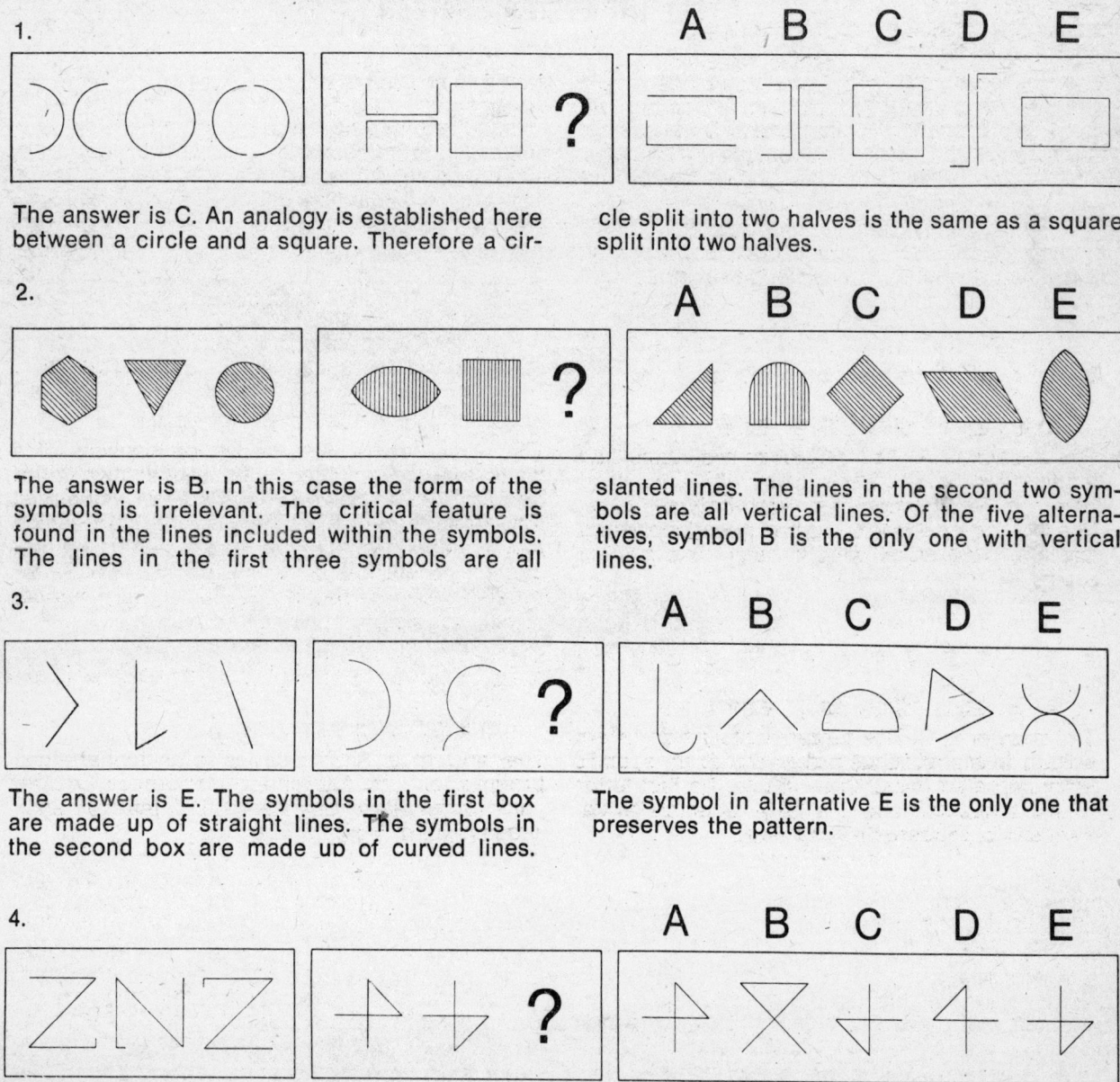

The answer is C. An analogy is established here between a circle and a square. Therefore a circle split into two halves is the same as a square split into two halves.

The answer is B. In this case the form of the symbols is irrelevant. The critical feature is found in the lines included within the symbols. The lines in the first three symbols are all slanted lines. The lines in the second two symbols are all vertical lines. Of the five alternatives, symbol B is the only one with vertical lines.

The answer is E. The symbols in the first box are made up of straight lines. The symbols in the second box are made up of curved lines. The symbol in alternative E is the only one that preserves the pattern.

The answer is C. The first three symbols are identical except for their orientation—the orientation of the second symbol is a 90° rotation of the first symbol. Likewise the third symbol is a 90° rotation of the second symbol. The symbols in the second box follow the same 90° rotation pattern. Alternative C is the only one that preserves the pattern.

Deriving Conclusions from Given Data

The tests in this section measure analytical and organizational ability. The first part consists of brief passages followed by questions that ask you to draw a logical conclusion about each passage based upon the facts given. The second part presents a jumble of ideas or events to be arranged in logical sequence.

TEST V. READ AND INFER

The development of plans, systems and procedures is an essential function of many Federal jobs. This function entails the ability to analyze given facts and discover their implications, as well as the ability to reason from general principles to the implications of these principles in specific situations. Question-type V tests these analytical abilities. Accordingly, each of the following questions consists of a statement which is to be accepted as true and should not be questioned for the purpose of this test. Following the statement are five alternatives. The correct alternative MUST derive from the information given in the original statement without drawing on additional information. By contrast, the four incorrect alternatives rest, to varying degrees, on the admission of new information.

1. No substantial alterations in the age structure took place between 1960-70 and life expectancy remained the same. A slight drop, nonetheless (from 38 to 37 per cent), is noted in the proportion of the population 20 years of age and younger.
   Therefore, between 1960-70
   A) the proportion of the productive-age population increased
   B) there was a slight decrease in fertility rates
   C) there was a decrease in emigration
   D) there was a slight increase in infant mortality
   E) production remained substantially the same

The correct alternative, A, follows from the data that there was a slight drop in the proportion of the population under 20 years of age and that life expectancy remained the same. Alternatives B and D are possible explanations of the slight decrease in the proportion of the younger population but do not derive from the original statement and would require additional evidence. Alternative C would likewise require additional information and would seem to apply more as a partial and possible explanation of a decrease in the productive-age population. Alternative E in no way derives from the given data since many factors affect production besides the age structure of the population.

2. A robot can take a walk in order to mail a letter; it can play chess, build other machines and generally exhibit rule-governed behavior. A robot can kill a person but, unlike a person, it cannot be ashamed. It can be annoying but not annoyed. It can *perhaps* exhibit behavior *as if* it were ashamed or annoyed.
   A) Robots are capable of thought.
   B) Robots can do things that people do but cannot be what people are.
   C) Robots and people are outwardly the same.
   D) Robots can make conscious decisions but have no moral consciousness.
   E) Robots never exhibit their inner thoughts and realities.

The correct alternative, B, derives its conclusion from the joint consideration of the actions enumerated in the original statement as actions that a robot can perform—mailing a letter, playing chess, killing a person—and the conscious states that are enumerated as impossible in a robot, i.e., being ashamed or annoyed. Furthermore, the last sentence in the original statement contrasts outward behaviors with the actual conscious states they represent. Alternative A rests on the assumption that thought can be equated with exhibited behavior and not with inner consciousness. Alternative C assumes not only that all exhibited behavior is the same but that the outward *appearance* of a robot and a person is the same. Alternative D correctly derives a section of its conclusion—the lack of moral consciousness—from the stated fact that a robot cannot be ashamed, but assumes that a robot can kill a person after making a *conscious* decision, which contradicts the original statement. Alternative E likewise affirms, in contradiction of the original statement, that robots have inner consciousness.

3. The Thirty Years' War, 1618 to 1648, established the principle of religious toleration among the German states, but it also reduced the German population by at least one-third, and much of the cultivated land became wilderness.
   Therefore, the Thirty Years' War
   A) altered the geographical boundaries of the German states
   B) was generally beneficial to the German states
   C) was fought on German soil
   D) established a large number of religions within the German states
   E) caused the German population to become widely scattered

The correct alternative, C, derives its conclusion from the given facts that the German population was reduced by one-third and much of the cultivated land became wilderness. Alternative A, on the other hand, assumes the establishment of new borders from the extraneous information that borders are usually changed by wars. Alternative B derives its conclusion from the assumption that religious tolerance creates a surrounding influence beneficial to all aspects of national life. Alternative D assumes an equation between religious tolerance and religious pluralism, and alternative E likewise assumes an equation between the reduction of the population and the scattering of the population.

4. Though easy to learn, backgammon is a surprisingly subtle and complex game to play very well. It is a game that calls for mastery of the laws of probability and the ability to weigh and undertake frequent shifts in strategy.
   Therefore, a necessary quality for playing backgammon very well is
   A) the ability to deceive the opponent
   B) a willingness to take calculated risks
   C) a high degree of manual dexterity
   D) the ability to make quick decisions
   E) a mastery of advanced mathematics

The correct alternative, B, derives its conclusion from the given fact that the game is based on decisions of probability. Thus the player must take calculated risks. The four incorrect alternatives, on the other hand, rest on assumptions that, to varying degrees, go beyond the original statement. Alternative E, for example, assumes that a mastery of the laws of probability entails a more generic mastery of advanced mathematics. Alternative D assumes that frequent shifts in strategy cannot be carried out slowly.

TEST VI. LOGICAL SEQUENCE

As in the previous section the questions in this section measure the ability to solve a problem when all the facts relevant to its solution are not given. More specifically, many Federal jobs require the employee to discover connections between events sometimes apparently unrelated. In order to do this the employee will find it necessary to correctly infer that unspecified events have probably occurred or are likely to occur. This ability becomes especially important when action must be taken on incomplete information. Accordingly, these questions require competitors to choose among five suggested alternatives, each of which presents a different sequential arrangement of five events. Competitors must choose the MOST logical of the five suggested sequences. In order to do so, they MAY be required to draw on general knowledge to infer missing concepts or events that are essential to sequencing the five given events. Competitors should be careful to infer only what is essential to the sequence. The plausibility of the wrong alternatives will always require the inclusion of unlikely events or of additional chains of events which are NOT essential to sequencing the five given events.

1.
   1. a body was found in the woods
   2. a man proclaimed innocence
   3. the owner of a gun was located
   4. a gun was traced
   5. the owner of a gun was questioned
      A) 4-3-5-2-1
      B) 2-1-4-3-5
      C) 1-4-3-5-2
      D) 1-3-5-2-4
      E) 1-2-4-3-5

2.
   1. a man was in a hunting accident
   2. a man fell down a flight of steps
   3. a man lost his vision in one eye
   4. a man broke his leg
   5. a man had to walk with a cane
      A) 2-4-5-1-3
      B) 4-5-1-3-2
      C) 3-1-4-5-2
      D) 1-3-5-2-4
      E) 1-3-2-4-5

The correct alternative, C, interrelates the events in the simplest and most logical sequence: if a body is found (1), it is probable that a weapon will be found and traced (4), that its owner will then be located (3) and questioned (5) and that he will proclaim his innocence (2). The plausibility of alternatives A and B rests on a more involved and less logical sequence because it requires the inclusion of an additional chain of events in order to make the discovery of a body (1) follow from a proclamation of innocence (2). The plausibility of alternative D likewise requires the inclusion of an additional chain of events to explain why a man would be located and questioned before the gun was traced. Sequence E rests on the assumption that the owner of the gun and the man proclaiming innocence are two persons. In this case the man proclaiming innocence loses his relation to the other events and becomes superfluous unless additional events are included.

The correct alternative, E, provides the most likely causal relationship for the five events. Accidents with weapons such as those used when hunting (1) can result in a loss of vision (3). One-eyed vision impedes depth perception and could result in a fall down a flight of steps (2) causing a broken leg (4) and necessitating the use of a cane (5). Alternatives A and B are less plausible because they establish a causal relationship between walking with a cane and having the type of hunting accident that results in loss of vision. In addition, it is less likely that a man with a broken leg would go hunting than that a man with impaired vision would have to go up or down steps. Alternative D is less plausible than E because a broken leg rather than impaired vision is likely to necessitate the use of a cane. Alternative C is less plausible than E because it is likely that a loss of vision will follow rather than precede a hunting accident. Also, a broken leg is more likely to result from a fall than from a hunting accident.

3.
1. a man is offered a new job
2. a woman is offered a new job
3. a man works as a waiter
4. a woman works as a waitress
5. a woman gives notice
   A) 4-2-5-3-1
   B) 4-2-5-1-3
   C) 2-4-5-3-1
   D) 3-1-4-2-5
   E) 4-3-2-5-1

The correct alternative, B, provides the best temporal sequence for the five events by establishing a causal relationship where the three events concerning the woman trigger the two events concerning the man. A woman works as a waitress (4); she is offered a new job (2); gives notice to her employer (5); who offers her job to a man (1); who begins work as a waiter (3) when the woman leaves. The other four alternatives describe plausible situations but do not establish a causal relationship between the two sets of events. Thus if the new job that is offered to the man is not the one vacated by the woman, there is no way to determine whether a woman works as a waitress (4) before a man works as a waiter (3) or vice versa unless additional events are included.

4.
1. a train left the station late
2. a man was late for work
3. a man lost his job
4. many people complained because the train was late
5. there was a traffic jam
   A) 5-2-1-4-3
   B) 5-1-4-2-3
   C) 5-1-2-4-3
   D) 1-5-4-2-3
   E) 2-1-4-5-3

The correct alternative, A, follows from the inference that the man who is late for work is essential to the departure of the train. This is the only assumption that leads to a logical and interrelated sequence for the five events. The other four alternatives do not really interrelate the events and become plausible only if numerous assumptions are made. In addition, the four alternatives sever the connection between the numerous complaints (4) and the lost job (3). Without this connection event 4 becomes superfluous.

Quantitative Ability

This test covers arithmetic computation and problem solving. The questions may involve fractions, percentages, decimals and algebra. In most cases, a single problem will require three or four computational operations—addition, subtraction, multiplication, and division—to reach the correct solution.

TEST VII. MATHEMATICS

DIRECTIONS: In the following multiple choice questions, choose the correct answer from the choices offered.

1. $113^{17}/_{52} - 33^{5}/_{13} =$
   A) $79^{49}/_{52}$
   B) $80^{3}/_{52}$
   C) $80^{12}/_{52}$
   D) $80^{49}/_{52}$
   E) None of these

The answer is A. First of all fractions are reduced to a common denominator. Additionally, since the fraction being subtracted is larger than the one it is to be subtracted from, a unit must be taken from the whole number, 113, reducing it ito 112. The borrowed unit is converted into fraction form and added to 17/52, i.e., $^{52}/_{52} + {}^{17}/_{52} = {}^{69}/_{52}$. The subtraction is then carried out: $112^{69}/_{52} - 33^{20}/_{52} = 79^{49}/_{52}$.

2. $\dfrac{16 \times 17}{(57 + 79)\,4} =$

   A) .50
   B) .72
   C) 1.9
   D) 8.0
   E) None of these

The answer is A. The numbers in parentheses are added, $57 + 79 = 136$ and 136 is then broken into $17 \times 2 \times 4$. Common factors are eliminated:

$$\dfrac{16 \times 17}{(57 + 79)4} = \dfrac{16 \times 17}{(136)4} = \dfrac{16 \times 17}{(17 \times 2 \times 4)4} =$$

$$\dfrac{16 \times 17}{17 \times 2 \times 4 \times 4} = \dfrac{1}{2} = .50$$

3. $221^{1}/_{19} \times 10^{11}/_{35} =$

   A) 80.3
   B) 2510.0
   C) 2510.1
   D) 2280
   E) None of these

The answer is D. Whole numbers are reduced to fractions: $\dfrac{4200}{19} \times \dfrac{361}{35}$. Fractions are broken into their component factors and common factors are eliminated: $\dfrac{7 \times 6 \times 100}{19} \times \dfrac{19 \times 19}{7 \times 5} =$

$\dfrac{7 \times 6 \times 5 \times 20 \times 19 \times 19}{19 \times 7 \times 5} =$
$6 \times 20 \times 19 = 2280$.

4. $\dfrac{(418 + 56 - 8)313}{77 + (50 + 9)7 - 24} =$

   A) -12378
   B) 310
   C) 313
   D) 1246.649
   E) None of these

The answer is C.
$\dfrac{(466)(313)}{77 + (59)7 - 24} = \dfrac{(466)(313)}{77 + 413 - 24} =$
$\dfrac{(466)(313)}{490 - 24} = \dfrac{(466)(313)}{466}$.

Common factors are eliminated and the result is 313.

5. An office supply store buys 100 reams of special quality paper for $400. If 1 ream = 500 sheets of paper, how much must the store receive per 100 sheets to obtain a 20% gain on its cost?

   A) 83¢
   B) 85¢
   C) 96¢
   D) 98¢
   E) None of these

The answer is C. Since 1 ream = 500 sheets, 100 reams = 50000 sheets. To discover the cost of 100 sheets we set up a proportion: $\frac{50000}{100} = \frac{400}{x}$; $50000x = 40000$; $x = \frac{40000}{50000} = 0.80$. The cost of 100 sheets is 80¢. To discover the amount that the store must receive per 100 sheets to obtain a 20% gain on the 80¢ cost, we find what 20% of 80¢ is and add the result: $80 + (0.20)(80) = 80 + 16 = 96¢$.

6. A vase is packed in a carton with a 10" diameter and is surrounded by packing 2" thick at the mouth. If the diameter of the base is ½ the diameter of the mouth, what is the diameter of the base?
    A) 3"
    B) 4"
    C) 6"
    D) 8"
    E) None of these

The answer is A. Since the vase is surrounded by packing 2" thick at the mouth and the diameter of the carton is 10", we subtract: $10 - (2 + 2) = 10 - 4 = 6"$ which is the diameter of the mouth. Since the diameter of the base is ½ the diameter of the mouth: $½(6) = 3"$.

7. Seventy 58" × 34" desks must be stored in a warehouse. If as many desks as possible are stored on the floor of a 15' × 25' room, how many desks will still require storage?
    A) 46
    B) 25
    C) 45
    D) 43
    E) None of these

The answer is C. First of all, the feet are reduced to inches: $15 \times 12 = 180$ and $25 \times 12 = 300$. Next we determine how many times the length of a desk fits into the length of the room and how many times the width of a desk fits into the width of the room: $\frac{180}{34} = 5\frac{10}{34}$ and $\frac{300}{58} = 5\frac{10}{58}$. We then multiply the whole numbers, which means multiplying the number of desks per row by the number of rows: $5 \times 5 = 25$. Since 25 desks fit in the room, 45 desks will still require storage $(70 - 25 = 45)$.

Alternative D is obtained by multiplying the width and length of the room and the width and length of a desk and dividing the total storage area by the total area of a desk: $180 \times 300 = 54000$ and $58 \times 34 = 1972$; $54000 \div 1972 = 27\frac{189}{493}$. Since $70 - 27 = 43$, more desks would fit in the same area. However, this solution is incorrect because it does not take into account that the storage space cannot be filled *completely* with desks. The shape of the desks is not adjustable to the shape of the room and there would always be unfilled spaces. Alternative A is obtained by determining how many times the width of a desk fits into the length of the room and the length of a desk fits into the width of the room: $\frac{300}{34} = 8\frac{14}{17}$ and $\frac{180}{58} = 3\frac{3}{29}$. The multiplication of the whole numbers yields 24, and $70 - 24 = 46$. One more desk actually fits into the storage area if we follow the process used to obtain the correct answer, alternative C.

8. A mechanic repairs 16 cars per 8-hour day. Another mechanic in the same shop repairs 1½ times this number in ¾ the time. Theoretically, how long will it take to repair 16 cars in the shop?
    A) 2⅔ hours
    B) 2⁹⁄₁₀ hours
    C) 3 hours
    D) 2½ hours
    E) None of these

The answer is A. For the second mechanic we obtain 1½ of 16 cars: $\frac{3}{2} \times 16 = 24$ and ¾ of 8 hours: $\frac{3}{4} \times 8 = 6$ hours. The second mechanic therefore repairs 24 cars per 6-hour day. Secondly we determine how many cars each mechanic repairs per hour—the first mechanic: 2 cars/hr. and the second mechanic 4 cars/hr. Therefore 6 cars are repaired every hour if both outputs are added. Lastly we determine how many hours are required to repair 16 cars: we divide the 16 cars by the 6 cars/hr. which yields 2⅔ hrs.

42 / P.A.C.E. Professional-Administrative Career Exam

TEST VIII. TABLE INTERPRETATION

DIRECTIONS: Read each question in this test carefully. Answer each one on the basis of the following table. Select the best answer among the given choices and blacken the proper space on the answer sheet at the end of the test.

TABLE I: GENERAL REVENUE OF STATE AND LOCAL GOVERNMENTS—STATES: 1970

REVENUE PER CAPITA (dollars) — Based on resident population

REVENUE (dollars) PER $1,000 OF PERSONAL INCOME IN CALENDAR YEAR, 1969:

STATE	Total amount (mil. dol.)	Total	From Federal Government	All taxes	Property tax	Other	Charges and miscellaneous	Total	From Federal Government	Total	Taxes	Charges and miscellaneous
Ala.	1,722	I	131	258	39	219	110	190	50	140	98	42
Alaska	1,259	4,168	358	417	102	315	3,393	1,001	86	915	II	815
Ariz.	1,172	662	121	426	166	260	115	206	38	168	132	36
Ark.	871	453	115	252	65	187	86	176	45	131	98	33
Calif.	17,028	853	164	559	262	297	130	204	39	165	134	31
Colo.	1,474	666	III	419	179	240	123	194	36	158	122	36
Conn.	1,970	649	85	484	238	246	80	144	19	125	107	18
Del.	379	692	88	450	84	366	154	172	22	150	112	38
D.C.	IV	953	359	517	169	348	77	192	72	120	104	16
Fla.	3,576	528	69	347	118	229	112	160	21	139	105	34

1. What is the value of I?
   A) 800
   B) 600
   C) 499
   D) 757
   E) None of these, or cannot be calculated from data provided

The answer is C. The figure represents the total Revenue per Capita which is obtained by adding the three major columns therein: Charges and miscellaneous, All taxes and Federal Government: 110 + 258 + 131 = 499. Alternative D represents an erroneous double addition of the Property tax and Other subcolumns, the amounts corresponding to which were already included in the All taxes column. Alternatives A and B are irrelevant values.

2. What is the value of II?
   A) 392
   B) 828
   C) 100
   D) 1814
   E) None of these, or cannot be calculated from data provided

The answer is C. It is obtained by subtracting Charges and miscellaneous from the Total Revenue from own sources: 915 − 815 = 100. Alternatives A, B and D are irrelevant values.

3. What is the value of III?
   A) 124
   B) 141
   C) 176
   D) 203
   E) None of these, or cannot be calculated from data provided

The answer is A. It is obtained by adding the two major columns for which values are given in the Revenue per Capita subdivision, All taxes and Charges and miscellaneous, and subtracting the result from the total Revenue per Capita: 419 + 123 = 542; 666 − 542 = 124. Alternatives B, C and D are irrelevant values.

4. What is the value of IV?
   A) 725
   B) 687
   C) 710
   D) 1144
   E) None of these, or cannot be calculated from data provided

The answer is E. The Total General Revenue cannot be calculated, since the total population figure is missing. This figure should be multiplied by the Per Capita Income to obtain the Total Revenue. Alternative D erroneously adds the totals for Revenue per Capita and Revenue per $1,000 of Personal Income: 192 + 953 = 1145. Alternatives A, B and C are irrelevant values.

Deriving Conclusions from Incomplete Data

This part of the exam provides a measure of your ability to solve a problem when all the necessary facts are not stated. To answer the questions correctly, you will have to supplement the facts from your store of general knowledge or make reasonable assumptions to fill in the missing information.

TEST IX. APPLYING GENERAL KNOWLEDGE

DIRECTIONS: For each question in this test, read carefully the stem and the five lettered choices that follow. Choose the answer which you consider correct or most nearly correct. Mark the answer sheet for the letter you have chosen: A, B, C, D, or E.

1. The development of a country's water power is advocated as a means of conserving natural resources CHIEFLY because such a hydroelectric policy would tend to
   A) stimulate the growth of industries in hitherto isolated regions
   B) encourage the substitution of machinery for hand labor
   C) provide a larger market for coal
   D) make cheap electricity available in rural areas
   E) lessen the use of irreplaceable fuel materials

Of the five alternatives, the correct alternative, E, derives from the fundamental or most essential reason for the endorsement of a hydroelectric policy, i.e., water is not a depletable energy resource. Alternatives A and D are plausible but are not as determinative as E. Alternative C is easily discarded since coal would have a larger market in the absence of hydroelectric power. Alternative B is also easily discarded since hydroelectric energy would increase the availability of both the fuel and/or electricity needed to run machinery.

2. Complaints by the owners of large cars that they cannot see an already-parked small car in a parking lot until they have begun to pull into a space, are BEST justified if
   A) there are few empty parking spaces in the lot
   B) the small car has been parked for a long time
   C) the owners of large cars have poor vision
   D) there is a designated parking area for small cars
   E) there are few other small cars in the lot

The correct alternative, D, hinges on the fact that strict *justification* for a complaint is more firmly rooted in legality than in individual situations or attitudes. Thus, for example, the owner of a large car who happens to find few empty parking spaces in a lot (alternative A), or who knows or assumes that a small car has been parked in a certain space for a long time (alternative B), can justify his or her annoyance only on the subjective level. On the other hand if a small car is parked in a space designated for large cars, the individual's annoyance and complaint acquire objective and formal justification.

3. A country that is newly settled usually produces very little art, music or literature. The MOST REASONABLE explanation of this fact is that
   A) its people have had few experiences to draw on
   B) there is little use for such work
   C) suitable materials for such work must be imported
   D) the physical development of the country absorbs most of the interest and energy of the people
   E) there is as yet no governmental encouragement of the arts

The correct alternative, D, presents the most basic explanation for the lack of artistic production in a newly-settled country. The development of a newly-settled country necessitates the undivided attention of its people, and manpower is thus basically unavailable for the production of art, music or literature. Alternative A is implausible since newly-settled people have many experiences which are eventually represented in the art, music and literature of later generations. Alternatives B, C and E make assumptions about conditions necessary for the production of art, music and literature which are only partially valid. Alternative B incorrectly assumes that art is always produced for utilitarian purposes. Alternative C partially applies to art and music but not at all to literature. Alternative E is only partially plausible. The government of a newly-settled country is likely to encourage the production of goods rather than the production of art, music or literature. However, artistic production can occur without governmental encouragement.

4. The CHIEF reason why every society has certain words and concepts that are never precisely translated into the language of another society is that
   A) the art of good translation is as yet not sufficiently developed
   B) there is too great a disparity between the intellectual levels attained by different societies
   C) every society possesses cultural elements which are unique to itself
   D) words and concepts never express the true nature of a society
   E) every society has some ideas which it does not wish to share with other societies

The correct alternative, C, is the most basic reason why certain concepts are never precisely translated. Languages express the socio-political contexts in which they are spoken and are bound to have expressions that are unique to these contexts. Alternative A fails to distinguish between the qualitative and the quantitative. Whereas the art of good translation appears to be as yet not sufficiently widespread, it is indeed available. Furthermore its total unavailability would still constitute a secondary explanation, over and against alternative C, for the impossibility of the precise translation of certain words. Alternative B rests on the assumption that *all* existing societies are substantially disparate in their level of development, which is known not to be the case. Alternative D assumes the truth of the postulate expounded by some philosophical theories that words and concepts have no referential value. Alternative E presents a farfetched ethical judgment whose plausibility rests on the assumption that social groups are secretive and that the function of language is to exclude communication beyond the social group.

Professional & Administrative Career Exam

TECHNIQUES OF STUDY AND TEST-TAKING

Although a thorough knowledge of the subject matter is the most important factor in succeeding on your exam, the following suggestions could raise your score substantially. These few pointers will give you the strategy employed on tests by those who are most successful in this not-so-mysterious art. It's really quite simple. Do things right . . . right from the beginning. Make successful methods a habit. Then you'll get the greatest dividends from the time you invest in this book.

PREPARING FOR THE EXAM

1. *Budget your time.* Set aside definite hours each day for concentrated study. Adhere closely to this budget. Don't fritter away your time with excessive "breaks." A cup of coffee, a piece of fruit, a look out of the window—they're fine, but not too often.

2. *Study with a friend or a group.* The exchange of ideas that this arrangement affords may be very beneficial. It is also more pleasant getting together in study sessions. Be sure, though, that you ban "socializing." Talk about friends, dates, trips, etc. at some other time.

3. *Eliminate distractions.* Psychologists tell us that study efforts will reap much more fruit when there is little or no division of attention. Disturbances caused by family and neighbor activities (telephone calls, chit-chat, TV programs, etc.) will work to your disadvantage. Study in a quiet, private room. Better still, use the library.

4. *Use the library.* Most colleges and universities have excellent library facilities. Some institutions have special libraries for the various subject areas: Physics library, Education library, Psychology library, etc. Take full advantage of such valuable facilities. The library is free from those distractions that may inhibit your home study. Moreover, research in your subject area is so much more convenient in a library since it can provide much more study material than you have at home.

5. *Answer all the questions in this book.* Don't be satisfied merely with the correct answer to each question. Do additional research on the other choices which are given. You will broaden your background to be adequately prepared for the "real" exam. It's quite possible that a question on the exam which you are going to take may require you to be familiar with the other choices.

6. *Get the "feel" of the exam.* The sample questions which this book contains will give you that "feel." Gestalt (meaning *configuration* or *pattern*) psychology stresses that true learning results in a grasp of the *entire situation.* Gestaltists also tell us that we learn by "insight." One of the salient facets of this type of learning is that we succeed in "seeing through" a problem as a consequence of experiencing *previous similar situations.* This book contains hundreds of "similar situations"—as you will discover when you take the actual exam.

7. *Take the Sample Tests as "real" tests.* With this attitude, you will derive greater benefit. Put yourself under strict examination conditions. Tolerate no interruptions while you are taking the sample tests. Work steadily. Do not spend too much time on any one question. If a question seems too difficult go to the next one. If time permits, go back to the omitted question.

8. *Tailor your study to the subject matter. Skim or scan.* Don't study everything in the same manner. Francis Bacon (1561-1626) expressed it this way: "Some books are to be tasted, others to be swallowed, and some few to be chewed and digested."

9. *Organize yourself.* Make sure that your notes are in good order—also, that your desk top is neat. Valuable time is consumed unnecessarily when you can't find quickly what you are looking for.

10. *Keep physically fit.* You cannot retain information well when you are uncomfortable, headachy, or tense. Physical health promotes mental efficiency. Guarding your health takes into account such factors as these:

a. Sufficient sleep
b. Daily exercise and recreation
c. Annual physical examination
d. A balanced diet
e. Avoidance of eyestrain
f. Mental health

HOW TO TAKE AN EXAM

1. *Get to the Examination Room about Ten Minutes Ahead of Time.* You'll start better when you are accustomed to the room. If the room is too cold, or too warm, or not well ventilated, call these conditions to the attention of the person in charge.

2. *Make Sure that you Read the Instructions Carefully.* In many cases, test-takers lose credits because they misread some important point in the given directions—example: the *incorrect* choice instead of the *correct* choice.

3. *Be Confident.* Statistics conclusively show that success is likely when you have prepared faithfully. It is important to know that you are not expected to answer every question correctly. The questions usually have a range of difficulty and differentiate between several levels of skill. It's quite possible that an "A" student might answer no more than 60% of the questions correctly.

4. *Skip Hard Questions and Go Back Later.* It is a good idea to make a mark on the question sheet next to all questions you cannot answer easily, and to go back to those questions later. First answer the questions you are sure about. Do not panic if you cannot answer a question. Go on and answer the questions you know. Usually the easier questions are presented at the beginning of the exam and the questions become gradually more difficult.

If you do skip ahead on the exam, be sure to skip ahead also on your answer sheet. A good technique is periodically to check the number of the question on the answer sheet with the number of the question on the test. You should do this every time you decide to skip a question. If you fail to skip the corresponding answer blank for that question, all of your following answers will be wrong.

Each student is stronger in some areas than in others. No one is expected to know all the answers. Do not waste time agonizing over a difficult question because it may keep you from getting to other questions that you can answer correctly.

5. *Guess If You Are Not Sure.* No correction is made for guessing when this exam is scored. Therefore, it is better to guess than to omit an answer.

6. *Mark the Answer Sheet Clearly.* When you take the examination, you will mark your answers to the multiple-choice questions on a separate answer sheet that will be given to you at the test center. If you have not worked with an answer sheet before, it is in your best interest to become familiar with the procedures involved. Remember, knowing the correct answer is not enough! If you do not mark the sheet correctly, so that it can be machine scored, you will not get credit for your answers!

In addition to marking answers on the separate answer sheet, you might also be asked to give your name and other information, including your social security number. As a precaution bring along your social security number for identification purposes.

Read the directions carefully and follow them exactly. If they ask you to print your name in the boxes provided, write only one letter in each box. If your name is longer than the number of boxes provided, omit the letters that do not fit. Remember, you are writing for a machine; it does not have judgment. It can only record the pencil marks you make on the answer sheet.

Use the answer sheet to record all your answers to questions. Each question, or item, has four or five answer choices labeled (A), (B), (C), (D), (E). You will be asked to choose the letter for the alternative that best answers each question. Then you will be asked to mark your answer by blackening the appropriate space on your answer sheet. Be sure that each space you choose and blacken with your pencil is *completely* blackened. If you change your mind about an answer, or mark the wrong space in error, you must erase the wrong answer. Erase as thoroughly and neatly as possible. The machine will "read" your answers in terms of spaces blackened. Make sure that only one answer is clearly blackened. If you erase an answer, erase it completely and mark your new answer clearly. The machine will give credit only for clearly marked answers. It does not pause to decide whether you really meant (B) or (C).

Make sure that the number of the question you are being asked on the question sheet corresponds to the number of the question you are answering on the answer sheet. It is a good idea to check the numbers of questions and answers frequently. If you decide to skip a question, but fail to skip the corresponding answer blank for that question, all your answers after that will be wrong.

7. *Read Each Question Carefully.* The exam questions are not designed to trick you through misleading or ambiguous alternative choices. On the other hand, they are not all direct questions of factual information. Some are designed to elicit responses that reveal your ability to reason, or to interpret a fact or idea. It's up to you to read each question carefully so you know what is being asked. The exam authors have tried to make the questions clear. Do not go too far astray in looking for hidden meanings.

8. *Don't Answer Too Fast.* The multiple-choice questions which you will meet are not superficial exercises. They are designed to test not only rote recall, but also understanding and insight. Watch for deceptive choices. Do not place too much emphasis on speed. The time element is a factor, but it is not all-important. Accuracy should not be sacrificed for speed.

9. *Materials and Conduct At The Test Center.* You need to bring with you to the test center your Admission Form, your social security number, and several No. 2 pencils. Arrive on time as you may not be admitted after testing has begun. Instructions for taking the tests will be read to you by the test supervisor and time will be called when the test is over. If you have questions, you may ask them of the supervisor. Do not give or receive assistance while taking the exams. If you do, you will be asked to turn in all test materials and told to leave the room. You will not be permitted to return and your tests will not be scored.

Professional & Administrative Career Exam

PART TWO

A Sample Exam For Practice

Understanding and Using Written Language

This part of the exam tests both reading comprehension and word knowledge. The reading test consists of brief paragraphs followed by one or more questions. In each case, the correct answer is either a restatement of the main concept of the passage, or a conclusion inherent in its content. The vocabulary questions require making fine distinctions in meaning among closely related words.

Deriving General Principles from Particular Data

This is a test of your ability to formulate and test hypotheses. The data presented may be a series of letters or a group of symbols. You must determine the relationship or analogy that exists among the letters or symbols given, and then predict what the next alternative will be.

Deriving Conclusions from Given Data

The tests in this section measure analytical and organizational ability. The first part consists of brief passages followed by questions that ask you to draw a logical conclusion about each passage based upon the facts given. The second part presents a jumble of ideas or events to be arranged in logical sequence.

Quantitative Ability

This test covers arithmetic computation and problem solving. The questions may involve fractions, percentages, decimals and algebra. In most cases, a single problem will require three or four computational operations—addition, subtraction, multiplication, and division—to reach the correct solution.

Understanding Charts and Tables

These tables and charts cover a variety of fields of work, and require of you no previous knowledge of the subject. Each set of questions is to be answered solely on the basis of the table or chart shown. Before answering each set of questions, look over the data given to you and get a good, general idea of what it means. Then, in answering the questions, refer back to the given data, and let who will be clever.

Deriving Conclusions from Incomplete Data

This part of the exam provides a measure of your ability to solve a problem when all the necessary facts are not stated. To answer the questions correctly, you will have to supplement the facts from your store of general knowledge or make reasonable assumptions to fill in the missing information.

Professional & Administrative Career Exam

FIRST SAMPLE EXAM FOR PRACTICE

To begin your studies, test yourself now to see how you measure up. This examination is similar to the one you'll get, and is therefore a practical yardstick for charting your progress and planning your course. Adhere strictly to all test instructions. Mark yourself honestly and you'll find where your weaknesses are and where to concentrate your study.

The time allowed for the entire examination is 3 ½ hours. In order to create the climate of the test to come, that's precisely what you should allow yourself ... no more, no less. Use a watch and keep a record of your time, especially since you may find it convenient to take the test in several sittings.

In constructing this Examination we tried to visualize the questions you are *likely* to face on your actual exam. We included those subjects on which they are *probably* going to test you.

Although copies of past exams are not released, we were able to piece together a fairly complete picture of the forthcoming exam.

A principal source of information was our analysis of official announcements going back several years.

Critical comparison of these announcements, particularly the sample questions, revealed the testing trend; foretold the important subjects, and those that are likely to recur.

In making up the Tests we predict for your exam, great care was exercised to prepare questions having just the difficulty level you'll encounter on your exam. Not easier; not harder, but just what you may expect.

The various subjects expected on your exam are represented by separate Tests. Each Test has just about the number of questions you may find on the actual exam. And each Test is timed accordingly.

The questions on each Test are represented exactly on the special Answer Sheet provided. Mark your answers on this sheet. It's just about the way you'll have to do it on the real exam.

As a result you have an Examination which simulates the real one closely enough to provide you with important training.

Proceed through the entire exam without pausing after each Test. Remember that you are taking this Exam under actual battle conditions, and therefore you do not stop until told to do so by the proctor.

Correct answers for all the questions in all the Tests of this Exam appear at the end of the Exam.

ANALYSIS AND FORECAST: SAMPLE EXAM FOR PRACTICE	
Since the number of questions for each test may vary on different forms of the actual examination, the time allotments below are flexible.	
SUBJECT TESTED	**Time Allowed**

UNDERSTANDING AND USING WRITTEN LANGUAGE
    Read and Deduce
    Synonyms
	35 Min. as follows:
	25 Minutes
	10 Minutes

DERIVING GENERAL PRINCIPLES FROM PARTICULAR DATA
    Letter Series
    Abstract Reasoning
	35 Min. as follows:
	20 Minutes
	15 Minutes

DERIVING CONCLUSIONS FROM GIVEN DATA
    Read and Infer
    Logical Sequence
	35 Min. as follows:
	20 Minutes
	15 Minutes

QUANTITATIVE ABILITY	35 Minutes
CHART AND TABLE INTERPRETATION	35 Minutes
DERIVING CONCLUSIONS FROM INCOMPLETE DATA PLUS GENERAL KNOWLEDGE	35 Minutes

A NOTE ABOUT TEST TIMES.

The time allotted for each Test in each Examination in this book is based on a careful analysis of all the information now available. The time we allot for each test, therefore, merely suggests in a general way approximately how much time you should expend on each subject when you take the actual Exam. We have not, in every case, provided precisely the number of questions you will actually get on the examination. It's just not possible to know what the examiners will finally decide to do for every Test in the Examination. It might be a good idea to jot down your "running" time for each Test, and make comparisons later on. If you find that you're working faster, you may assume you're making progress. Remember, we have timed each Test uniformly. If you follow all our directions, your scores will all be comparable.

/ First Sample Exam / 53

ANSWER SHEET FOR SAMPLE EXAMINATION I.

Consolidate your key answers here just as you would do on the actual exam. Using this type of Answer Sheet will provide valuable practice. Tear it out along the indicated lines and mark it up correctly. Use a No. 2 (medium) pencil. Make only ONE mark for each answer. Additional and stray marks may be counted as mistakes. In making corrections erase errors COMPLETELY. Make glossy black marks.

TEST I. READ AND DEDUCE

(Answer grid: items 1–24, options A B C D E)

TEST II. SYNONYMS

(Answer grid: items 1–24, options A B C D E)

TEST III. LETTER SERIES

(Answer grid: items 1–24, options A B C D E)

TEST IV. ABSTRACT REASONING

(Answer grid: items 1–16, options A B C D E)

TEST V. READ AND INFER

(Answer grid: items 1–16, options A B C D E)

TEST VI. LOGICAL SEQUENCE

(Answer grid: items 1–16, options A B C D E)

TEST VII. MATHEMATICS

TEST VIII. ARITHMETIC COMPUTATION

TEST IX. DATA INTERPRETATION

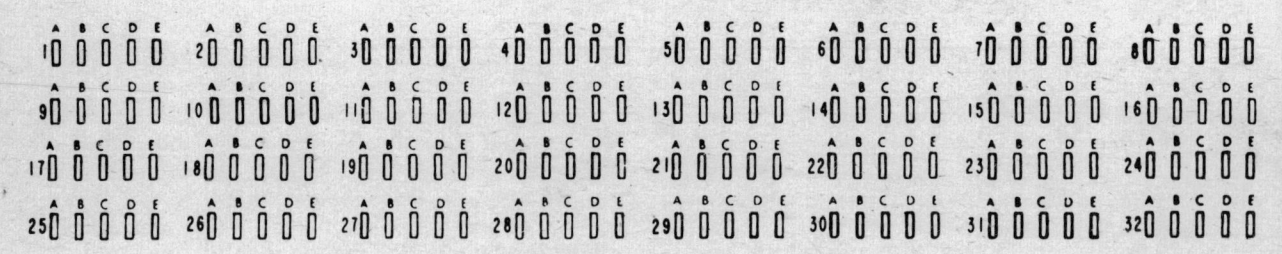

TEST X. APPLYING GENERAL KNOWLEDGE

Understanding and Using Written Language

TEST I. READ AND DEDUCE

TIME: 25 Minutes. 20 Questions.

This test of reading interpretation consists of a number of brief passages. One question is based on each passage. A question consists of an incomplete statement about the passage. The statement is followed by five choices lettered (A) (B) (C) (D) (E). For each question, mark your answer sheet with the letter of that choice which best conveys the meaning of the passage, and which best completes the statement.

Correct answers for these questions appear at the end of this examination, together with the answers to all the other tests.

1. "Iron is used in making our bridges and skyscrapers, subways and steamships, railroads and automobiles, and nearly all kinds of machinery—besides millions of small articles varying from the farmer's scythe to the woman's needle."

    The paragraph best supports the statement that iron
    A) is the most abundant of the metals
    B) has many different uses
    C) is the strongest of all metals
    D) is the only material used in building skyscrapers and bridges
    E) is the most durable of the metals

2. "Some fire-resistant buildings, although wholly constructed of materials that will not burn, may be completely gutted by the spread of fire through their contents by way of hallways and other openings. They may even suffer serious structural damage by the collapse of metal beams and columns."

    The paragraph best supports the statement that some fire-resistant buildings
    A) suffer less damage from fire than from collapse of metal supports
    B) can be damaged seriously by fire
    C) have specially constructed halls and doors
    D) afford less protection to their contents than would ordinary buildings
    E) will burn readily

3. "Life is too short for one person to do very many things well. The person who determines fairly early what he can do that he likes to do, and who goes at it hard and stays with it, is likely to do the best work and find the most peace of mind."

    The paragraph best supports the statement that the reason the average man does not master many different jobs is that he
    A) desires peace of mind
    B) seldom has more than a few interests
    C) is unable to organize his ideas
    D) lacks the necessary time
    E) has a natural tendency to specialize

4. "Both the high school and the college should take the responsibility for preparing the student to get a job. Since the ability to write a good application letter is one of the first steps toward this goal, every teacher should be willing to do what he can to help the student learn to write such letters."

    The paragraph best supports the statement that
    A) inability to write a good letter often reduces one's job prospects
    B) the major responsibility of the school is to obtain jobs for its students
    C) success is largely a matter of the kind of work the student applies for first
    D) every teacher should teach a course in the writing of application letters
    E) letter writing is more important than most subjects taught in high schools and colleges

5. "'White collar' is a term used to describe one of the largest groups of workers in American industry and trade. It distinguishes those who work with the pencil and the mind from those who depend on their hands and the machine. It suggests occupations in which physical exertion and handling of materials are not primary features of the job."

The paragraph best supports the statement that "white collar" workers are
A) the most powerful labor group because of their numbers
B) not so strong physically as those who work with their hands
C) those who supervise workers handling materials
D) all whose work is entirely indoors
E) not likely to use machines so much as are other groups of workers

6. "The location of a railway line is necessarily a compromise between the desire to build the line with as little expense as possible and the desire to construct it so that its route will cover that over which trade and commerce are likely to flow."

The paragraph best supports the statement that the route selected for a railway line
A) should be the one over which the line can be built most cheaply
B) determines the location of commercial centers
C) should always cover the shortest possible distance between its terminals
D) cannot always be the one involving the lowest construction costs
E) is determined chiefly by the kind of production in the area

7. "A survey to determine the subjects that have helped students most in their jobs shows that typewriting leads all other subjects in the business group. It also leads among the subjects college students consider most valuable and would take again if they were to return to high school."

The paragraph best supports the statement that
A) the ability to type is an asset in business and in school
B) students who return to night school take typing
C) students with a knowledge of typing do superior work in college
D) every person should know how to type
E) success in business is assured those who can type

8. "It is a common assumption that city directories are prepared and published by the cities concerned. However, the directory business is as much a private business as is the publishing of dictionaries and encyclopedias. The companies financing the publication make their profits through the sales of the directories themselves and through the advertising in them."

The paragraph best supports the statement that
A) the publication of a city directory is a commercial enterprise
B) the size of a city directory limits the space devoted to advertising
C) many city directories are published by dictionary and encyclopedia concerns
D) city directories are sold at cost to local residents and businessmen
E) the preparation of a city directory, but not the printing, is a responsibility of the local government

9. "Since duplicating machines are being changed constantly, the person who is in the market for such a machine should not purchase offhand the kind with which he is most familiar or the one recommended by the first salesman who calls on him. Instead he should analyze his particular equipment situation and then investigate all the possibilities."

The paragraph best supports the statement that, when duplicating equipment is being purchased,
A) the purchaser should choose equipment that he can use with the least extra training
B) the latest models should always be bought
C) the needs of the purchaser's office should determine the selection
D) the buyer should have his needs analyzed by an office-equipment salesman
E) the recommendations of salesmen should usually be ignored

10. "There has been a slump in first-aid training in the industries, and yet one should not fall into the error of thinking there is less interest in first aid in industry. The falling off has been in the number of new employees needing such training. It appears that in industries interested in first-aid training there is now actually a higher percentage so trained than there ever was before."

The paragraph best supports the statement that first-aid training is
A) a means of avoiding the more serious effects of accidents
B) being abandoned because of expense
C) helpful in every line of work
D) of great importance to employees
E) sometimes given new workers in industry

11. "There exists a false but popular idea that a clue is a mysterious fact which most people overlook but which some very keen investigator easily discovers and recognizes as having, in itself, a remarkable meaning. The clue is most often an ordinary fact which an observant person picks up—something which gains its significance when, after a long series of careful investigations, it is connected with a network of other clues."

    The paragraph best supports the statement that to be of value clues must be
    A) discovered by skilled investigators
    B) found under mysterious circumstances
    C) connected with other facts
    D) discovered soon after the crime
    E) observed many times

12. "It is wise to choose a duplicating machine that will do the work required with the greatest efficiency and at the least cost. Users with a large volume of business need speedy machines that cost little to operate and are well made."

    The paragraph best supports the statement that
    A) most users of duplicating machines prefer low operating cost to efficiency
    B) a well-built machine will outlast a cheap one
    C) a duplicating machine is not efficient unless it is sturdy
    D) a duplicating machine should be both efficient and economical
    E) in duplicating machines speed is more usual than low operating cost

13. "Any business not provided with capable substitutes to fill all important positions is a weak business. Therefore a foreman should train each man not only to perform his own particular duties but also to do those of two or three positions."

    The paragraph best supports the statement that
    A) dependence on substitutes is a sign of a weak organization
    B) training will improve the strongest organization
    C) the foreman should be the most expert at any particular job under him
    D) every employee can be trained to perform efficiently work other than his own
    E) vacancies in vital positions should be provided for in advance

14. "The coloration of textile fabrics composed of cotton and wool generally requires two processes, as the process used in dyeing wool is seldom capable of fixing the color upon cotton. The usual method is to immerse the fabric in the requisite baths to dye the wool and then to treat the partially dyed material in the manner found suitable for cotton."

    The paragraph best supports the statement that the dyeing of textile fabrics composed of cotton and wool
    A) is less complicated than the dyeing of wool alone
    B) is more successful when the material contains more cotton than wool
    C) is not satisfactory when solid colors are desired
    D) is restricted to two colors for any one fabric
    E) is usually based upon the methods required for dyeing the different materials

15. "The Federal investigator must direct his whole effort toward success in his work. If he wishes to succeed in each investigation, his work will be by no means easy, smooth, or peaceful; on the contrary, he will have to devote himself completely and continuously to a task that requires all his ability."

    The paragraph best supports the statement that an investigator's success depends most upon
    A) ambition to advance rapidly in the service
    B) persistence in the face of difficulty
    C) training and experience
    D) willingness to obey orders without delay
    E) the number of investigations which he conducts

16. "Honest people in one nation find it difficult to understand the viewpoint of honest people in another. State departments and their ministers exist for the purpose of explaining the viewpoints of one nation in terms understood by another. Some of their most important work lies in this direction."

    The paragraph best supports the statement that
    A) people of different nations may not consider matters in the same light
    B) it is unusual for many people to share similar ideas
    C) suspicion prevents understanding between nations
    D) the chief work of state departments is to guide relations between nations united by a common cause
    E) the people of one nation must sympathize with the viewpoints of others

17. "Economy once in a while is just not enough. I expect to find it at every level of responsibility, from cabinet member to the newest and youngest recruit. Controlling waste is something like bailing a boat; you have to keep at it. I have no intention of easing up on my insistence on getting a dollar of value for each dollar we spend."

The paragraph best supports the statement that
A) we need not be concerned about items which cost less than a dollar
B) it is advisable to buy the cheaper of two items
C) the responsibility of economy is greater at high levels than at low levels
D) economy becomes easy with practice
E) economy is a continuing responsibility

18. "On all permit imprint mail the charge for postage has been printed by the mailer before he presents it for mailing and pays the postage. Such mail of any class is mailable only at the post office that issued a permit covering it. Since the postage receipts for such mail represent only the amount of permit imprint mail detected and verified, employees in receiving, handling, and outgoing sections must be alert constantly to route such mail to the weighing section before it is handled or dispatched."

The paragraph best supports the statement that, at post offices where permit mail is received for dispatch,
A) dispatching units make a final check on the amount of postage payable on permit imprint mail
B) employees are to check the postage chargeable on mail received under permit
C) neither more nor less postage is to be collected than the amount printed on permit imprint mail
D) the weighing section is primarily responsible for failure to collect postage on such mail
E) unusual measures are taken to prevent unstamped mail from being accepted

19. "Education should not stop when the individual has been prepared to make a livelihood and to live in modern society. Living would be mere existence were there no appreciation and enjoyment of the riches of art, literature, and science."

The paragraph best supports the statement that true education
A) is focused on the routine problems of life
B) prepares one for full enjoyment of life
C) deals chiefly with art, literature and science
D) is not possible for one who does not enjoy scientific literature
E) disregards practical ends

20. "Insured and c.o.d. air and surface mail is accepted with the understanding that the sender guarantees any necessary forwarding or return postage. When such mail is forwarded or returned, it shall be rated up for collection of postage; except that insured or c.o.d. air mail weighing 8 ounces or less and subject to the 10 cents an ounce rate shall be forwarded by air if delivery will be advanced, and returned by surface means, without additional postage."

The paragraph best supports the statement that the return postage for undeliverable insured mail
A) is included in the original prepayment on air mail parcels
B) is computed but not collected before dispatching surface parcel post mail to sender
C) is not computed or charged for any air mail that is returned by surface transportation
D) is included in the amount collected when the sender mails parcel post
E) is collected before dispatching for return if any amount due has been guaranteed

END OF TEST

Go on to do the following Test in this Examination, just as you would be expected to do on the actual exam.

TEST II. SYNONYMS

TIME: 10 Minutes. 20 Questions.

DIRECTIONS: Each of the numbered words given below is followed by four lettered words. For each numbered word, select the lettered word which most nearly defines it.

Correct answers for these questions appear at the end of this examination.

1. CORROBORATION
   - (A) expenditure
   - (B) compilation
   - (C) confirmation
   - (D) reduction.

2. IMPERATIVE
   - (A) impending
   - (B) impossible
   - (C) compulsory
   - (D) logical.

3. FEASIBLE
   - (A) simple
   - (B) practicable
   - (C) visible
   - (D) lenient.

4. SALUTARY
   - (A) popular
   - (B) urgent
   - (C) beneficial
   - (D) forceful.

5. ACQUIESCE
   - (A) endeavor
   - (B) discharge
   - (C) agree
   - (D) inquire.

6. DIFFIDENCE
   - (A) shyness
   - (B) distinction
   - (C) interval
   - (D) discordance.

7. HEINOUS
   - (A) flagrant
   - (B) habitual
   - (C) awful
   - (D) Hellenic.

8. ACCESS
   - (A) too much
   - (B) extra
   - (C) admittance
   - (D) arrival.

9. SUBSEQUENT
   - (A) preceding
   - (B) early
   - (C) following
   - (D) winning.

10. HERITAGE
    - (A) will
    - (B) unbeliever
    - (C) legend
    - (D) inheritance.

11. COHERENT
    - (A) not clear
    - (B) logically related
    - (C) specific
    - (D) courteous.

12. OBESITY
    - (A) bestial
    - (B) corpulence
    - (C) obstinacy
    - (D) instrument.

13. MAIL
    - (A) armor
    - (B) seaside
    - (C) rapid travel
    - (D) wool.

14. PROXIMITY
    - (A) nearness
    - (B) declivity
    - (C) worldliness
    - (D) adherence.

15. HAGGLE
    - (A) dicker
    - (B) nag
    - (C) quarrel
    - (D) buy.

16. AMENABLE
    - (A) pleasant
    - (B) tractable
    - (C) amiable
    - (D) bloodless.

17. PALPABLE
    - (A) savory
    - (B) obvious
    - (C) paltry
    - (D) easy.

18. FLORID
    - (A) seedy
    - (B) flowery
    - (C) ruddy
    - (D) overflowing.

19. FALLACIOUS
    - (A) faltering
    - (B) stumbling
    - (C) deceptive
    - (D) foolish.

20. DOGMA
    - (A) canine
    - (B) creed
    - (C) truth
    - (D) prophecy.

END OF TEST

Deriving General Principles from Particular Data

TEST III. LETTER SERIES

TIME: 20 Minutes. 20 Questions.

DIRECTIONS: Each question consists of a series of letters or numbers (or both) which follow some definite order. Study each series to determine what the order is. Then look at the answer choices. Select the one answer that will complete the set in accordance with the pattern established.

Suggestions: In solving alphabetic series, it is helpful to write out the alphabet and keep it in front of you as you work. This makes it easier to spot the key to a letter series.

Correct answers for these questions appear at the end of this examination, together with the answers to all other tests.

```
A  B  C  D  E  F  G  H  I  J  K  L  M  N  O  P  Q  R  S  T  U  V  W  X  Y  Z
1  2  3  4  5  6  7  8  9 10 11 12 13 14 15 16 17 18 19 20 21 22 23 24 25 26
```

1. B A C A D A E A F A G A
   (A) H A   (B) A H
   (C) K A   (D) L A

2. A B D B B D C B D D B D E B D F B
   (A) H D   (B) Q X
   (C) D B   (D) D G

3. J I H G F E D C
   (A) B C   (B) Q P
   (C) B A   (D) N P

4. Z Y X W V U T S R
   (A) P Q   (B) Q P
   (C) O P   (D) D H

5. X X W X V X U X T X S X R
   (A) X O   (B) X Y
   (C) X Q   (D) Q X

6. K L N M O P R Q S T
   (A) V U   (B) U V
   (C) W V   (D) V W

7. A B C F E D G H I L K J M
   (A) O N   (B) N O
   (C) O M   (D) M O

8. Z Y W X V U S T R Q O P N M
   (A) K J   (B) J K
   (C) K L   (D) L K

9. Y Z X W U V T S Q R P O M N
   (A) K J   (B) L K
   (C) K L   (D) J K

10. Z Y X U V W T S R O P Q N M L
    (A) I K   (B) K I
    (C) I J   (D) K J

11. A C E G I K M O Q
    (A) S U   (B) S T
    (C) R S   (D) R T

12. Z X V T R P N L
    (A) K L   (B) K J
    (C) L J   (D) J H

13. Z W T Q N K H
    (A) E B   (B) E C
    (C) F B   (D) F C

14. A D G J M P S
    (A) V W   (B) U W
    (C) U V   (D) V Y

S1487   60

15. A D F I K N P S
    (A) W U   (B) U W
    (C) U X   (D) U V

16. A C E D G I H K M L
    (A) O P   (B) O Q
    (C) Q P   (D) P Q

17. Z X V T R P N
    (A) J K   (B) K J
    (C) L K   (D) L J

18. B A D C F E H G J I L
    (A) K N   (B) K M
    (C) N K   (D) L K

19. Y Z W X U V S T Q R O P M
    (A) L K   (B) K L
    (C) N L   (D) N K

20. A B D C E F H G I J L K M N
    (A) R P   (B) P O
    (C) O P   (D) P Q

END OF TEST

Go on to do the following Test in this Examination, just as you would be expected to do on the actual exam.

62 / *P.A.C.E. Professional-Administrative Career Exam*

TEST IV. ABSTRACT REASONING

TIME: 15 Minutes. 16 Questions.

DIRECTIONS: In each of these questions, look at the symbols in the first two boxes. Something about the three symbols in the first box makes them alike; something about the two symbols in the other box with the question mark makes them alike. Look for some characteristic that is common to all symbols in the same box, yet makes them different from the symbols in the other box. Among the five answer choices, find the symbol that can best be substituted for the question mark, because it is like the symbols in the second box, and, for the same reason, different from those in the first box.

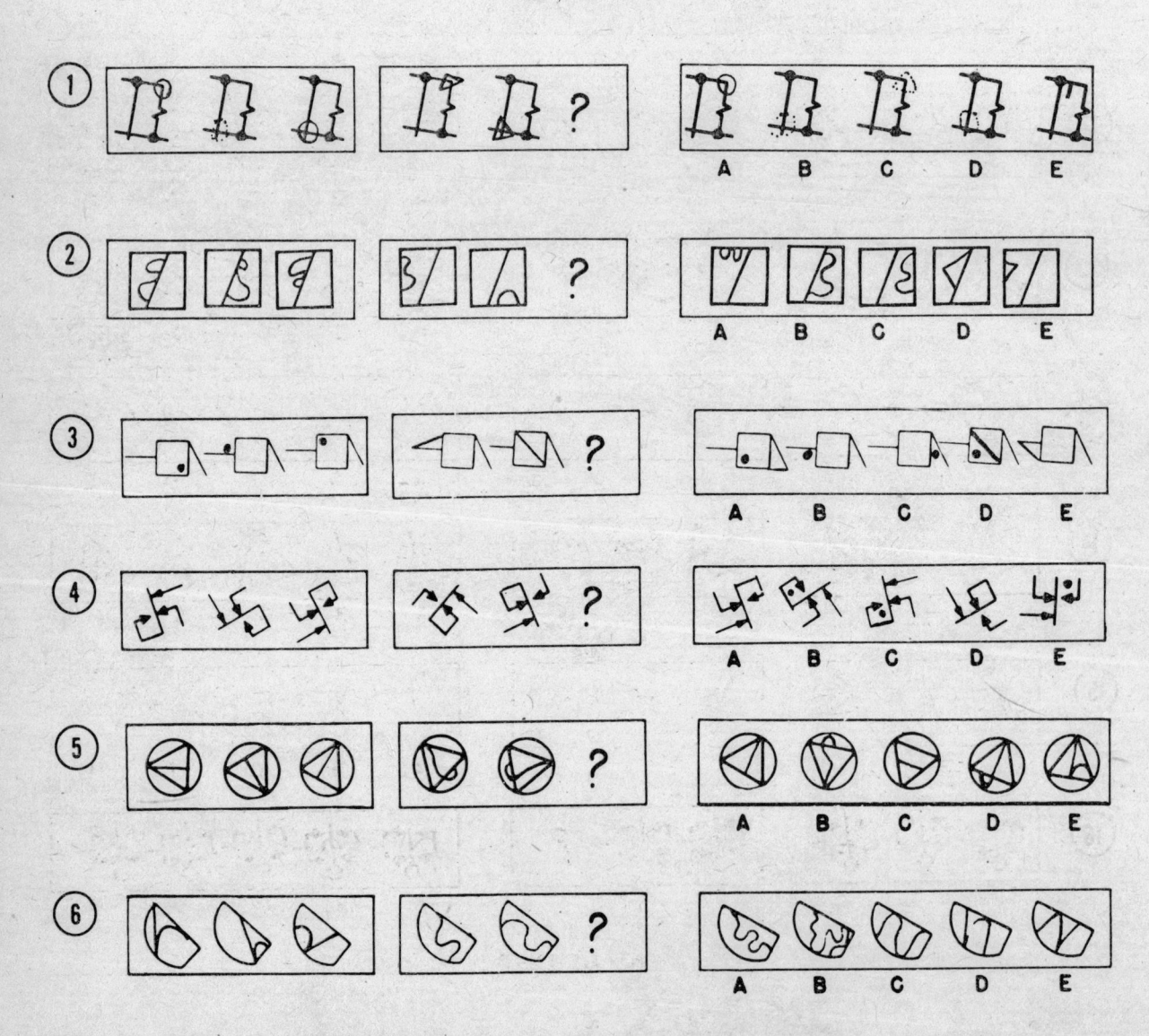

First Sample Exam / 63

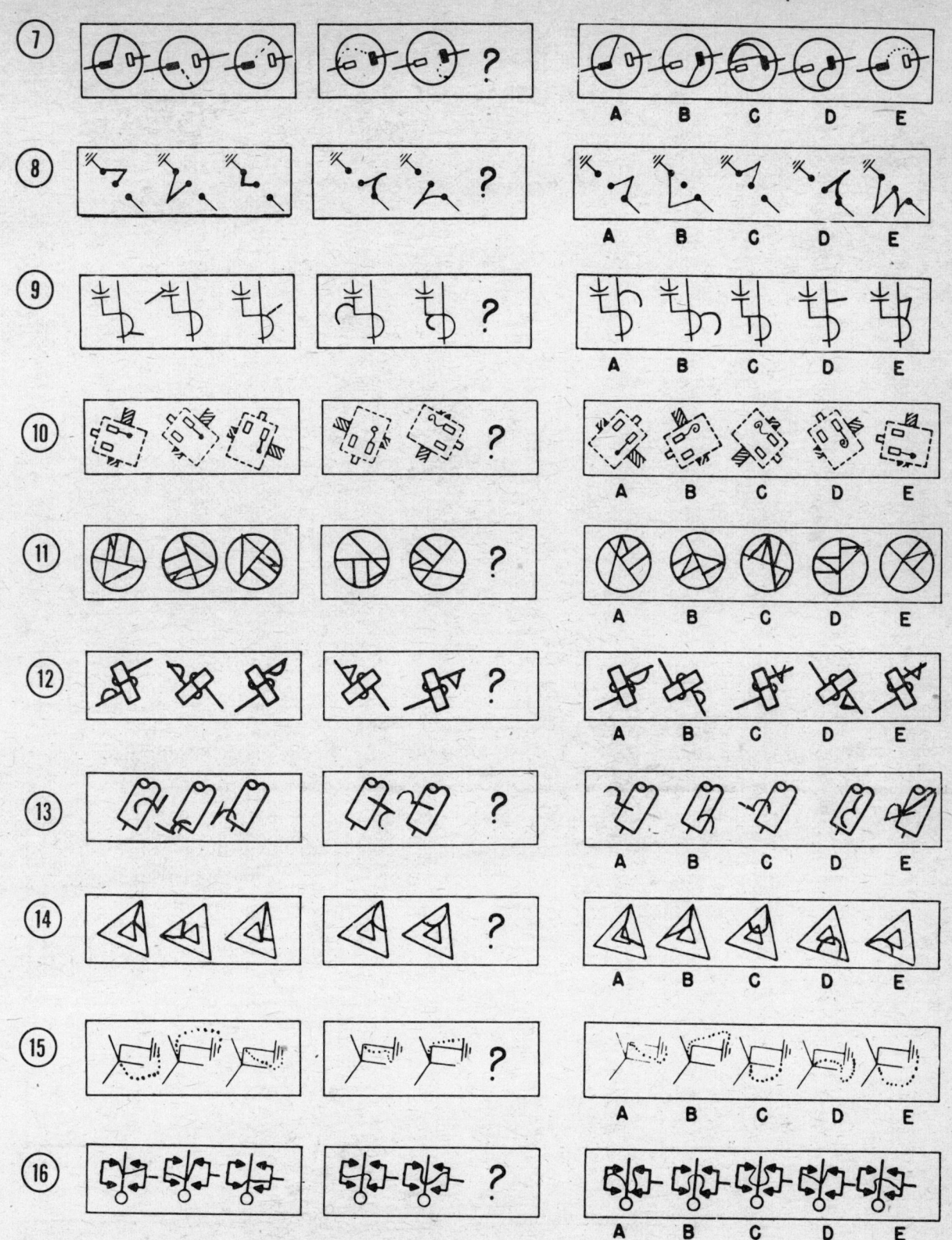

END OF TEST

Deriving Conclusions from Given Data

TEST V. READ AND INFER

TIME: 20 Minutes. 16 Questions.

This reading comprehension test consists of a number of different passages. One or more questions are based on each passage. The questions are composed of incomplete statements about the passage. Each incomplete statement is followed by five choices lettered (A) (B) (C) (D) (E). Mark your answer sheet with the letter of that choice which best completes the statement, and which best conveys the meaning of the passage.

Correct answers for these questions appear at the end of this examination, together with the answers to all other tests.

Reading Passage

Poverty in itself is seldom the cause of revolution. It is the sense of inequality in the distribution of wealth that breeds discontent. When the rich are indifferent to this inequality, and no effort is made to ease the economic burden of the poor, the sense of inequality grows into enmity.

The chief task of good administration is to secure internal peace through orderly growth. Many factors contribute to the economic growth or decay of a country; climate, natural resources, agriculture, and industry to mention a few. To insure that economic growth benefits all citizens, not just a few, government must deal with and regulate those factors.

1. The title that best epitomizes this passage is

    (A) Changes in the early society of our country
    (B) The monopoly of wealth by a special class
    (C) Insuring internal peace
    (D) Enmity resulting from social burdens
    (E) Governmental regulations

2. Good administration should

    (A) distribute wealth equally
    (B) regulate those factors which affect the economy
    (C) control economic life
    (D) help the poor by promoting government economy
    (E) make the poorer citizens happy

3. Discontent is chiefly the result of
    (A) poverty
    (B) inevitable social and economic changes
    (C) increase in wealth of the country
    (D) class competition
    (E) uneven distribution of wealth

Reading Passage

I suppose that I might connect this with another myth: that since most Chinese are illiterate they are, therefore, ignorant. Actually there is surprisingly little connection between illiteracy and ignorance. I learned this in my forty years in China from many friends who, though illiterate, were wise and sophisticated. I learned it again in my own country, where I found literacy and ignorance in frequent combination. Knowing how to read does not mean that one reads or thinks. Wisdom is the essential element of civilization, and of wisdom the Chinese have much.

4. The title below that best expresses the idea of this passage is

    (A) Illiteracy, a myth   (B) Illiteracy and wisdom
    (C) Forty years in China   (D) Characteristics of the illiterate
    (E) Wisdom through reading

5. The writer considers the Chinese on the whole

    (A) ignorant but friendly   (B) literate
    (C) wise   (D) satisfied with their illiteracy
    (E) less mythical than Americans

Reading Passage

Television has just about reached in 20 years the goal toward which print has been working for 500: to extend its audience to include the entire population. In 1973 in the United States, nine out of ten families watched 45 million sets going an average of five hours a day.

6. According to the above paragraph

   (A) the entire nation has TV sets
   (B) nine out of ten individuals watch an average of five hours a day
   (C) the TV viewing public grew much more rapidly than did the reading public
   (D) there are more TV sets in the United States than in other countries
   (E) the total possible TV audience is larger than the reading public

Reading Passage

The problem in adult education seems to be not the piling up of facts but practice in thinking.

7. According to the above paragraph

   (A) educational methods for adults and young people should differ
   (B) adults do not seem to retain new facts
   (C) adults seem to think more than young people
   (D) a well-educated adult is one who thinks but does not have a store of information
   (E) adult education should stress ability to think

Reading Passage

Approximately 19,000 fatal accidents in 1972 were sustained in industry. There were approximately 130 non-fatal injuries to each fatal injury.

8. According to the above paragraph, the number of non-fatal accidents during 1972 was approximately

   (A) 146,000   (B) 190,000   (C) 1,150,000
   (D) 2,500,000   (E) 3,200,000

Reading Passage

The capacity of banks to grant loans depends, in the long run, on the amount of money deposited with them by the public. In the short run, however, it is a well known fact that banks not only can, but do lend more than is deposited with them. If such lending is carried to excess, it leads to inflation.

9. On the basis of the preceding paragraph it is most reasonable to conclude that

   (A) banks often indulge in the vicious practice of lending more than is deposited with them
   (B) in the long run, a sound banking policy operates for the mutual advantage of the bankers and the public
   (C) inflation is usually the result of excess lending by the banks
   (D) the public must guard against inflation
   (E) bank lending is always in direct ratio with bank deposits

Reading Passage

Neither the revolution in manufacturing nor that in agriculture could have proceeded without those brilliant inventions in transportation and communication which have bound country to city, nation to nation, and continent to continent.

10. Judging from the contents of the preceding paragraph it can most precisely be indicated that

    (A) nations have been brought together more closely by transportation than by manufacturing and agriculture
    (B) progress in communication and transportation has been essential to progress in manufacturing and agriculture
    (C) changes in manufacturing and agriculture are characterized by a revolutionary process
    (D) industrial changes must be preceded by brilliant inventions in communication
    (E) both industry and transportation serve to bind country to city, nation to nation, and continent to continent

68 / P.A.C.E. Professional-Administrative Career Exam

Reading Passage

Of the 300 cars owned in 1895, only four were manufactured in this country. Of the 100 million registered in 1973, most were manufactured in American plants.

11. The paragraph notes that cars registered in this country in 1973

    (A) were far in excess of those manufactured abroad in 1895
    (B) were manufactured in the United States
    (C) increased considerably over the preceding decade
    (D) improved greatly in construction over the 1895 model
    (E) were largely of domestic construction

Reading Passage

The labor required to produce a bushel of wheat in 1830 was three hours. Today it takes less than ten minutes. Further, it has been estimated that fifty men, employing modern farm machinery and agricultural methods, can do the work of five hundred peasants toiling under the conditions of the eighteenth century.

12. On the basis of the facts presented above, one could best conclude that

    (A) the increase of efficiency in agriculture is almost as great as that in manufacturing
    (B) peasants in the eighteenth century worked much harder than today's farmers
    (C) modern farm machinery has resulted in serious unemployment among farmers
    (D) more than 18 times as much wheat is produced today than in 1830
    (E) modern farm machinery is labor-saving

Reading Passage

The railroads, building trades, mineral industries, and automotive works normally take two-thirds of our annual production of steel. The remaining third has been around 16 million tons. For this last third of our output the farmers have been the best customers with farm machinery, tools, and wire constituting their chief demands.

13. Judging from the above facts it would be most reasonable to assume that

   (A) there is an increasing demand for the newer and more efficient farm machinery and tools
   (B) the growth of the steel industry has made possible the growth of all of our basic industries that depend upon steel
   (C) the farmers are our best steel customers
   (D) our normal annual steel output is about 48 million tons
   (E) only one-third of our steel output is exported with the remaining two-thirds consumed by our own industries

Reading Passage

Although rural crime reporting is spottier and less efficient than city and town reporting, sufficient data is collected to support the statement that rural crime rates are lower than those of urban communities.

14. According to the above paragraph

   (A) better reporting of crime occurs in rural areas than in cities
   (B) there appears to be a lower proportion of crime in rural areas than in cities
   (C) cities have more crime than towns
   (D) crime depends on the amount of reporting
   (E) no conclusions can be drawn regarding crime in rural areas because of inadequate reporting

Reading Passage

Prior to the Civil War, the steamboat was the center of life in the thriving Mississippi towns. With the war came the railroads. River traffic dwindled and the white-painted vessels rotted at the wharves. During World War I, the government decided to relieve rail congestion by reviving the long-forgotten waterways. Today, steamers, diesels, and barges ply the Mississippi.

15. According to the above paragraph

   (A) the railroads were once the center of thriving river towns on the Mississippi River
   (B) the volume of river transportation was greater than the volume of rail transportation during World War I
   (C) growth of river transportation greatly increased the congestion on the railroads
   (D) business found river transportation more profitable than railroad transportation during World War I
   (E) since the Civil War, the volume of transportation on the Mississippi has varied

Reading Passage

In a recent questionnaire circulated among college students, a majority held that the greatest single benefit derived from the movies was a better understanding of people and customs in other parts of the world. One-third more students agreed with this statement than with the runner-up, that the movies promoted the desire for greater freedom in social relations.

16. According to the paragraph above, the questionnaire revealed that the students felt movies had most significantly influenced their lives through

   (A) an emphasis on crime and crime prevention
   (B) improved facility in foreign languages
   (C) creation of a desire for greater freedom of social relations among college students
   (D) dissemination of the broad cultural aspects of lands other than our own
   (E) the graphic presentation of foreign folklore

END OF TEST

Go on to do the following Test in this Examination, just as you would be expected to do on the actual exam.

TEST VI. LOGICAL SEQUENCE

TIME: 15 Minutes. 15 Questions.

DIRECTIONS: In these questions, four given sentences may or may not be arranged in the order in which they would logically appear in a paragraph. Following the four given sentences are five suggested sequences, lettered A, B, C, D, and E, from which you are to select the sequence that indicates the best arrangement of the sentences. For example: If, in the first question, you find that the fourth sentence should come first, the first sentence should be second, the second sentence should be third, and the third sentence should be fourth, you would look among the five choices for the answer 4-1-3-2, and designate the letter which precedes that sequence as your answer.

(1) 1. There is also good reason for careful attention to internal communication.
2. Effective communication with those inside the organization makes for fewer misunderstandings, and fewer disgruntled employees.
3. Harmony within the business carries over into public relations with outsiders.
4. In the area of office communication, primary attention is usually centered upon relations with outsiders - customers, suppliers, and others.
 (A) 2-3-1-4 (B) 4-1-2-3
 (C) 3-2-1-4 (D) 1-3-2-4
  (E) 4-2-3-1

(2) 1. The underlying theory of dictation is that it enables the executive to pass on to others his mature judgment on important matters in a minimum of time, leaving him free to exercise executive direction in other phases of management.
2. What are the characteristics of an efficient dictator, an inefficient dictator?
3. How does one go about dictating?
4. Research studies and personal experiences tell us that sometimes only time and effort in practicing good dictation procedure can turn a poor dictator into a good one.

 (A) 2-1-4-3 (B) 4-2-1-3
 (C) 1-3-4-2 (D) 2-4-3-1
  (E) 3-2-1-4

(3) 1. A systematic plan for handling the mail will speed up the performance of office work.
2. Regardless of the volume of mail, competent supervision and control are necessary.
3. The provision of facilities for handling mail will depend largely upon the volume to be handled.
4. The number of persons forming the mailroom staff, in turn, varies with the volume of correspondence to be handled and the degree to which mechanical equipment is used.
 (A) 1-3-4-2 (B) 2-1-3-4
 (C) 3-1-4-2 (D) 4-3-2-1
  (E) 2-4-1-3

(4) 1. A budget is a plan of financial requirements during a given time period.
2. It necessarily is based upon analysis of the situation which faces the enterprise.
3. It develops a course of action to be followed.

4. The general uses of any budget are those of planning financial needs in advance and providing a basis for controlling current expenditures.
   (A) 3-2-4-1   (B) 4-2-3-1
   (C) 2-4-3-1   (D) 1-2-3-4
   (E) 2-1-3-4

(5) 1. The employee has little control over any of them.

2. The cost of the training period and its effectiveness will depend upon the degree to which these conditions are properly controlled by the employer.

3. The conditions under which the employee must learn will materially affect the length of the training period.

4. These conditions can be controlled by the employer.
   (A) 1-2-4-3   (B) 4-2-1-3
   (C) 3-4-2-1   (D) 2-4-3-1
   (E) 1-4-3-2

(6) 1. But once that point is reached, reappraisal and modification should be made in light of the skill and experience of the work force and the cost of perfectionism.

2. The second caution is that the development effort should be aimed at creating a simple, workable procedure as distinct from a perfect procedure.

3. As one speaker put it, "Hire a few workers to mop the floor so that you don't have to develop a perfect system that will keep 400 people from dropping things on the floor."

4. To be sure, the initial effort should be directed toward developing the ideal.
   (A) 4-1-3-2   (B) 3-1-4-2
   (C) 2-1-3-4   (D) 2-4-1-3
   (E) 1-2-4-3

(7) 1. They include computation and rate tables, codes, charts, price lists, wiring diagrams, account titles and definitions, and the like.

2. The use and usefulness of these devices should be fully explored during the survey of work methods.

3. In general, the analyst's objective should be to find out if all special data required to perform any part of the routine are readily available, conveniently arranged, and kept up to date.

4. Work aids are the nonmechanical devices of many kinds used to facilitate repetitive clerical operations.
   (A) 1-2-3-4   (B) 4-1-2-3
   (C) 3-1-4-2   (D) 2-1-4-3
   (E) 3-2-4-1

(8) 1. This is just another way of stating the important principle that duplication is not always avoidable or wasteful.

2. On this whole matter of combining forms, one point of caution needs to be stressed: The analyst must be careful not to go beyond the point of diminishing returns.

3. In some situations it may be the simplest way of meeting the requirements.

4. He must not fall into the error of seeking combination for its own sake.
   (A) 2-4-1-3   (B) 3-4-1-2
   (C) 4-1-2-3   (D) 1-3-4-2
   (E) 3-1-2-4

(9) 1. The big risk, of course, in funneling all proposed procedure instructions through a single point is that the adoption of worthwhile changes will be unnecessarily delayed.

2. The approvals required must be clearly specified and held to a minimum, and the procedures staff must be geared to process recommended changes quickly.

3. Unless this is done, operating personnel will soon become discouraged from submitting recommendations through the prescribed channels and will revert to making its own changes as the need arises.

4. To avoid this danger, the path of revision must be short, easy to follow, and well understood by everyone.
   (A) 4-1-3-2   (B) 3-1-2-4
   (C) 1-4-2-3   (D) 2-4-1-3
   (E) 4-3-2-1

10. 1. For one man, everything he does falls under the heading of administration.
2. To a large extent, what the administrative functions of your job are depend on what you say they are.
3. You can talk to a dozen executives without getting two to agree.
4. Another executive will tell you only planning and decision making belong there.
    (A) 1-2-4-3   (B) 2-1-3-4
    (C) 3-2-4-1   (D) 4-1-2-3
        (E) 3-1-4-2

11. 1. The importance of communications is axiomatic.
2. When the phrase "two-way" precedes the word "communications," there is the feeling in some quarters that we have said everything there is to say on the subject.
3. But communications may proceed in two directions and still not be inclusive enough to make it possible for you to do a thorough communications job.
4. The fact is, the communications load of many executives tends to be decidedly uneven.
    (A) 4-3-1-2   (B) 2-3-4-1
    (C) 3-4-1-2   (D) 1-2-3-4
        (E) 4-1-2-3

12. 1. In actuality, this isn't the case at all.
2. The trouble with many approaches to problem solving is the mistaken idea that problems come to you spelled out in clear and simple terms.
3. For example, a problem may grow so imperceptibly that it may actually have been around for years before it begins to take on the aspects of a problem.
4. Or the facts of a case may be indistinguishable from the fancies.
    (A) 3-4-1-2   (B) 2-1-3-4
    (C) 1-3-2-4   (D) 4-2-1-3
        (E) 2-3-4-1

13. 1. Regardless of the reason, the effects of the vacuum range from the disheartening to the deadly.
2. Men in management, more often than you might think, find themselves "in solitary."
3. It's seldom calculated, but the fact remains, they have no one to talk to.
4. Lack of direct channels to colleagues may reflect anything from poor personal relationships to faulty organizational setup.
    (A) 4-1-3-2   (B) 2-4-1-3
    (C) 2-3-4-1   (D) 3-1-4-2
        (E) 1-4-3-2

14. 1. They must operate to accomplish any one of the primary tasks.
2. These processes are planning, doing, and controlling.
3. They cause the organization to function.
4. Three processes are at work in an organization.
    (A) 4-2-3-1   (B) 1-2-3-4
    (C) 3-1-4-2   (D) 2-4-1-3
        (E) 4-1-3-2

15. 1. Difficulty in the application of the principle of unity of command arises principally from its blind application to a static organization structure to meet a need that fluctuates with conditions and situations.
2. The relationships shown on an organization chart seem as inflexible and static as the structure of the organization itself.
3. If the organization is to serve its purpose, however, it cannot be entirely static because it is dealing with moving and changing situations.
4. The relationships between the component units of the organization enable it to become a flexible, living organism.
    (A) 2-4-3-1   (B) 4-1-3-2
    (C) 3-4-1-2   (D) 2-1-3-4
        (E) 1-2-3-4

END OF TEST

Go on to do the following Test in this Examination, just as you would be expected to do on the actual exam.

Quantitative Ability

TEST VII. MATHEMATICS

TIME: 30 Minutes. 25 Questions.

DIRECTIONS: Study each of the following problems and work out your answers in the blank space at the right. Below each problem you will find a number of suggested answers. Select the one that you have figured out to be right and mark its letter on the answer sheet. In the sample questions provided, the correct answers are: S1 = A; S2 = C.

Correct answers for these questions appear at the end of this examination, together with the answers to all other tests.

Samples:

S1. If the area of a square is 62 square inches, find to the nearest tenth of an inch the length of one side.
  A. 7.9
  B. 9.7
  C. 6.2
  D. 2.6.

S2. Solve the following equation for a:
  $5a + 3b = 14$
  A. $14 - 3b + 5$
  B. $3b - 14 \times 5$
  C. $\dfrac{14 - 3b}{5}$
  D. $3b - 14$.

DO YOUR FIGURING HERE

1. Solve for x and y.
   $$5x - 2y = 19$$
   $$7x - 4y = 29$$
   A. $x = -3, y = -2$
   B. $x = 2, y = 3$
   C. $x = 3, y = -2$
   D. $x = -2, y = -3$.

2. Mr. Brown makes deposits and writes checks as follows:

   May 1, $375 deposit
   May 6, $150 check
   May 10, $35 check
   May 11, $42 deposit
   May 20, $140 check
   May 26, $18 check.

   Mr. Brown's bank balance on April 30 was $257. What is his balance on May 31?

   A. $465
   B. $331
   C. $185
   D. $165.

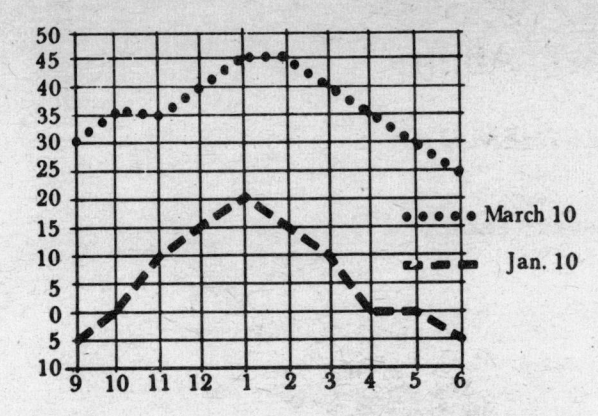

3. The above graph shows the temperatures in a certain city for 2 different dates. How many degrees higher was the lowest temperature on March 10 than the lowest temperature on January 10?

   A. 35°
   B. 30°
   C. 25°
   D. 45°.

4. From the same graph estimate the temperature at 3:30 on March 10.

   A. 37-1/2°
   B. 42-1/2°
   C. 30°
   D. 5°.

5. From the same graph determine the times on January 10 when the temperature was 5°.

   A. 11:30 and 3:30
   B. 10:30 and 2:30
   C. 10:30 and 3:30
   D. 11:30 and 2:30.

6. A student had averages of 87, 90, 80, 85, and 75 for the first 5 terms in school. What must be his average for the sixth term in order for his overall average for the six terms to be 85%?

   A. 93%
   B. 85%
   C. 87%
   D. 90%.

7. In a class of 36 students, 28 passed an examination, 4 failed and the rest were absent. What percent of the class was absent?

   A. 14-2/7%
   B. 11-1/9%
   C. 75%
   D. 33-1/3%.

76 / P.A.C.E. Professional-Administrative Career Exam

8. How many digits are there to the right of the decimal point in the square root of 74859.2401?

    A. 4
    B. 2
    C. 3
    D. 1.

9. The scale of a map is 3/8"=100 miles. How far apart are 2 cities 2-1/4" apart on the map?

    A. 1200 miles
    B. 300 miles
    C. 600 miles
    D. 150 miles.

10. Tom is preparing a circle graph to show that 1/12 of the local income tax is spent in payment of public debts. How big an angle must he measure at the center of the circle to represent this fact?

    A. 30°
    B. 15°
    C. 12°
    D. 60°.

11. The diagram at the right shows the side view of a house. What is the distance from E to AB?

    A. 41'
    B. 25'
    C. 20'
    D. 39'.

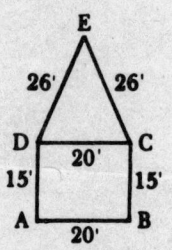

12. A weather bureau reported the following temperatures on a certain day:

    1 A.M. —5°
    5 A.M. —2°
    9 A.M.   0°
    1 P.M. 10°
    5 P.M. 10°
    9 P.M.   5°

    What was the average temperature for the day?

    A. −3°
    B. 0°
    C. +3°
    D. +6°

DO YOUR FIGURING HERE

13. If you have 3 hrs. and 20 minutes to travel 150 miles, what is the average speed at which you must travel?

    A. 60 mph C. 50 mph
    B. 45 mph D. 70 mph.

14. What is the square root of .0004?

    A. .0002 C. .16
    B. .002   D. .02.

15. The side of a square is 18". What is its area in square feet?

    A. 324 C. 2.25
    B. 9   D. 3/2.

16. Reduce to its simplest form: $\dfrac{x^2 - y^2}{(x-y)^2}$

    A. $x+y$ C. $x-y$
    B. $\dfrac{x-y}{x+y}$ D. $\dfrac{x+y}{x-y}$

17. Find ∠x, where the central angles are as shown

    A. 15° C. 30°
    B. 70° D. 35°

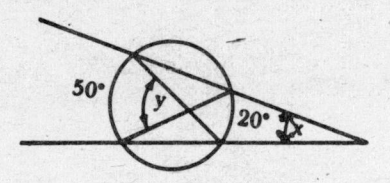

18. In the same diagram, find ∠y.

    A. 15° C. 30°
    B. 70° D. 35°.

19. If the sides of a parallelogram are 8" and 10" and the included angle is 60°, find its area.

    A. 80 square inches
    B. 40 $\sqrt{2}$ square inches
    C. 40 square inches
    D. 40 $\sqrt{3}$ square inches.

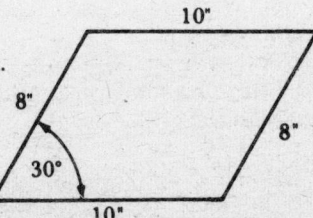

DO YOUR FIGURING HERE

20. If the numerical value of the circumference of a circle is equal to the numerical value of its area, find its radius.

    A. 4
    B. 1
    C. 8
    D. 2.

21. A tower casts a shadow of 40' at the same time that a yardstick casts a shadow of 2'. How high is the tower?

    A. 80'
    B. 40'
    C. 60'
    D. 100'.

22. How high must a box be if its base is 5" by 6", and its contents must be 135 cubic inches?

    A. 9"
    B. 4"
    C. 5"
    D. 4-1/2".

23. What is the probability that a random selection from a box containing 6 black balls and 4 white balls will be a white ball?

    A. 4:6
    B. 6:10
    C. 4:10
    D. 6:4.

24. What common fraction is the equivalent of .625?

    A. 3/5
    B. 5/8
    C. 4/5
    D. 2/3.

25. What is the value of the following expression when reduced to its simplest form?

    $$\left(\frac{x}{y} - \frac{y}{x}\right) \div \left(\frac{x-y}{xy}\right)$$

    A. 1
    B. x−y
    C. y−x
    D. x+y

END OF TEST

Go on to do the following Test in this Examination, just as you would be expected to do on the actual exam.

TEST VIII. ARITHMETIC COMPUTATIONS

TIME: 5 Minutes. 10 Questions.

DIRECTIONS: Each question has five suggested answers lettered A, B, C, D, and E. Suggested answer E is NONE OF THESE. Blacken space E only if your answer for a question does not exactly agree with any of the first four suggested answers. When you have finished all the questions, compare your answers with the correct answers at the end of the examination.

ANSWERS

1) Multiply:
    896
  × 708
(A) 643,386
(B) 634,386
(C) 634,368
(D) 643,368
(E) None of these

2) Divide:
9 / 4266
(A) 447
(B) 477
(C) 474
(D) 475
(E) None of these

3) Add:
  $125.25
     .50
   70.86
+   6.07
(A) $201.68
(B) $202.69
(C) $200.68
(D) $202.68
(E) None of these

4) Subtract:
 $1,250.37
−   48.98
(A) $1,201.39
(B) $1,201.49
(C) $1,200.39
(D) $1,201.38
(E) None of these

5) Divide:
29 / 476.92
(A) 16.4445
(B) 17.4445
(C) 16.4555
(D) 17.4455
(E) None of these

ANSWERS

6) Multiply:
 7962.27
×   .06
(A) 4777.362
(B) 477.6732
(C) 4787.632
(D) 477.7362
(E) None of these

7) Add:
  28
  19
  17
+ 24
(A) 87
(B) 88
(C) 90
(D) 89
(E) None of these

8) Divide:
3.7 / 2339.86
(A) 632.4
(B) 62.34
(C) 642.3
(D) 63.24
(E) None of these

9) Add:
  4 ½
  5 ¾
+ 3 ⅔
(A) 13 10/13
(B) 12 ¾
(C) 13 ⅔
(D) 12 ½
(E) None of these

10) Multiply:
  45,286
×   4 1/5
(A) 190,021 1/5
(B) 190,234
(C) 190,201 1/5
(D) 190,202 2/5
(E) None of these

END OF TEST

Understanding Charts and Tables

TEST IX. DATA INTERPRETATION

TIME: 35 Minutes. 25 Questions.

DIRECTIONS: This test consists of data presented in graphic form followed by questions based on the information contained in the graph, chart or table shown. After studying the data given, choose the best answer for each question and blacken the corresponding space on the answer sheet. Answer each group of questions solely on the basis of the information given or implied in the data preceding it.

Questions 1 to 17

In the table that follows lettered entries have been substituted for some of the numbers. In answering the questions about the lettered entries, you are to compute the number that should be in the space where the lettered entry appears. In those questions which concern tokens, consider the worth of a token as 35 cents.

DAILY FARE REPORT

Date: 3/12/76　　　　　　　　　　　　　　　　　　　　　　　Booth No. S-50

Name: John Brown　　　　　　　　　　　　　　　　　　　　　Name: Mary Smith
Time: From 7 A.M. to 3 P.M.　　　　　　　　　　　　　　　　Time: From 3 P.M. to 11 P.M.

TURNSTILES

Turn-stile	Opening Reading	Closing Reading	Difference	Opening Reading	Closing Reading	Difference
1	5123	5410	287	5410	6019	609
2	3442	Entry F	839	4281	4683	402
3	8951	9404	453	Entry G	9757	353
4	7663	8265	602	8265	8588	Entry H

Totals:	Entry I	27360	2181	27360	Entry J	1687
	Total Fares		2181	Total Fares		1687
	Deduct: Slugs, Foreign Coins		12	Deduct: Slugs, Foreign Coins		Entry K
	Deduct: Test Rings-Turnstile #		0	Deduct: Test Rings-Turnstile #3		3
	Net Fares		2169	Net Fares		1680
(a)	Net Fares at Token Value		Entry L	(a) Net Fares at Token Value		$588.00
	Token Reserve at Start		4200	Token Reserve at Start		5000
	Add: Tokens Received		2200	Add: Tokens Received		Entry M
	Deduct: Tokens Transferred Out		1400	Deduct: Tokens Transferred Out		0
	Total Token Reserve		Entry N	Total Token Reserve		6450
	Deduct: Total Reserve at End		4330	Deduct: Total Reserve at End		5674
	No. of Reserve Tokens Sold		670	No. of Reserve Tokens Sold		Entry O
(b)	Value of Reserve Tokens Sold		Entry P	(b) Value of Reserve Tokens Sold		$271.60
	Net Amount Due: (a) + (b)		$993.65	Net Amount Due: (a) + (b)		Entry Q

First Sample Exam / 81

1. Entry F for Brown's tour of duty should be a closing reading of
   (A) 2603   (B) 3873   (C) 4281   (D) 4671

2. Entry G for Smith's tour of duty should be an opening reading of
   (A) 8642   (B) 3932   (C) 9404   (D) 9857

3. Entry H for Smith's tour of duty should be a difference of
   (A) 303   (B) 323   (C) 344   (D) 402

4. Entry I for Brown's tour of duty should be a total of
   (A) 24299   (B) 25179   (C) 26288   (D) 27168

5. Entry J for Smith's tour of duty should be a total of
   (A) 28036   (B) 29047   (C) 29556   (D) 30437

6. Entry K for Smith's tour of duty should indicate that the number of slugs and foreign coins is
   (A) 0   (B) 2   (C) 4   (D) 7

7. Entry L for Brown's tour of duty should indicate that the net fares at token value amount to
   (A) $493.80   (B) $542.25   (C) $650.70   (D) $759.15

8. Entry M for Smith's tour of duty should indicate that the tokens received number
   (A) 674   (B) 1000   (C) 1200   (D) 1450

9. Entry N for Brown's tour of duty should indicate a total token reserve of
   (A) 670   (B) 5000   (C) 6400   (D) 7800

10. Entry O for Smith's tour of duty should indicate that the number of reserve tokens sold was
    (A) 776   (B) 1450   (C) 3250   (D) 12124

11. Entry P for Brown's tour of duty should indicate that the value of reserve tokens sold should be
    (A) $210.00 (B) $234.50   (C) $490.00   (D) $523.35

12. Entry Q for Smith's tour of duty should indicate that the net amount due is
    (A) $859.60 (B) $478.30   (C) $317.10   (D) $270.90

13. The number of passengers using Turnstile No. 2 from 7 A.M. to 11 P.M. is
    (A) 1241   (B) 839   (C) 402   (D) 287

14. The turnstile showing the greatest use from 7 A.M. to 3 P.M. is

    (A) No. 1   (B) No. 2   (C) No. 3   (D) No. 4

15. The total fares for all turnstiles from 7 A.M. to 11 P.M. amounted to

    (A) 1687   (B) 2181   (C) 3868   (D) 4275

16. The total net fares from 7 A.M. to 11 P.M. amounted to

    (A) 1680   (B) 2169   (C) 3849   (D) 3868

17. Net fares at token value from 7 A.M. to 11 P.M. amounted to

    (A) $993.65   (B) $588.00   (C) $1353.80   (D) $1347.15

Questions 18 to 22

Questions 18 to 22 are based on the chart of HOURLY TURNSTILE READINGS shown below. Refer to this chart when answering these questions.

HOURLY TURNSTILE READINGS					
TURNSTILE NO.	7:00 AM	8:00 AM	9:00 AM	10:00 AM	11:00 AM
1	37111	37905	38342	38451	38485
2	78432	79013	79152	79237	79306
3	45555	45921	45989	46143	46233
4	89954	90063	90121	90242	90299

18. The total number of passengers using Turnstile No. 1 from 7:00 A.M. to 11:00 A.M. is

    (A) 580   (B) 794   (C) 1374   (D) 1594

19. The turnstile which registered the largest number of fares from 7:00 A.M. to 8:00 A.M. is

    (A) No. 1   (B) No. 2   (C) No. 3   (D) No. 4

20. The total number of passengers using all four turnstiles between 10:00 A.M. and 11:00 A.M. is

    (A) 57   (B) 250   (C) 396   (D) 3271

21. Turnstile No. 4 registered the highest number of passengers between

    (A) 7:00 A.M. and 8:00 A.M.   (B) 8:00 A.M. and 9:00 A.M.
    (C) 9:00 A.M. and 10:00 A.M.   (D) 10:00 A.M. and 11:00 A.M.

22. The turnstile which registered the lowest number of passengers between 8:00 A.M. and 9:00 A.M. is

    (A) No. 1   (B) No. 2   (C) No. 3   (D) No. 4

Questions 23 to 25

In the graph below, the lines labeled "A" and "B" represent the cumulative progress in the work of two file clerks, each of whom was given 500 consecutively numbered applications to file in the proper cabinets over a five-day work week. Answer questions 23 to 25 solely upon the data provided in the graph.

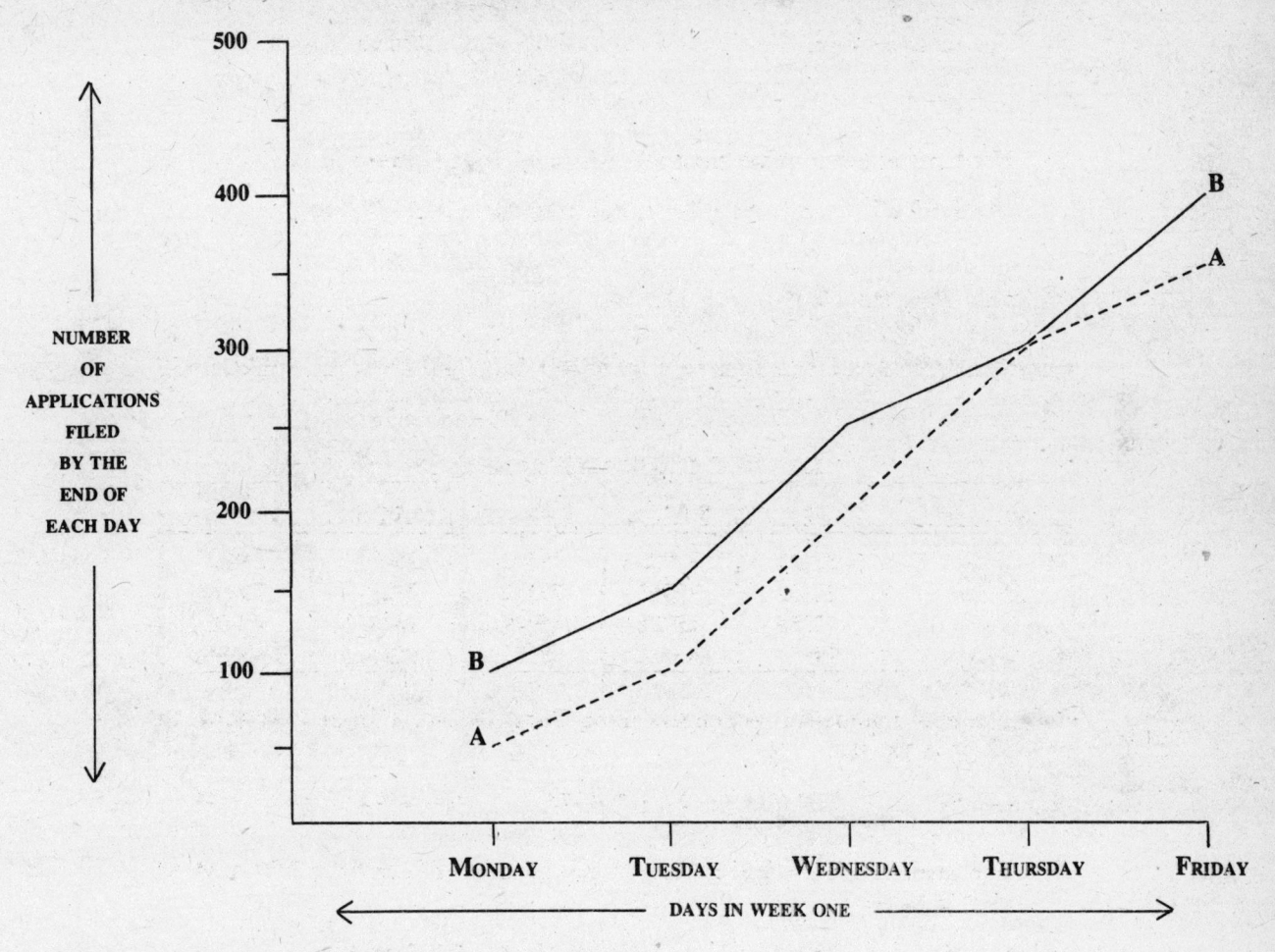

23. The day during which the largest number of applications was filed by both clerks was
    (A) Monday (B) Tuesday
    (C) Wednesday (D) Friday

24. At the end of the second day, the percentage of applications still to be filed was
    (A) 25% (B) 50%
    (C) 66% (D) 75%

25. Assuming that the production pattern is the same the following week as the week shown in the chart, the day on which the file clerks will finish this assignment will be
    (A) Monday (B) Tuesday
    (C) Wednesday (D) Friday

Deriving General Principles from Particular Data

TEST X. APPLYING GENERAL KNOWLEDGE

TIME: 35 Minutes. 30 Questions.

DIRECTIONS: For each question in this test, read carefully the stem and the five lettered choices that follow. Choose the answer which you consider correct or most nearly correct. Mark the answer sheet for the letter you have chosen: A, B, C, D, or E.

Correct answers for these questions appear at the end of this examination, together with the answers to all other tests.

1. The average span of life has increased chiefly because
   (A) modern civilization exerts less pressure on the individual
   (B) the individual does not have to work as hard as formerly
   (C) modern inventions conserve the individual's energy
   (D) advances in the field of medicine have made possible control of many formerly fatal diseases
   (E) the human body over a period of centuries has built up greater resistance to disease.

2. Zoning has been introduced for residential districts in order to
   (A) keep the district residential, thereby preventing confusion and unnecessary movement
   (B) maintain real estate values
   (C) fix the growth of the city in definite patterns
   (D) keep unwanted populations out of exclusive districts
   (E) reduce friction between communities.

3. The rate of increase of the farm population in the United States has been greater than that of cultivated farm land. We may conclude from this that
   (A) there will be more farmers than city dwellers in a short time
   (B) the rural population will shortly become too many for the available land
   (C) we may soon expect a movement from the farms to the cities
   (D) there will be more people to cultivate the same land
   (E) too many people are cultivating too little land.

4. An automobile can pick up speed more quickly than a locomotive train chiefly because it
   (A) has a less complicated mechanism than the locomotive
   (B) runs on rubber tires instead of on tracks
   (C) the automobile uses gasoline instead of steam as fuel
   (D) the automobile is lighter in weight than the locomotive
   (E) the automobile is capable of operating at a higher speed than the locomotive.

5. Replacement of obsolete machinery by modern equipment is often a benefit to the manufacturer in that it
   (A) relieves the strain on the workers
   (B) lowers the selling price of his product
   (C) lowers his overhead
   (D) produces a better product at a lower unit cost
   (E) reduces taxes.

6. Which of the following would be the surest indication that a druggist may have violated the legal requirement that narcotic drugs be dispensed only on a physician's prescription?
   (A) a number of people known to have purchased other drugs from him are believed to possess narcotics, but no prescriptions issued to these persons are in the druggist's file
   (B) he is himself an addict
   (C) his wholesaler refuses to sell him narcotics

(D) the total of his present narcotics stock and the amount legally accounted for is much less than his purchases
  (E) the supply of narcotics in stock is less than the amount he recently reported.

7. Stars are invisible in the daytime principally because
  (A) the distance between the earth and the stars increases during the night
  (B) the relative brightness of the sun is greater than that of the stars during the day
  (C) the earth's rotation places them on the opposite side of the earth
  (D) they do not reflect the light of the sun during the day
  (E) they are really still visible as they can be seen from the bottom of a deep well.

8. Sculpture predated painting as an art because
  (A) it is more important than painting
  (B) it is simpler than painting
  (C) it was used as an adjunct in construction
  (D) it is more interesting to the primitive mind
  (E) it requires primitive strength.

9. Custom regulations concerning the importation of fruit trees exist primarily in order to
  (A) prevent the smuggling of fruit trees into the country
  (B) aid farmers in maintaining high prices for their fruits
  (C) prevent the introduction into the United States of foreign destructive fruit insects
  (D) prevent foreign products from flooding the American market
  (E) aid in the introduction of new varieties of fruit trees into the United States.

10. In starting a load, a horse has to pull harder than he does to keep it moving because
  (A) the load weighs less when it is moving
  (B) there is no friction after the load is moving
  (C) the horse becomes accustomed to pulling the load
  (D) the wheels stick to the axles
  (E) the horse has to overcome the tendency of the wagon to remain at rest.

11. The best reason for the rule in criminal cases requiring that the defendant's guilt be established beyond a reasonable doubt is
  (A) in a civil case the plaintiff must prove his claim in the same way
  (B) a fair preponderance of the credible evidence is necessary in a civil suit
  (C) the District Attorney has his own investigators, the Police Department and other official assistance in preparing his case whereas the defendant has to rely mainly on his own lawyer
  (D) it is so provided in the State or Federal Constitutions
  (E) because it is one of the strongest safeguards under our system of law against unjust convictions.

12. From 1930 to 1940 there was a 7% rise in the population of the United States. During the same period there was a rise of 60% in the numbers of married people. The increase in the number of married people may be attributed to
  (A) an increased birth rate
  (B) a natural increase in the population of the country
  (C) a large number of marriages from 1930 to 1940
  (D) unrest in the world
  (E) previous population increases.

13. The price of a two-pound can is less than double that of a one-pound can because
  (A) packaging costs are not proportional to the quantity of material in a package
  (B) a cheaper grade of merchandise is always included in larger packages
  (C) the manufacturer would rather sell small packages
  (D) more expensive merchandise is usually in smaller packages
  (E) large packages are a good advertisement.

14. Men work chiefly because they must
  (A) support the state
  (B) support themselves
  (C) enjoy themselves
  (D) utilize leisure time
  (E) broaden their viewpoint on life.

15. Mass production results in lower prices chiefly because
  (A) the cost of making each unit is lowered
  (B) a larger amount of material is used
  (C) competition becomes keener
  (D) demand for the product increases
  (E) the articles produced are of an inferior quality.

16. Your superior directs you to find certain papers. You know the purpose for which the papers are to be used. In the course of your search for the papers, you come across certain material which would be very useful for the purpose to be served by the papers. You should
    (A) bring the papers to your superior and ask whether he wishes the other materials
    (B) go to your superior immediately and ask whether he wishes both the papers and the materials
    (C) bring to your superior the other materials together with the papers
    (D) bring only the other materials and point out to your superior how these materials are of greater value than the papers
    (E) bring only the papers and say nothing about the other materials.

17. The purpose of new regulations requiring that the use of any excessive flavoring or coloring matter in whiskey be noted on the label is to
    (A) keep people from buying such whiskey
    (B) make the taste of whiskey less pleasant
    (C) let the buyer know the exact quality of his purchases
    (D) decrease the number of different blends of whiskey
    (E) keep distillers from using any such matters.

18. The fact that ships leaving shore seem to drop below the horizon proves chiefly that
    (A) the ocean and the horizon merge at a certain point
    (B) the farther from shore, the lower the ship
    (C) the earth is round
    (D) the distance between the ship and the shore is increased
    (E) the ship gradually fades out.

19. The individual distinguishes differences in colors primarily because colors
    (A) have different chemical compositions
    (B) have different wave-lengths
    (C) are all part of the color spectrum
    (D) reflect light
    (E) are visible except to those who are color blind.

20. The various forms of social insurance are aimed at
    (A) eradicating unhappiness
    (B) effecting a radical change in our social system
    (C) eliminating the causes of dependency
    (D) spreading the cost of maintaining those in need over as many people and as wide a period of time as possible
    (E) getting the most good to the greatest number.

21. The fact that fossil fish are found on a mountain indicates that
    (A) fishes once lived on land
    (B) the mountain-top was once below sea-level
    (C) fish were one of the first organisms existent upon the earth
    (D) the level of the sea and the mountain was once equal
    (E) fossil fish are valuable as relics of prehistoric life.

22. The Government does not allow pictures to be made of its paper money because in that way
    (A) it preserves the bills
    (B) discourages counterfeiting
    (C) it stabilizes the currency
    (D) it prevents paper money from being used in preference to coins
    (E) it conceals the infinite detail in the currency.

23. "All minors everywhere are highly emotional, for they are adolescents." This statement assumes most nearly that
    (A) all adolescents who are highly emotional are minors
    (B) all adolescents are minors
    (C) few minors are not emotional
    (D) any person who is an adolescent is highly emotional
    (E) some adolescents are not highly emotional.

24. Rare manuscripts are reproduced on photographic film
    (A) to reduce the possibility of loss by fire
    (B) so that the text may be available without any disturbance to the original manuscript
    (C) so that they may be stored in smaller space
    (D) to facilitate ready reference
    (E) to aid scholars in research.

25. The chief reason why a bank can extend its loans beyond the volume of the cash in its possession is that
    (A) it takes a long time for checks drawn upon it to be cashed
    (B) checks drawn upon it are likely to be deposited with it instead of being cashed
    (C) checks drawn upon it are likely to be deposited in another bank
    (D) the bank does not have to supply the required loan immediately
    (E) the bank can extend its loan thirty per cent beyond cash at hand by federal law.

26. Water from a spring in the woods should generally be boiled before being used for drinking purposes chiefly because
    (A) it may contain dirt
    (B) boiling will remove any taste of clay
    (C) any sediment contained in the water will settle to the bottom after boiling
    (D) it may contain harmful bacteria
    (E) the minerals in it will be eliminated by boiling.

27. The air is cool at the bottom of an unused chimney because it is
    (A) undisturbed
    (B) under pressure
    (C) farther from the outside air
    (D) heavier and cool air settled there
    (E) away from the sun's rays.

28. If the earth were made of lead, objects would
    (A) weigh more
    (B) weigh less
    (C) retain their present weight
    (D) tend to decrease in dimension
    (E) corrode.

29. The relative position of stars in the sky is continually changing because
    (A) of the stellar "drift"
    (B) the earth moves eastward around the sun once a year
    (C) of the semi-annual increase in the earth's velocity
    (D) of changes in the relative distance between the earth and the stars
    (E) of phenomena as yet unexplained.

30. Leverage is most useful in
    (A) multiplying energy
    (B) decreasing work
    (C) reducing friction
    (D) gaining mechanical advantage
    (E) bending heavy bars.

END OF EXAMINATION

Now that you have completed the last Test in this Examination, use your available time to make sure that you have written in your answers correctly on the Answer Sheet. Then, after your time is up, check your answers with the Correct Answers we have provided for you. Derive your scores for each Test Category and determine where you are weak so as to plan your study accordingly.

CORRECT ANSWERS FOR SAMPLE EXAMINATION I.

Now compare your answers with these Correct Answers to the Practice Questions. If your answers differ from these, go back and study those questions to see where and how you made your mistakes.

TEST I. READ AND DEDUCE

1.B	4.A	7.A	10.E	13.E	16.A	19.B
2.B	5.E	8.A	11.C	14.E	17.E	20.B
3.D	6.D	9.C	12.D	15.B	18.B	

TEST II. SYNONYMS

1.C	4.C	7.A	10.D	13.A	16.B	19.C
2.C	5.C	8.C	11.B	14.A	17.B	20.B
3.B	6.A	9.C	12.B	15.A	18.C	

TEST III. LETTER SERIES

1.A	4.B	7.B	10.C	13.A	16.B	19.D
2.D	5.C	8.C	11.A	14.D	17.D	20.B
3.C	6.A	9.B	12.D	15.C	18.A	

TEST IV. ABSTRACT REASONING

1.C	3.E	5.B	7.D	9.A	11.A	13.A	15.C
2.C	4.D	6.A	8.D	10.C	12.D	14.E	16.E

TEST V. READ AND INFER

1.C	3.E	5.C	7.E	9.C	11.E	13.D	15.E
2.B	4.B	6.C	8.D	10.B	12.E	14.B	16.D

TEST VI. LOGICAL SEQUENCE

1.B	4.D	7.B	10.E	13.C
2.E	5.C	8.A	11.D	14.A
3.A	6.D	9.C	12.B	15.E

TEST VII. MATHEMATICS

1.C	5.C	8.B	11.D	14.D	17.A	20.D	23.C
2.B	6.A	9.C	12.C	15.C	18.D	21.C	24.B
3.B	7.B	10.A	13.B	16.D	19.D	22.D	25.D
4.A							

TEST VIII. ARITHMETIC COMPUTATIONS

1.C	3.D	5.E	7.B	9.E
2.C	4.A	6.D	8.A	10.C

TEST IX. DATA INTERPRETATION

1. C	5. B	9. B	13. A	17. D	21. C	25. B
2. C	6. C	10. A	14. B	18. C	22. D	
3. B	7. D	11. B	15. C	19. A	23. C	
4. B	8. D	12. A	16. C	20. B	24. D	

TEST IX. EXPLANATORY ANSWERS

1. **(C)** It is possible to answer this question by careful reading of the two reports shown, without any computation at all. John Brown's report covers Turnstiles 1, 2, 3, and 4 from 7 AM to 3 PM, and Mary Smith's report covers the same Turnstiles from 3 PM to 11PM. Therefore, the Closing Reading for Turnstile 2 on John Brown's report (Entry F) will be the same figure as the Opening Reading for Turnstile 2 on Mary Smith's report.

    To compute the Closing Reading, simply add the Difference shown for Turnstile 2 to the Opening Reading given:
    $$3442 + 839 = 4281$$

2. **(C)** As in Question 1, this figure can be supplied by simply reading the report. The Opening Reading for Turnstile 3 (Entry G) on Mary Smith's report will be the same as the Closing Reading for Turnstile 3 on John Brown's report.

    To compute the Opening Reading, subtract the Difference (or number of turns made) from the Closing Reading given:
    $$9757 - 353 = 9404$$

3. **(B)**
    ```
    8588 Closing Reading
   -8265 Opening Reading
     323 Difference or Entry H
    ```

4. **(B)** Entry I is the sum of all opening Readings
    ```
     5123
     3442
     8951
     7663
    25179
    ```

5. **(B)** Entry J is the sum of all closing readings
    ```
     6019
     4683
     9757
     8588
    29047
    ```

90 / *P.A.C.E. Professional-Administrative Career Exam*

6. **(C)** The difference between Total Fares and Net Fares = 1687 − 1680 = 7
Since Test Rings = 3, the remainder of the difference must be made up of Slugs and Foreign Coins.

      7 Difference between Total Fares and Net Fares
     −3 Test Rings
      4 Slugs and Foreign Coins

7. **(D)**   2169 Net Fares
     ×   .35 Token Value
   $759.15 Net Fares at Token Value or Entry L

8. **(D)** Since no tokens were transferred out, Mary Smith's Total Token Reserve = Tokens at Start + Tokens Received.

    6450 Total Token Reserve
 −5000 Token Reserve at Start
    1450 Tokens Received or Entry M

9. **(B)**   4200 Token Reserve at Start
  +2200 Tokens Received
    6400
  −1400 Tokens transferred Out
    5000 Total Token Reserve or Entry N

10. **(A)**   6450 Total Token Reserve
  −5674 Total Reserve at End
     776 No. of Reserve Tokens Sold or Entry O

11. **(B)**   670 No. of Reserve Tokens Sold
   ×.35 Value of Each Token
  $234.50 Value of Reserve Tokens Sold or Entry P

12. **(A)**   588.00 Net Fares at Token Value (a)
  +271.60 Value of Reserve Tokens Sold (b)
  $ 859.60 Net Amount Due

13. **(A)** The Difference between the Opening Reading and the Closing Reading for each Turnstile = the number of times the Turnstile has turned or the number of passengers who have passed through the Turnstile. Therefore, the total number of passengers using Turnstile 2 = Number of Passengers (Difference) from 7 AM to 3 PM + Number of Passengers (Difference) from 3 PM to 11 PM.

$$839 + 402 = 1241$$

14. **(B)** Examination of the chart shows that Turnstile 2 had a Difference (which is the number of turns made or the number of passengers using the turnstile) of 839 between Opening and Closing Readings. This is greater than the Difference shown for Turnstiles 1, 3, or 4.

First Sample Exam / 91

15. **(C)**   2181 Total Fares 7 AM to 3 PM
             +1687 Total Fares 3 PM to 11 PM
              3868 Total Fares 7 AM to 11 PM

16. **(C)**   2169 Net Fares 7 AM to 3 PM
             +1680 Net Fares 3 PM to 11 PM
              3849 Total Net Fares 7 AM to 11 PM

17. **(D)**   2169 Net Fares 7 AM to 3 PM
             +1680 Net Fares 3 PM to 11 PM
              3849 Total Net Fares 7 AM to 11 PM
             × .35 Value of Tokens
          $1347.15 Net Fares at Token Value 7 AM to 11 PM

18. **(C)** To find the total number of passengers using Turnstile No. 1 from 7 AM to 11 AM, subtract the 7 AM reading at Turnstile 1 from the 11 AM reading at Turnstile 1:

    38485 11 AM Reading
    −37111 7 AM Reading
     1374 Total Number of Passengers using Turnstile No. 1

19. **(A)** To find the number of fares registered between 7 AM and 8 AM, subtract the 7 AM Reading from the 8 AM Reading for each Turnstile. Then compare the results to see which is the greatest.

    Turnstile 1   37905 8 AM Reading
                   −37111 7 AM Reading
                     794 Number of fares registered

    Turnstile 2   79013 8 AM Reading
                   −78432 7 AM Reading
                     581 Number of Fares Registered

    Turnstile 3   45921 8 AM Reading
                   −45555 7 AM Reading
                     366 Number of Fares Registered

    Turnstile 4   90063 8 AM Reading
                   −89954 7 AM Reading
                     109 Number of Fares Registered

20. **(B)** To find the number of passengers using all turnstiles from 10 AM to 11 AM, subtract the 10 AM reading from the 11 AM reading for each turnstile, then add the resulting figures.

    Turnstile 1   38485 11 AM Reading
                   −38451 10 AM Reading
                      34 Passengers Registered

    Turnstile 2   79306 11 AM Reading
                   −79237 10 AM Reading
                      69 Passengers Registered

Turnstile 3 46233 11 AM Reading
     −46143 10 AM Reading
       90 Passengers Registered

Turnstile 4 90299 11 AM Reading
     −90242 10 AM Reading
       57 Passengers Registered

34·+ 69 + 90 + 57 = 250 Total number of passengers using all turnstiles between 10 and 11 AM.

21. **(C)** To find the number of passengers registered per hour, subtract the earlier reading from the latter reading as follows:

  90063 8 AM Reading
  −89954 7 AM Reading
   109 Number of Passengers between 7 AM and 8 AM

  90121 9 AM Reading
  −90063 8 AM Reading
   58 Number of Passengers between 8 AM and 9 AM

  90242 10 AM Reading
  −90121 9 AM Reading
   121 Number of Passengers between 9 AM and 10 AM

  90299 11 AM Reading
  −90242 10 AM Reading
   57 Number of Passengers between 10 AM and 11 AM

Comparison of the resulting figures shows that the greatest number of passengers at Turnstile 4 was registered between 9 AM and 10 AM.

22. **(D)** Find the number of passengers for each Turnstile by subtracting the 8 AM Reading from the 9 AM Reading, then compare the results to see which is lowest.

Turnstile 1 38342 9 AM Reading
     −37905 8 AM Reading
      437 Passengers between 8 AM and 9 AM

Turnstile 2 79152 9 AM Reading
     −79013 8 AM Reading
      139 Passengers between 8 AM and 9 AM

Turnstile 3 45989 9 AM Reading
     −45921 8 AM Reading
      68 Passengers between 8 AM and 9 AM

Turnstile 4 90121 9 AM Reading
     −90063 8 AM Reading
      58 Passengers between 8 AM and 9 AM

Turnstile 4, with only 58 passengers registered, had the lowest number of passengers between 8 AM and 9 AM.

23. **(C)** The progress of Clerk A is as follows:

   Mon.   1 to 50   =   50 Applications Filed
   Tues. 50 to 100 =   50
   Wed.   100 to 200 = 100
   Thur. 200 to 300 = 100
   Fri.   300 to 350 = 50

   The progress of Clerk B is as follows:

   Mon.   1 to 100 = 100 Applications Filed
   Tues. 100 to 150 = 50
   Wed.   150 to 250 = 100
   Thur. 250 to 300 = 50
   Fri.   300 to 400 = 100

   Combined Totals of Applications Filed by both clerks =
   Mon.   50 + 100 = 150
   Tues. 50 + 50 = 100
   Wed. 100 + 100 = 200
   Thur. 100 + 50 = 150
   Fri.   50 + 100 = 150

   Therefore, the largest number of applications filed by both clerks was 200 applications, which were filed on Wednesday.

24. **(D)** Using the calculations above, it can be seen that by the end of the second day, Clerks A and B had filed 150 + 100 or 250 applications. Since they each had 500 applications to file, there are 1000 applications to be filed.
   1000 − 250 = 750 applications still to be filed after second day

   $\frac{750}{1000}$ = .75 or 75% of applications still to be filed.

25. **(B)** Using the calculations made above, it can be seen that the two clerks filed 750 applications from Monday to Friday
   (150 + 100 + 200 + 150 + 150 = 750)

   1000 − 750 = 250 applications left to be filed in the following week.

   At the rate of 100 to 150 applications filed per day, they will finish the job on Tuesday of the following week.

TEST X. APPLYING GENERAL KNOWLEDGE

1.D	5.D	9.C	13.A	17.C	21.D-B	25.B	29.B
2.A	6.D	10.E	14.B	18.C	22.B	26.D	30.D
3.D	7.B	11.E	15.A	19.B	23.D	27.D	
4.D	8.C	12.C	16.A	20.D	24.B	28.A	

Professional & Administrative Career Exam

PART THREE

Practice With Subjects on Which You Are Likely To Be Tested

THE GIST OF TEST STRATEGY

HOW TO BE A MASTER TEST TAKER

- APPROACH THE TEST CONFIDENTLY. TAKE IT CALMLY.
- REMEMBER TO REVIEW, THE WEEK BEFORE THE TEST.
- DON'T "CRAM." BE CAREFUL OF YOUR DIET AND SLEEP...ESPECIALLY AS THE TEST DRAWS NIGH.
- ARRIVE ON TIME...AND READY.
- CHOOSE A GOOD SEAT. GET COMFORTABLE AND RELAX.
- BRING THE COMPLETE KIT OF "TOOLS" YOU'LL NEED.
- LISTEN CAREFULLY TO ALL DIRECTIONS.
- APPORTION YOUR TIME INTELLIGENTLY WITH AN "EXAM BUDGET."
- READ ALL DIRECTIONS CAREFULLY. TWICE IF NECESSARY. PAY PARTICULAR ATTENTION TO THE SCORING PLAN.
- LOOK OVER THE WHOLE TEST BEFORE ANSWERING ANY QUESTIONS.
- START RIGHT IN, IF POSSIBLE. STAY WITH IT. USE EVERY SECOND EFFECTIVELY.
- DO THE EASY QUESTIONS FIRST; POSTPONE HARDER QUESTIONS UNTIL LATER.
- DETERMINE THE PATTERN OF THE TEST QUESTIONS. IF IT'S HARD-EASY ETC., ANSWER ACCORDINGLY.
- READ EACH QUESTION CAREFULLY. MAKE SURE YOU UNDERSTAND EACH ONE BEFORE YOU ANSWER. RE-READ, IF NECESSARY.
- THINK! AVOID HURRIED ANSWERS. GUESS INTELLIGENTLY.
- WATCH YOUR WATCH AND "EXAM BUDGET," BUT DO A LITTLE BALANCING OF THE TIME YOU DEVOTE TO EACH QUESTION.
- GET ALL THE HELP YOU CAN FROM "CUE" WORDS.
- REPHRASE DIFFICULT QUESTIONS FOR YOURSELF. WATCH OUT FOR "SPOILERS."
- REFRESH YOURSELF WITH A FEW, WELL-CHOSEN REST PAUSES DURING THE TEST.
- USE CONTROLLED ASSOCIATION TO SEE THE RELATION OF ONE QUESTION TO ANOTHER AND WITH AS MANY IMPORTANT IDEAS AS YOU CAN DEVELOP.
- NOW THAT YOU'RE A "COOL" TEST-TAKER, STAY CALM AND CONFIDENT THROUGHOUT THE TEST. DON'T LET ANYTHING THROW YOU.
- EDIT, CHECK, PROOFREAD YOUR ANSWERS. BE A "BITTER ENDER." STAY WORKING UNTIL THEY MAKE YOU GO.

Professional & Administrative Career Exam

TOP SCORES ON READING TESTS

In the following pages you'll find every proven technique for succeeding with the reading comprehension question, the pitfall of many a test-taker. These methods have worked beautifully for thousands of ambitious people and they are certain to help you. They are well worth all the time you can afford to devote to them.

Students must be able to read the paragraphs quickly, and still be able to answer questions correctly. The more correct answers you can give, the better your score will be. But if there are twenty paragraphs, and you are able to finish only ten because you read slowly, obviously, you are going to get a score of 50 percent, even if you answer all the questions correctly. On the other hand, if you finish all the paragraphs but can only answer half of the questions correctly, you will still get only 50 percent. Your goal, then, is to build up enough speed to finish all the paragraphs, and at the same time give as many correct answers as possible.

Our goal is to help you reach your goal—and then some. We want you to get the best score possible on any test of reading comprehension; and we also want you to be able to read with enough speed and understanding so that your studying time is cut in half, and your pleasure reading time is multiplied.

You *can* upgrade your reading ability—but you must have a plan—a procedure—a method. First, let us understand that there are two aspects of success in reading interpretation:
1. READING SPEED
   and
2. UNDERSTANDING WHAT YOU READ.

But these two aspects are not separate. As a matter of fact, they are totally dependent on each other. You can improve your speed by improving your comprehension—and then your comprehension will improve further because you have improved your speed. What you are improving, therefore, is your *speed of comprehension*. Your eyes and your mind must work together. As your mind begins to look for ideas rather than words, your eyes will begin to obey your mind. Your eyes will start to skim over words, looking for the ideas your mind is telling them to search for. Good reading is good thinking—and a good thinker will be a good reader. Speed and comprehension work together.

For convenience, however, let us divide our discussion into two parts—increasing reading speed and improving reading comprehension.

Increasing Reading Speed

A great many people read very slowly and with little comprehension, yet are completely unaware of just how badly they do read. Some people pronounce the words to themselves as they read, saying each word almost as distinctly as though reading aloud; or they think each one separately.

The reason for this is that many people have not gone quite far enough in their "learning to read" process. When you were first taught to read, you learned the sounds of each letter. Then you learned that if you put the letters together, they would make words. But that is where many people stop. Reading, to them, is reading words. But try reading a sentence out loud, saying each word as though it were a separate unit. How does it sound? Pretty meaningless! A more mature reader will put words together to make phrases. And the most mature reader will put phrases together to make ideas. A writer uses words to state ideas—and that is what a good reader looks for—those ideas. This will affect the way his eyes work. Let's see how.

HOW YOUR EYES WORK IN READING

As you learn to read phrases and thoughts, you will find that your eyes are increasing their *span*. This means that your eyes are seeing several words at a time as you are reading, not just one.

S771

Your eyes work as a camera does. When you want to take a picture, you hold the camera still and snap the shutter. If you move the camera, the picture will blur. When you read, your eyes take pictures of words—and, like a camera, when they are "photographing," they are standing still. Each time your eyes "picture" words in a line of print, they stop—and each stop is called a *fixation*. Watch someone read, and you will see how his eyes make very quick stops across the line. You know he has finished a line when you see his eyes sweep back to the beginning of the next line.

EYE SPAN AND FIXATION

The more words your eyes take in with one fixation, the larger the eye span. And the larger the eye span, the fewer stops your eyes will have to make across the line. Thus, you will be reading faster.

For example, let's divide a sentence the way a slow, word-by-word reader would:

You/ will/ find/ that/ you/ can/ read/ faster/ if/ you/ per/ mit/ your/ eyes/ to/ see/ large/ thought/ units/.

The reader's eyes have made at least nine stops on each line.

This is the way a fast reader would divide the same sentence:

You will find that/ you can read faster/ if/ you permit/ your eyes to see/ large thought/ units.

This reader's eyes have stopped only three times on each line, so of course he will be able to read much faster. Also, reading thought units will enable him to grasp the meaning more effectively. Now here are some exercises to help you increase your eye span.

EXERCISES FOR INCREASING EYE-SPAN

1.
```
0............0............0............0
0............0............0............0
0............0............0............0
0............0............0............0
0............0............0............0
0............0............0............0
```

In the above "paragraph," the dots stand for letters and each 0 is one eye fixation. "Read" a line, forcing your eyes to shift from 0 to 0. When you finish the first line, let your eyes swing back to the next line. Try to get an even rhythm. Now you can feel what your eyes should be doing as they read a line in four fixations. Is this different from the way they usually feel when you read? Keep practicing this "paragraph" until it feels comfortable, and then try to read a line of print in the same way. You can make up your own "paragraph" with only three fixations and practice.

2. Here is a list of three-word phrases, with a line drawn down the center. Focus your eyes on the line, and look at the three words at once. Remember, only *one* fixation. Do not read each word separately. If you have trouble at first, read the phrases through once in your usual way, and then practice the one fixation.

at the store
day and night
box of candy
come with me
in the house
bring my paper
time to finish
make every effort
all the questions
read very fast

3. Choose a newspaper column on a subject that interests you, and read it through. Then draw two vertical lines equally distant from each other down the center. Reread the column fixating on first one vertical line, then the next—two fixations per line. When you get very good at this, try drawing just one line down the center and fixating once. You can practice this daily.

VOCALIZING CAN SLOW YOU DOWN

Some readers move their lips or whisper while they read "silently." This habit is called vocalizing. It is caused by the fact that your earliest reading was done aloud, and the habit of hearing each word as you read it, persists.

It would be physically impossible for you to speak at the rate of speed at which a good reader can read—say 350 words per minute. And if you could, no one could understand you. If you read only as fast as you can talk, you will never be a fast reader.

Obviously, then, you must stop vocalizing. Your

lips and vocal cords must not be permitted to interfere in the exchange of ideas between eyes and mind. Even if you are not obviously vocalizing, you may be subvocalizing. Your lips are not moving, your vocal cords are not involved, but you are hearing each word as you read it. This is as much a deterrent to reading speed as actual vocalizing. Most people *do* subvocalize.

HOW TO STOP VOCALIZING

1. Put your fingers on your lips. Make sure your lips do not move as you read. If they do, put a pencil or a rubber eraser between your teeth. Then read. If you start to vocalize, the pencil will drop out. If you are reading in public you might be embarrassed to appear with a pencil in your mouth. In that case, just clench your teeth hard—and keep reading.

2. Only *you* will know if you are subvocalizing—and be honest with yourself. If you are subvocalizing (and you probably are) try this exercise. Before you start to read, repeat these nonsense syllables to yourself for 30 seconds: da-rum, da-rum, da-rum, da-rum, etc. Now begin to read and continue to repeat da-rum as you read. If you are doing this, then you cannot subvocalize what you are reading. At first you will find this extremely difficult to do, but if you keep practicing, soon you will find that there is a direct connection between written word and thought—with no intervening vocalizing.

VARY YOUR READING SPEED

One should adjust his reading speed to what he is reading. Some paragraphs will be easier for you than others, possibly because you are more interested in the subject matter, or know something about it. Other paragraphs, particularly those that deal with factual or technical material, may have to be read more slowly.

Flexibility should be employed so that the reader will change his speed from paragraph to paragraph—even from sentence to sentence, just as a driver would vary his driving speed depending on where he is driving. Some passages are open highways while others are crowded city thoroughfares.

For example, read the following passage:

It was a sunny Sunday afternoon in December. Some people were at the movies; some were out walking; and some were at home listening to the radio. Suddenly an announcement was broadcast—and the United States was plunged into war.

On December 7, 1941, the Japanese Air Force attacked Pearl Harbor, destroying battleships, aircraft carriers, planes, and a strategic military base, leaving the United States without the military arsenals needed for anti-aircraft activity and civilian protecton.

Which of these paragraphs is the "highway"? Which is the crowded city thoroughfare? Where can you breeze through? Where will you need to slow down to absorb every detail. You're right! The first paragraph is a simple introduction. A glance should suffice. The second paragraph is fact-packed, so you will need to slow down.

OTHER PHYSICAL FACTORS

Don't neglect the obvious reading aids. Good eyesight is essential. When was your last eye checkup? If glasses were prescribed, are you using them? Make sure that you are physically comfortable, sitting erect wlth head slightly inclined. You should have good direct and indirect light, with the direct light coming from behind you and slightly above your shoulder. Hold your reading matter at your own best reading distance so that you don't have to stoop or squint.

FORCE YOURSELF TO FASTER READING

Now that you know the elements that make for fast reading, you must continue to force yourself to read as quickly as you can. Use a stop-watch to time yourself. You can figure your rate of speed by dividing the number of words on a page into the number of seconds it took you to read it, and then multiplying by 60. This will give you your rate in words-per-minute. Since no one rate of speed is possible for all reading material, your rate will vary. But an average reading speed of 350 words-per-minute should be possible for uncomplicated, interesting, straightforward material. If you are already reading that fast, then try for 500 words-per-minute. You should be able to answer correctly at least 80 per cent of the questions following a reading passage.

Practice reading quickly. Move your eyes rapidly across the line of type, skimming it. Don't permit your eyes to stop for individual words. Proceed quickly through the paragraph without backtracking. If you think you don't understand what you are reading, then reread two or three times—but always read quickly. You will be amazed to discover how much you actually do understand.

Improving Reading Comprehension

Many readers are afraid of not understanding what they read quickly. But the old idea that slow readers make up for their slowness by better comprehension of what they read has been proven untrue. Your ability to comprehend what you read will keep pace with your increase in speed. You will absorb as many ideas per page as before, and get many more ideas per unit of reading time.

It has been demonstrated that those who read quickly also read best. This is probably due to the fact that heavier concentration is required for rapid reading; and concentration is what enables a reader to grasp important ideas contained in the reading material.

GETTING THE MAIN IDEA

A good paragraph generally has one central thought—and that thought is usually stated in one sentence. That sentence, the *topic sentence,* is often the first sentence of the paragraph, but it is sometimes buried in the middle, or it can be at the end. Your main task is to locate that sentence and absorb the thought it contains while reading the paragraph. The correct interpretation of the paragraph is based on that thought *as it is stated,* and not on your personal opinion, prejudice, or preference about that thought.

Here are several examples of paragraphs. Read them quickly and see if you can pick out the topic sentence. It is the key sentence. The rest of the paragraph either supports or illustrates it. The answers follow the paragraphs.

1. Pigeon fanciers are firmly convinced that modern inventions can never replace the carrier pigeon. "A pigeon gets through when everything else fails," they say. In World War II, one pigeon flew twenty miles in twenty minutes to cancel the bombing of a town. Radios may get out of order and telephone lines may get fouled up, but the pigeon is always ready to take off with a message.
2. When a piece of paper burns, it is completely changed. The ash that is left behind does not look like the original piece of paper. When dull-red rust appears on a piece of tinware, it is quite different from the gleaming tin. The tarnish that forms on silverware is a new substance unlike the silver itself. Animal tissue is unlike the vegetable substance from which it is made. A change in which the original substance is turned into a different substance is called a chemical change.
3. A child who stays up too late is often too tired to be successful in school. A child who is allowed to eat anything he wishes may have bad teeth and even suffer from malnutrition. Children who are rude and disorderly often suffer pangs of guilt. Children who are disciplined are happy children. They blossom in an atmosphere where they know exactly what is expected of them. This provides them with a sense of order, a feeling of security.

Answers: In paragraph 1, the first sentence is the topic sentence. In paragraph 2, the last sentence is the topic sentence. In paragraph 3, it is the fourth sentence—"Children who are disciplined. . . . .".

If a selection consists of two or more paragraphs, the correct interpretation is based on the central idea of the entire passage. The ability to grasp the central idea of a passage can be acquired by practice—practice that will also increase the speed with which you read.

Reading for a Purpose—The Survey Method

Many readers don't know what they are looking for when they read. They plunge into a page full of words, and often that is what they end up with—just words. It's like walking into a supermarket without having made a list of what you want to buy. You wander aimlessly up and down the aisles and end up with a basketful of cookies and fruit and pickles—and nothing for a main dish.

It is extremely important to have a purpose in mind *before* you start to read—to make a "list" before you start shopping. Good readers use the *survey* method. By "survey" we mean a quick over-view of what you are going to read before you actually start reading. It is like looking at a road map before you start on a trip. If you know in what direction you are going, you are apt to get there sooner, and more efficiently. This is what you do.

1. Read the title. Think about what the selection will probably be about. What kind of information can you expect to obtain? Gear your mind to look for the central thought.

2. Think about the kind of vocabulary you will meet. Will it be technical? Are you familiar with the subject, or will you have to prepare yourself to meet many new words? After a quick glance, you may decide to skip this selection and go back to it later. (Remember, on a timed reading test you want to give yourself a chance to sample *all* the selections. The one at the end may be easier for you than the one in the middle, but you won't know if you never get to the end.) The difficulty of the vocabulary may be the deciding factor.

3. If there are subheadings, read them. They can provide a skeleton outline of the selection.

4. Read the first sentence of each paragraph. It usually contains the most important ideas in the selection. The topic sentence is more often found in the beginning of a paragraph than in any other position.

5. READ THE QUESTIONS BASED ON THE SELECTION. The questions are there to test whether or not you understand the most important ideas in the selection. If you read them first, they will steer you through your reading in the most effective way possible. Now you really know what to look for! In any kind of reading, whether on test or in texts, always look at the questions first (unless you are directed not to do so).

The survey method can be applied to all kinds of reading, particularly textbook reading. In addition to the above, you should include the following in your textbook survey:

(a) Read the preface quickly. It states the author's purpose in writing the book.

(b) Look at the publication date (on the copyright page). This can tell you if the information is up-to-date.

(c) Look through the table of contents. See what the author has included, and the order in which it appears. Some tables of contents can serve as an outline for the book.

(d) If there are chapter or part summaries, read through them quickly. They'll give you a forecast of what's to come.

(e) Look at illustrations, maps, graphs, etc. These are meant to help you visualize essential information. Remember, one picture can be worth a thousand words.

Increase Your Vocabulary

In order to understand what you are reading, you must know the meaning of the words that are used. Very often you can guess at the meaning from the rest of the sentence, but that method is not completely reliable. The sentence itself is important for determining which of the word's several meanings is intended, but you usually have to have some idea of the word itself.

How can you build a larger vocabulary? You could sit down with a long list of words and try to memorize it, or perhaps go through the dictionary page by page. This would be very time consuming—and very boring! Memorizing words is probably the *least* successful way of building a vocabulary.

Words are best remembered when they are understood and used, when they are part of your own experience. Here are some ways in which you can do this.

1. Learn a little etymology. You already know a lot, because approximately 70 per cent of the words we use consist of roots and prefixes de-

rived from Latin and Greek. There are 84 roots and 44 prefixes that are the mainstay of our language. If you learn those you will have a clue to the meaning of thousands of words. For example, the Latin root *voc* (meaning "to call") appears in the words advocate, vocation, irrevocable, vociferous, etc. The root *port* (meaning "to carry") is found in the words report, export, support, porter, etc.

Learn to look for the roots of words, and for familiar parts of words you meet.

2. Read—everything, anything. Even signs and posters sometimes have new words in them. Try to find at least one new word every day.

3. Use the dictionary—frequently and extensively. Look up the meaning of a word you don't know, and see if you can identify its root.

4. Play word games—like Anagrams, Scrabble. And do Crossword Puzzles.

5. Listen to people who speak well. Don't be afraid to ask them the meaning of a word they use that is unfamiliar to you. They'll be flattered.

6. Make a personal word list of your new words. Make it on index cards so that you can play a "flash-card" game with yourself.

7. Look for special word meanings in special subject areas. Since most reading comprehension passages deal with science, literature, or social studies, a weakness in the vocabulary used in these subjects can put you at a great disadvantage. Be sure you know the meaning of the terms that are frequently used.

8. Use the new words you learn each day. Don't save them for a rainy day—by then they may be lost. When you talk or write, try to use as many new words as you can. A word used is a word remembered!

Cues and Clues For Readers

Examination points may be unnecessarily lost by ignoring the author's hints as to what *he* thinks is most important. Be on the lookout for such phrases as "Note that . . ." "Of importance is . . ." "Don't overlook . . ." These give clues to what the writer is stressing. Beware of negatives and all-inclusive statements. They are often put in to trip you up. Words like *always, never, all, only, every, absolutely, completely, none, entirely, no,* can sometimes turn a reasonable statement into an untrue statement. For example look at the following sentence:

When you get caught in the rain, you catch cold.
True? Of course. Now look at this sentence:
When you get caught in the rain, you *always* catch cold.
Different, isn't it? Not *always* true.

PUNCTUATION

Other hints which you should also watch for are those given by punctuation. Here are a few points to keep in mind:

1. QUOTATION MARKS—When a statement is quoted, it may not necessarily represent the author's opinion, or the main thought of the passage. Be sure you make this distinction if it is called for.

2. EXCLAMATION POINT—This mark is often used to indicate an *emphatic* or *ironical* comment. It's the author's way of saying, "This is important!"

3. COMMAS—Watch those commas. They can change the meaning of a sentence. For example:

As I left the room, in order to go to school John called me.

As I left the room in order to go to school, John called me.

In each sentence, a different person is going to school.

4. PARENTHESES—These are often used to set off a part of the sentence that is not absolutely necessary to the sentence. But don't ignore them in reading comprehension tests. Sometimes they give vital information. For example:

Shakespeare (whose life spanned the sixteenth and seventeenth centuries) was a great dramatist.

5. COLON—Often used to emphasize a sequence in thought between two independent sentences. For example:

Science plays an important role in our civilization: thus we should all study physics, chemistry, and biology.

6. ELLIPSES—Three dots often found in quoted material which indicates that there has been an omission of material from the original quotation. Often the material omitted is not important, but a good, critical reader should be aware of the omission.

TEN SUCCESS STEPS

Here are proven techniques for getting the right answer to *any* Reading Interpretation question.

Survey Selection

1. Read the selection through quickly to get the general sense.
2. Reread the selection, concentrating on the central idea.
3. Can you now pick out the *topic sentence* in each paragraph?
4. If the selection consists of more than one paragraph, determine the *central idea* of the entire selection.

Survey Stems
Concentrate on Each Question

5. Examine the five choices carefully, yet rapidly. Eliminate immediately those choices which are *far-fetched, ridiculous, irrelevant, false,* or *impossible*.
6. Eliminate those choices which may be true, but which have nothing to do with the sense of the selection.
7. Check those few choices which now remain as possibilities.

Reread Selectively
Shuttle Back to Selection

8. Refer back to the original selection and determine which one of these remaining possibilities is best in view of

    a) specific information in the selection
    or
    b) implied information in the selection

Reread only the part of the selection that applies to the question, and make your decision as to the correct choice based on these considerations:

(a) A choice must be based on fact actually given or definitely understood (and not on your personal opinion or prejudice.) Some questions require making a judgment—and this judgment also must be based on the facts as given.

(b) In questions involving the central thought of the passage (for example: "The best title for this selection . . .") the choice must accurately reflect the entire thought—not too narrow, and not too general.

9. Be sure to consider only the facts *given* or *definitely understood* some place in the selection.

10. Be especially careful of trick expressions or "catch-words" which sometimes destroy the validity of a seemingly acceptable answer. These include the expressions: "under all circumstances," "at all times," "never," "always," "under no conditions," "absolutely," "completely," and "entirely."

AVOID THE TRAPS

Trap #1—Sometimes the question cannot be answered on the basis of the stated facts. You may be required to make a deduction from the facts given.
Trap #2—Eliminate your personal opinions.

Trap #3—Search out significant details that are nestled in the paragraph. Reread the paragraph as many times as necessary (with an eye on your watch).

104 / P.A.C.E. Professional-Administrative Career Exam

USING THE "SUCCESS STEPS" WITH A PRACTICE PASSAGE

HERE'S HOW YOU SHOULD ANSWER THESE READING QUESTIONS. Each one is made up of a paragraph, followed by four or five statements based on the paragraph. You may never have seen the paragraph before, but you must now read it carefully so that you understand it. Then read the statements following. Any one of them might be right. You have to choose the one that is most correct. Try to pick the one that's most complete, most accurate . . . the one that is best supported by and necessarily flows from the paragraph. Be sure that it contains nothing false so far as the paragraph itself is concerned. After you've thought it out, write the capital letter preceding your best choice in the margin next to the question. When you've answered all the questions, score yourself faithfully by checking with our answers that follow the last question. But please don't look at those answers until you've written your own. You just won't be helping yourself if you do that. Besides, you'll have ample opportunity to do the questions again, and to check with our answers, in the event that your first try results in a low score.

DESCRIPTION OF THE TEST AND SAMPLE QUESTIONS

Here are some sample questions for you to do. Mark your answers on the Sample Answer Sheet, making sure to keep your mark inside the correct box. If you want to change an answer, erase the mark you don't want to count. Then mark your new answer. Use a No. 2 (medium) pencil.

CONSOLIDATE YOUR KEY ANSWERS HERE

```
   A B C D E      A B C D E      A B C D E      A B C D E      A B C D E
1 [ ][ ][ ][ ][ ]  2 [ ][ ][ ][ ][ ]  3 [ ][ ][ ][ ][ ]  4 [ ][ ][ ][ ][ ]  5 [ ][ ][ ][ ][ ]
```

Let us, now, demonstrate with an actual exam-type reading interpretation selection how to apply the ten "success steps":

Reading Passage

Vacations were once the prerogative of the privileged few, even as late as the 19th century. Now they are considered the right of all, except for such unfortunate masses as, for example, the bulk of China's and India's population, for whom life, save for sleep and brief periods of rest, is uninterrupted toil.

They are more necessary now than once because the average life is less well-rounded and has become increasingly departmentalized. I suppose the idea of vacations, as we conceive it, must be incomprehensible to primitive peoples. Rest of some kind has of course always been a part of the rhythm of human life, but earlier ages did not find it necessary to organize it in the way that modern man has done. Holidays, feast days, were sufficient.

With modern man's increasing tensions, with the stultifying quality of so much of his work, this break in the year's routine became steadily more necessary. Vacations became mandatory for the purpose of renewal and repair. And so it came about that in the United States, the most self-indulgent of nations, the tensest and most departmentalized, vacations have come to take a predominant place in domestic conversation.

STEP-BY-STEP EXPLANATIONS

STEP 1—We read the selection through quickly to get the general sense.
STEP 2—We reread the selection concentrating on the central idea.
STEP 3—We discover that the topic sentence of each paragraph of this selection is the first sentence of each paragraph. This order is almost always the case: the topic sentence is the first sentence of a paragraph.
STEP 4—The central idea of the selection consists of various aspects of vacations.

① The title below that best expresses the ideas of this passage is:
    a. Vacation Preferences
    b. Vacations: the Topic of Conversation
    c. Vacations in Perspective
    d. The Well-Organized Vacation
    e. Renewal, Refreshment and Repair

Explanation of Question

STEP 5—Question 1. . . . We eliminate Choice D immediately because it is irrelevant. The selection refers in no way to organization of a vacation.
STEP 6—Eliminate Choice B. Vacations are often a topic of conversation—not so in this selection, however.
STEP 7—Since Choices A, C, and E remain as possible correct choices, we check them.
STEP 8—Choice C is an all-inclusive title. Choices A and E are not all-inclusive. Therefore, C is the correct choice as the best title for the passage.
STEP 9—In arriving at the correct answer, we have considered only the facts given or definitely understood.
STEP 10—We were on the alert for trick expressions and "catch-words." There were none in Question 1.

....

Proceed in the same "10-Step" manner in answering questions 2, 3 and 4 of the sample selection.

② We need vacations now more than ever before because we have
    A. a more carefree nature
    B. much more free time
    C. little diversity in our work
    D. no emotional stability
    E. a higher standard of living

Explanation of Question

We concentrate on Question 2 and its five possible answers. We remember that first reading indicated that the answer to this question is in the beginning of paragraph 2, so we reread just that part of the selection, which deals with the necessity for vacations. Choice A is irrelevant and ridiculous, and we eliminate it. Choice B may be a true statement, but it does not pertain to the *need* for vacations. Choice C looks like a good possibility, because a less well-rounded life that is increasingly departmentalized indicates little diversity—but better to check further. We eliminate Choice D immediately because of the word "no," one of our trick expressions. Choice E, like Choice B, does not refer to need. So we return to Choice C as the best possible answer.

③ It is implied in the passage that the lives of Americans are very
    A. habitual   C. patriotic
    B. ennobling   D. varied
               E. independent

Explanation of Question

We concentrate on Question 3 with its five possible answers, remembering that the answer is to be found in paragraph 3—so we go directly to that paragraph. The word "implied" in the stem of the question tells us that we may not find a direct answer but will have to do some thinking. The paragraph tells us that much work is stultifying, that there is much routine, and that vacations are necessary for renewal and repair. We can conclude, then, that life is pretty dull and we will look at the choices to find a word that is synonymous with "dull." Choice A is certainly a possibility, but we look quickly at the remaining choices just to be sure, and discover that there is no other possible choice; B, C, and E are irrelevant, and D is the exact opposite. Choice A is our answer.

④ As used in the passage, the word "prerogative" (line 1) most nearly means
    A. habit   C. request
    B. distinction D. demand
               E. hope

Explanation of Question

Concentrating on Question 4 we find that it calls for the definition of a word which is located in line 1, so we go to that portion of the paragraph. Word definitions can often be answered by a careful reading of the sentence in which the word appears, and often the following sentence as well. If we read the sentence in which "prerogative" appears and look at the five possible answers, any one of them might be correct. However, if we read the first part of the second sentence in paragraph 1, we see the clue word *now*. In other words, at this time, as contrasted with the past, vacations are the right of all instead of the right of a few. We can thus conclude that the word "prerogative" is synonymous with the word "right." We look at the five possible choices in this light. We can eliminate A and E immediately since they are in no way synonymous with "right."

Choice C, while a possible synonym, is really too mild a word if we substitute it in the sentence. Choices B and D are possible, with Choice D seeming to be the most likely. But if we substitute it in the sentence for the word prerogative, it does not make as much sense as does Choice B, for vacations were not actually a demand of the privileged few—but more a distinction. Since the stem of our question asks for the nearest meaning, we can be most comfortable in choosing B.

STEP 8—*Shuttle back to the selection*. We check to see that we have answered each question and marked the answer in accordance with the directions specified at the beginning of the examination.

If you follow the outlined procedure for answering reading comprehension questions, you will find that you are answering questions correctly and quickly. Most passages will require at least two readings—one for general sense and one for answering the questions. The important thing is to know where to spot the answers, and to remain calm and collected when examining the possible choices. Don't panic—you can be pretty sure that if a question is hard for you it will be hard for everyone else, too.

A SAMPLE QUESTION ANALYZED

Here is a sample question followed by an analysis. Try to understand the process of arriving at the correct answer.

Reading Passage

"Too often, indeed, have scurrilous and offensive allegations by underworld creatures been sufficient to blast the career of irreproachable and incorruptible executives who, because of their efforts to serve the people honestly and faithfully, incurred the enmity of powerful political forces and lost their positions."

5) Judging from the contents of the preceding paragraph, you might best conclude that

(A) the larger majority of executives are irreproachable and incorruptible

(B) criminals often swear in court that honest officials are corrupt in order to save themselves

(C) political forces are always clashing with government executive

(D) underworld creatures make scurrilous and offensive allegations against incorruptible executives

(E) false statements by criminals sometimes cause honest officials the loss of their positions or the ruin of their careers.

Analysis of Choices

(A) can generally be said to be a true statement, but it cannot be derived from the paragraph. Nothing is said in the paragraph about "the larger majority" of executives.

(B) may also be a true statement and can to a certain extent be derived from the paragraph. However, the phrase "in order to save themselves" is not relevant to the sense of the paragraph, and even if it were, this choice does not sum up its central thought.

(C) cannot be derived from the paragraph. The catch-word "always" makes this choice entirely invalid.

(D) This choice is true as derived from the sense of the paragraph. It is open, however, to two exceptions. First, this choice is in the form of a general statement whereas the paragraph starts with the restrictive phrase "too often," thereby precluding a generality. Secondly, this choice does not summarize the central idea of the paragraph which may be better expressed in the remaining choice.

(E) is the *best* conclusion that could be drawn from the contents of the paragraph in the light of the five choices given. It is open to no exceptions and adequately sums up the central thought of the paragraph.

TEST I. READING COMPREHENSION

TIME: 20 Minutes. 15 Questions.

This reading comprehension test consists of a number of different passages. One or more questions are based on each passage. The questions are composed of incomplete statements about the passage. Each incomplete statement is followed by five choices lettered (A) (B) (C) (D) (E). Mark your answer sheet with the letter of that choice which best completes the statement, and which best conveys the meaning of the passage.

Correct key answers to these sample questions are given at the conclusion of the test. Please don't peek at our key answers until you've answered all the questions on your own.

Reading Passage

Next morning I saw for the first time an animal that is rarely encountered face to face. It was a wolverine. Though relatively small, rarely weighing more than 40 pounds, he is, above all animals, the one most hated by the Indians and trappers. He is a fine tree climber and a relentless destroyer. Deer, reindeer, and even moose succumb to his attacks. We sat on a rock and watched him come, a bobbing rascal in blackish-brown. Since the male wolverine occupies a very large hunting area and fights to the death any other male that intrudes on his domain, wolverines are always scarce, and in order to avoid extinction need all the protection that man can give. As a trapper, Henry wanted me to shoot him, but I refused, for this is the most fascinating and little known of all our wonderful predators. His hunchback gait was awkward and ungainly, lopsided yet tireless.

1. Wolverines are very scarce because

   (A) they suffer in the survival of the fittest
   (B) they are afraid of all humankind
   (C) they are seldom protected by man
   (D) trappers take their toll of them
   (E) their food supply is limited

2. The wolverine ran headlong into everything in his path because of his

   (A) pursuit by the trappers
   (B) helplessness in the face of danger
   (C) snow blindness
   (D) ferocious courage
   (E) anxiety and curiosity

3. The author of this selection is most probably

   (A) a conscientious naturalist
   (B) an experienced hunter
   (C) an inexperienced trapper
   (D) a young Indian
   (E) a farmer

Reading Passage

It's not necessary to travel great distances to other lands to find interesting, valuable scientific results. Here in the United States there are treasures to be found, which may be gone in a few years. Although the frontier has disappeared, there are still vast areas along the Atlantic seaboard and in the Mississippi Valley that are practically unexplored. Museums and universities sponsor expeditions for photographs of native wild birds and recordings of their voices. They are particularly interested in species endangered by encroaching civilization.

4. The writer points out that the Atlantic states provide

   (A) a rich field for scientific investigation
   (B) a high level of civilization
   (C) opportunities for travel
   (D) great museums and universities
   (E) vast areas

5. The writer mentions museum expeditions sent out to

   (A) create bird sanctuaries
   (B) domesticate wild birds
   (C) kill and retrieve birds for exhibits
   (D) take pictures of rare birds
   (E) capture native birds

6. The kind of treasure this paragraph refers to is

   (A) buried gold
   (B) new territory
   (C) museum collections
   (D) exact knowledge of wildlife
   (E) natural beauty

Reading Passage

Using new tools and techniques, scientists, almost unnoticed, are remaking the world of plants. They have already remodeled 65 sorts of flowers, fruits, vegetables, and trees, giving us among other things tobacco that resists disease, cantaloupes that are immune to the blight, and lettuce with crisper leaves. The chief new tool they are using is colchicine, a poisonous drug, which has astounding effects upon growth and upon heredity. It creates new varieties with astonishing frequency, whereas such mutations occur but rarely in nature. Colchicine has thrown new light on the fascinating jobs of the plant hunters. The Department of Agriculture sends men all over the world to find plants already here. Scientists have crossed these foreign plants with those at home, thereby adding many desirable characteristics to our farm crops. The colchicine technique has enormously facilitated their work because hybrids so often can be made fertile and because it takes so few generations of plants now to build a new variety with the qualities desired.

7. The title below that best expresses the idea of this paragraph is

   (A) Plant growth and heredity
   (B) New plants for old
   (C) Remodeling plant life
   (D) A more abundant world
   (E) The fascination of plant hunting

8. Mutation in plant life results in

   (A) diseased plants
   (B) hybrids
   (C) new varieties
   (D) fertility
   (E) larger and stronger plants

9. Colchicine speeds the improvement of plant species because it

   (A) makes possible the use of foreign plants
   (B) makes use of natural mutations
   (C) makes hybrid plants fertile
   (D) can be used with 65 different vegetables, fruits, and flowers
   (E) makes plants immune to disease and blight

Reading Passage

In a lightning-like military advance, similar to that used by the Germans, the use of persistent chemicals is unnecessary. It might even be a considerable detriment to a force advancing over a broad front.

10. According to the above paragraph

    (A) chemicals should not be used by a defending army
    (B) the Germans advanced in a narrow area
    (C) an advancing army may harm itself through the use of chemicals
    (D) chemicals are unnecessary if warfare is well-organized
    (E) chemical warfare is only effective if used by an advancing army

Reading Passage

The X-ray has gone into business. Developed primarily to aid in diagnosing human ills, the machine now works in packing plants, in foundries, in service stations, and in a dozen ways contributes to precision and accuracy in industry.

11. According to the above paragraph, the X-ray

    (A) was first developed to aid business
    (B) is more of a help to business than to medicine
    (C) is being used to improve the functioning of industry
    (D) is more accurate for packing plants than for foundries
    (E) increases the output of such industries as service stations

Reading Passage

For the United States, Canada has become the most important country in the world, yet there are few countries about which Americans know less. Canada is the third largest country in the world; only Russia and China are larger. The area of Canada is more than a quarter of the whole British Empire.

12. According to the above paragraph
    (A) the British Empire is smaller than Russia or China
    (B) the territory of China is greater than that of Canada
    (C) Americans know more about Canada than about China or Russia
    (D) the United States is the most important nation in the world as far as Canada is concerned
    (E) the Canadian population is more than one quarter the population of the British Empire.

Reading Passage

Whether or not the nerve impulses in various nerve fibers differ in kind is a question of great interest in physiology. The usually accepted view is that they are identical in character in all fibers and vary only in intensity.

13. Judging from the information contained in the foregoing paragraph it could be most correctly assumed that
    (A) nerve fibers are the product of neural impulses
    (B) nerve fibers are usually accepted as differing in kind
    (C) the nature of neural impulses is still a moot question
    (D) the student of physiology accepts the view that nerve impulses sometimes differ in intensity
    (E) the character of nerve fibers is accepted as being constant

Reading Passage

In humid climates a thick growth of vegetation with a mattress of interlacing roots usually protects the moist soil from wind. But in arid regions vegetation is either wholly lacking, or scant growths are found huddled in detached clumps, leaving patches of unprotected ground. Since there is little or no moisture present to make the soil particles cohere, they are readily lifted and scattered by the wind.

14. According to the passage
    (A) vegetation is always present in humid climates
    (B) lack of moisture decreases cohesion
    (C) moisture is an important element in soil and rock erosion
    (D) wind is the chief agent in the dispersal of topsoil
    (E) tree roots are closely associated with the thick growth of vegetation in moist climates

Reading Passage

When a classification of facts results in a simple principle describing the relationship and sequences of any group, that principle usually leads to the discovery of a wider range of phenomena in the same or related fields.

15. Which phrase most adequately describes the preceding paragraph?

    (A) relationship between group classifications
    (B) establishment of principles derived from group relationships and sequences
    (C) association of phenomena in a wide range of varied fields
    (D) establishment of general laws in hitherto undiscovered fields
    (E) discovery of hitherto unregarded phenomena in their relationships and sequences to varied groups

CONSOLIDATE YOUR KEY ANSWERS HERE

Practice using Answer Sheets. Make ONE mark for each answer. Additional and stray marks may be counted as mistakes. In making corrections erase errors COMPLETELY. Make glossy black marks. To arrive at an accurate estimate of your ability and progress cover the Correct Answers with a sheet of white paper while you are taking this test.

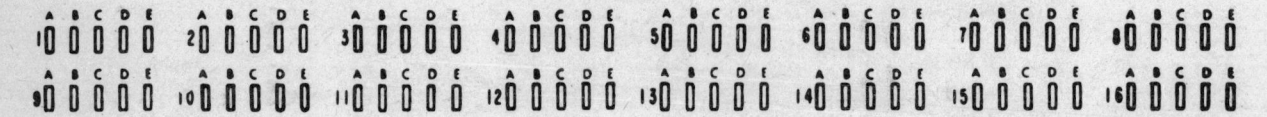

CORRECT ANSWERS TO THE FOREGOING PRACTICE QUESTIONS

Now compare your answers with these Correct Answers to the Practice Questions. If your answers differ from these, go back and study those questions to see where and how you made your mistakes.

1.A	3.A	5.D	7.C	9.C	11.C	13.C	15.B
2.E	4.A	6.D	8.C	10.C	12.B	14.B	

TEST II. READING COMPREHENSION

TIME: 15 Minutes. 10 Questions.

This test of reading interpretation consists of a number of brief passages. One question is based on each passage. A question consists of an incomplete statement about the passage. The statement is followed by five choices lettered (A) (B) (C) (D) (E). For each question, mark your answer sheet with the letter of that choice which best conveys the meaning of the passage, and which best completes the statement.

Correct key answers to these sample questions are given at the conclusion of the test. Please don't peek at our key answers until you've answered all the questions on your own.

Reading Passage

During the last century and a half the economic life of the western world has been transformed by a series of remarkable inventions and the general application of science to the productive process. A revolution, more profound in its effects than any armed revolt that ever shook the foundations of a political state, has been achieved in the three realms of manufacturing, agriculture, and communication.

1. The paragraph notes that science

    (A) has revolutionized the productive process
    (B) has shaken the foundations of manufacturing, agriculture and communication
    (C) is the tool of the inventor
    (D) has been an important factor in the founding of the agricultural process
    (E) is becoming more and more the determining factor in modern civilization

Reading Passage

Scientific judgments as opposed to legal judgments are more impartial, objective, and precise. They are more subject to verification by any competent observer.

2. According to the passage, scientific judgments

 (A) can be verified by competent observers
 (B) can be tested by advanced laboratory methods
 (C) accept no opinion until validated
 (D) accept no truth a priori
 (E) are usually propounded by experts in their fields

Reading Passage

A scientific law is the brief expression of relationships and sequences observed in any given group. It is the product of the perceptive and reasoning faculties in man, and can be formulated by man alone.

3. According to this passage, scientific law

 (A) may have meaning apart from the human mind if it is a summation of related scientific facts
 (B) is essentially a product of the human mind
 (C) may be related to man's reasoning faculties and yet not be based on experience
 (D) is as variable as the human mind
 (E) may exist without the human mind, but has no meaning until perceived

Reading Passage

We find many instances in early science of "a priori" scientific reasoning. Scientists thought it proper to carry generalizations from one field to another. It was assumed that the planets revolved in circles because of the geometrical simplicity of the circle. Even Newton assumed that there must be seven primary colors corresponding to the seven tones of the musical scale.

4. According to the paragraph one might best conclude that

   (A) Newton sometimes used the "a priori" method of investigation
   (B) scientists no longer consider it proper to carry over generalizations from one field to another
   (C) the planets revolve about the earth in ellipses rather than in circles
   (D) even great men like Newton sometimes make mistakes
   (E) the number of notes in the musical scale has no connection with the number of primary colors

Reading Passage

From analyses of the composition of food we have been able to determine caloric values. From such analyses we have also discovered vitamins, and have succeeded in measuring them, and in identifying their components.

5. From reading the passage one knows that

   (A) the composition of food materials has been greatly enlarged
   (B) food value per unit weight has added greatly to our knowledge of vitamins
   (C) quantitative estimation of fuel value in individual foods has added to our knowledge of their composition
   (D) investigation of the composition of foods has been aided by detailed analytical studies of their individual components
   (E) the determination of the unit weight in individual foods has increased our knowledge of the composition of foods

Reading Passage

It was formerly thought that whole wheat and graham breads were far superior to white bread made from highly refined wheat flour. However, it is now believed that the general use of milk solids in white bread significantly narrows the nutritional gap between the two types of bread. About the only dietary advantages now claimed for whole wheat bread are higher content of iron and vitamin B, both easily obtainable in many other common foods.

6. The paragraph notes that

   (A) white bread is fattening because of its milk content
   (B) whole wheat bread is not much more nutritious than white bread
   (C) whole wheat bread contains roughage
   (D) white bread contains neither iron nor vitamin B
   (E) contrary to popular misconception, white bread is not inferior in quality to bread made from graham or whole wheat flour

Reading Passage

The view is widely held that butter is more digestible and better absorbed than other fats because of its low melting point. There is little scientific authority for such a view. As margarine is made today, its melting point is close to that of butter, and tests show only the slightest degree of difference in digestibility of fats of equally low melting points.

7. According to the paragraph one could most reasonably conclude that

   (A) butter is more easily digested than margarine
   (B) the concept that butter has a lower melting point than other fats is a common misconception, disproved by scientists
   (C) there is not much difference in the digestibility of butter and margarine
   (D) most people prefer butter to margarine
   (E) it sometimes becomes necessary to use a substitute for butter

Reading Passage

More produce is artificially ripened by treatment with ethylene gas, which makes possible shipment in "the firm green condition," and the sale of fruits and vegetables before they would naturally be in season. This method of ripening is prohibited only when it is applied to oranges so unripe as to contain less than 8 parts of sugar to 1 of acid.

8. It can be reasonably concluded from the preceding paragraph that

   (A) artificial ripening is not harmful unless applied to oranges containing less than 8 parts of sugar to 1 of acid
   (B) fruits and vegetables are usually shipped in the firm green condition
   (C) oranges are ripe when they contain more than 8 parts of sugar to 1 of acid
   (D) the law does not prohibit the use of ethylene ripening in most cases
   (E) it is dangerous to eat fruits and vegetables out of season, since they are often artificially ripened

Reading Passage

Salt has always been important in our diet as a flavoring for food, but recently doctors have come to recognize it as an absolute necessity. Most living things contain salt and it is almost impossible to eat a normal diet without getting some. However, that "some" may not be enough. Now doctors recommend that those who normally use little salt step up their salt consumption in hot weather, when more than the usual salt intake is required by the body.

9. According to the preceding paragraph one could assume most correctly that

   (A) salt is necessary if life is to be maintained
   (B) people living on a normal diet have an intake of salt which is sufficient to maintain good health
   (C) the body needs more salt in summer than in winter
   (D) all organic life contains salt in one form or another
   (E) up to very recently, the most important function of salt has been its use in the flavoring of foods

Reading Passage

In a general way, the size and form of the brain is determined by the size and form of the cranial cavity. Some skulls are relatively long and narrow, others short and broad. But conformation of the skull, as seen from the outside, is not an accurate indication of the conformation of the brain within.

118 / P.A.C.E. Professional-Administrative Career Exam

10. The paragraph notes that
    (A) intelligence in humans is, in a general way, correlated with the volume of the cranial cavity
    (B) the size and form of the external skull is not an accurate indication of the conformation of the cranial cavity
    (C) as we go up the rungs of the ladder of evolution, we note a gradual increase in the size of the brain
    (D) there is no connection between the size of the skull and the size of the brain
    (E) the size and form of the brain is an inherited trait, just as is the conformation of the cranial cavity.

CONSOLIDATE YOUR KEY ANSWERS HERE

Practice using Answer Sheets. Make ONE mark for each answer. Additional and stray marks may be counted as mistakes. In making corrections erase errors COMPLETELY. Make glossy black marks. To arrive at an accurate estimate of your ability and progress cover the Correct Answers with a sheet of white paper while you are taking this test.

CORRECT ANSWERS TO THE FOREGOING PRACTICE QUESTIONS

Now compare your answers with these Correct Answers to the Practice Questions. If your answers differ from these, go back and study those questions to see where and how you made your mistakes.

| 1. A | 3. B | 5. E | 7. C | 9. C |
| 2. A | 4. A | 6. B | 8. D | 10. B |

Professional & Administrative Career Exam

TOP SCORES ON VOCABULARY TESTS

Although questions on vocabulary may not actually appear on your test, it is advisable to practice with the kind of material you have in this chapter. Words and their meanings are quite important in pushing up your score on tests of reading, comprehension, effective writing and correct usage. By broadening your vocabulary, you will definitely improve your marks in these and similar subjects.

INCREASE YOUR VOCABULARY

How is your vocabulary? Do you know the meanings of just about every word you come upon in your reading—or do you find several words that stump you? You must increase your vocabulary if you want to read with understanding. Following are steps that you can take in order to build up your word power:

(a) Read as much as you have the time for. Don't confine yourself to one type of reading either. Read all kinds of newspapers, magazines, books. Seek variety in what you read—different newspapers, several types of magazines, all types of books (novels, poetry, essays, plays, etc.). If you get into the habit of reading widely, your vocabulary will grow by leaps and bounds. You'll learn the meanings of words *by context*.

(b) Take vocabulary tests. There are many practice books which have word tests. We suggest one of these: *2300 Steps to Word Power* — (Arco Publishing Co.). These tests are fun to take—and they will build up your vocabulary fast.

(c) Listen to lectures, discussions, and talks by people who speak well. There are some worthwhile TV programs that have excellent speakers. Listen to such people—you'll learn a great many words.

(d) Use a dictionary. Whenever you don't know the meaning of a word, make a note of it. Then, when you get to a dictionary, look up the meaning of the word. Keep your own little notebook—call it "New Words." In a month or two, you will have added a great many words to your vocabulary. If you do not have a dictionary at home, you should buy one. A good dictionary is not expensive.

BASIC LETTER COMBINATIONS

One of the most efficient ways in which you can build up your vocabulary is by a systematic study of the basic word and letter combinations which make up the greater part of the English language.

Etymology is the science of the formation of words, and this somewhat frightening-sounding science can be of great help to you in learning new words and identifying words which may be unfamiliar to you. You will also find that the progress you make in studying the following pages will help to improve your spelling.

A great many of the words which we use every day have come into our language from the Latin and Greek. In the process of being absorbed into English, they appear as parts of words, many of which are related in meaning to each other.

For your convenience, this material is presented in easy-to-study form. Latin and Greek syllables and letter-combinations have been categorized into three groups:

1. *Prefixes:* letter combinations which appear at the beginning of a word.
2. *Suffixes:* letter combinations which appear at the end of a word.
3. *Roots or stems:* which carry the basic meaning and are combined with each other and with prefixes and suffixes to create other words with related meanings.

With the prefixes and suffixes, which you should study first, we have given examples of word formation with meanings, and additional examples. If you find any unfamiliar words among the samples, consult your dictionary to look up their meanings.

The list of roots or stems is accompanied by words in which the letter combinations appear. Here again, use the dictionary to look up any words which are not clear in your mind.

Remember that this section is not meant for easy reading. It is a guide to a program of study that will prove invaluable if you do your part. Do not try to swallow too much at one time. If you can put in a half-hour every day, your study will yield better results.

After you have done your preliminary work and have gotten a better idea of how words are formed in English, schedule the various vocabulary tests and quizzes we have provided in this chapter. They cover a wide variety of the vocabulary questions commonly encountered on examinations. They are short quizzes, not meant to be taken all at one time. Space them out. Adhere closely to the directions which differ for the different test types. Keep an honest record of your scores. Study your mistakes. Look them up in your dictionary. Concentrate closely on each quiz . . . and watch your scores improve.

HINTS FOR IMPROVING YOUR VOCABULARY

Vocabulary tests are really just tests of your knowledge of the meaning of words.

Would you like to increase your vocabulary so that you will do better on this kind of test?

Here are some things that you can do:

1. Some newspapers and magazines print quizzes, or little tests, on the meaning of words. Try these quizzes when you see them. Write down the words that you miss and try to learn what they mean.
2. Read newspapers and magazines and write down all the words that you don't know. Then look them up in a dictionary. The library has dictionaries.
3. Anytime you look up a word, write a sentence using it or try to use it when you talk.
4. Borrow a book to help build up your vocabulary from your library. Then do what the book tells you to do.

To increase your knowledge of words, remember to—

1. Read more.
2. Look up words you aren't sure of.
3. Use new words often so that they will become a part of your vocabulary.

ETYMOLOGY - A KEY TO WORD RECOGNITION

PREFIXES

PREFIX	MEANING	EXAMPLE
ab, a	away from	absent, amoral
ad, ac, ag, at	to	advent, accrue, aggressive, attract
an	without	anarchy
ante	before	antedate
anti	against	antipathy
bene	well	beneficent
bi	two	bicameral
circum	around	circumspect
com, con, col	together	commit confound, collate
contra	against	contraband
de	from, down	descend
dis, di	apart	distract, divert
ex, e	out	exit, emit
extra	beyond	extracurricular
in, im, il, ir, un	not	inept, impossible, illicit
inter	between	interpose
intra, intro, in	within	intramural, introspective

PREFIX	MEANING	EXAMPLE
mal	bad	malcontent
mis	wrong	misnomer
non	not	nonentity
ob	against	obstacle
per	through	permeate
peri	around	periscope
poly	many	polytheism
post	after	post-mortem
pre	before	premonition
pro	forward	propose
re	again	review
se	apart	seduce
semi	half	semicircle
sub	under	subvert
super	above	superimpose
sui	self	suicide
trans	across	transpose
vice	instead of	vice-president

SUFFIXES

SUFFIX	MEANING	EXAMPLE
able, ible	capable of being	capable, reversible
age	state of	storage
ance	relating to	reliance
ary	relating to	dictionary
ate	act	confiscate
ation	action	radiation
cy	quality	democracy

SUFFIX	MEANING	EXAMPLE
ence	relating to	confidence
er	one who	adviser
ic	pertaining to	democratic
ious	full of	rebellious
ize	to make like	harmonize
ment	result	filament
ty	condition	sanity

LATIN AND GREEK STEMS

STEM	MEANING	EXAMPLE
ag, ac	do	agenda, action
agr	farm	agriculture
aqua	water	aqueous
cad, cas	fall	cadence, casual
cant	sing	chant
cap, cep	take	captive, accept
capit	head	capital
cede	go	precede
celer	speed	celerity
cide, cis	kill, cut	suicide, incision
clud, clus	close	include, inclusion
cur, curs	run	incur, incursion
dict	say	diction
duct	lead	induce
fact, fect	make	factory, perfect
fer, lat	carry	refer, dilate
fring, fract	break	infringe, fracture
frater	brother	fraternal
fund, fus	pour	refund, confuse
greg	group	gregarious
gress, grad	move forward	progress, degrade
homo	man	homicide
ject	throw	reject
jud	right	judicial
junct	join	conjunction
lect, leg	read, choose	collect, legend
loq, loc	speak	loquacious, interlocutory
manu	hand	manuscript
mand	order	remand
mar	sea	maritime
mater	mother	maternal
med	middle	intermediary
min	lessen	diminution
mis, mit	send	remit, dismiss
mort	death	mortician
mote, mov	move	remote, remove
naut	sailor	astronaut
nom	name	nomenclature
pater	father	paternity
ped, pod	foot	pedal, podiatrist
pend	hang	depend
plic	fold	implicate
port	carry	portable
pos, pon	put	depose, component
reg, rect	rule	regicide, direct
rupt	break	eruption
scrib, scrip	write	inscribe, conscription
anthrop	man	anthropology

STEM	MEANING	EXAMPLE
arch	chief, rule	archbishop
astron	star	astronomy
auto	self	automatic
biblio	book	bibliophile
bio	life	biology
chrome	color	chromosome
chron	time	chronology
cosmo	world	cosmic
crat	rule	autocrat
dent, dont	tooth	dental, indent
eu	well, happy	eugenics
gamos	marriage	monogamous
ge	earth	geology
gen	origin, people	progenitor
graph	write	graphic
gyn	women	gynecologist
homo	same	homogeneous
hydr	water	dehydrate
logy	study of	psychology
meter	measure	thermometer
micro	small	microscope
mono	one	monotony
onomy	science	astronomy
onym	name	synonym
pathos	feeling	pathology
philo	love	philosophy
phobia	fear	hydrophobia
phone	sound	telephone
pseudo	false	pseudonym
psych	mind	psychic
scope	see	telescope
soph	wisdom	sophomore
tele	far off	telepathic
theo	god	theology
thermo	heat	thermostat
sec	cut	dissect
sed	remain	sedentary
sequ	follow	sequential
spect	look	inspect
spir	breathe	conspire
stat	stand	status
tact, tang	touch	tactile, tangible
ten	hold	retentive
term	end	terminal
vent	come	prevent
vict	conquer	evict
vid, vis	see	video, revise
voc	call	convocation
volv	roll	devolve

TEST I. VOCABULARY: SYNONYMS

TIME: 6 Minutes. 20 Questions.

DIRECTIONS: For each question in this test, select the appropriate letter preceding the word which is most nearly the same in meaning as the italicized word in each sentence.

Correct Answers for this Test are consolidated after the last question.

1. The person who is *diplomatic* in his relations with others is, most nearly
   (A) well dressed (B) very tactful
   (C) somewhat domineering (D) deceitful and tricky
   (E) verbose.

2. Action at this time would be *inopportune*. The word "inopportune" means most nearly
   (A) untimely (B) premeditated
   (C) sporadic (D) commendable
   (E) fortunate.

3. The word *appraise* means most nearly
   (A) consult (B) attribute
   (C) manage (D) honor
   (E) judge.

4. The word *cognizant* means most nearly
   (A) rare (B) reluctant
   (C) aware (D) haphazard
   (E) correlated.

5. *Probity* is an important requirement of many positions. The word "probity" means most nearly
   (A) analytical ability (B) vision
   (C) tried integrity (D) clear insight
   (E) perseverence.

6. The word *denote* means most nearly
   (A) encumber (B) evade
   (C) furnish (D) indicate
   (E) reduce in rank.

7. The competent employee should know that a method of procedure which is *expedient* is most nearly
   (A) unchangeable (B) based upon a false assumption
   (C) unduly harmful (D) difficult to work out
   (E) suitable to the end in view.

8. An incentive which is *potent* is most nearly
   (A) impossible (B) highly effective
   (C) not immediately practicable (D) a remote possibility
   (E) universally applicable.

9. An employer who is *judicious* is most nearly
   (A) domineering (B) argumentative
   (C) sincere (D) arbitrary
   (E) wise.

10. He presented a *controversial* plan. The word "controversial" means most nearly
    (A) subject to debate (B) unreasonable
    (C) complex (D) comparable
    (E) well formulated.

11. "He sent the irate employee to the personnel manager." The word *irate* means most nearly
    (A) irresponsible (B) untidy
    (C) insubordinate (D) angry.

12. An *ambiguous* statement is one which is
    (A) forceful and convincing
    (B) capable of being understood in more than one sense
    (C) based upon good judgment and sound reasoning processes
    (D) uninteresting and too lengthy.

13. To *extol* means most nearly to
    (A) summon (B) praise
    (C) reject (D) withdraw.

14. The word *proximity* means most nearly
    (A) similarity (B) exactness
    (C) harmony (D) nearness.

15. "His friends had a detrimental influence on him." The word *detrimental* means most nearly
    (A) favorable (B) lasting
    (C) harmful (D) short-lived.

16. "The chief inspector relied upon the veracity of his inspectors." The word *veracity* means most nearly
    (A) speed (B) assistance
    (C) shrewdness (D) truthfulness.

17. "There was much diversity in the suggestions submitted." The word *diversity* means most nearly
    (A) similarity (B) value
    (C) triviality (D) variety.

18. "The survey was concerned with the problem of indigence." The word *indigence* means most nearly
    (A) poverty (B) corruption
    (C) intolerance (D) morale.

19. "The investigator considered this evidence to be extraneous." The word *extraneous* means most nearly
    (A) significant (B) pertinent but unobtainable
    (C) not essential (D) inadequate.

20. "He was surprised at the temerity of the new employee." The word *temerity* means most nearly
    (A) shyness (B) enthusiasm
    (C) rashness (D) self-control.

CONSOLIDATE YOUR KEY ANSWERS HERE

Practice using Answer Sheets. Make ONE mark for each answer. Additional and stray marks may be counted as mistakes. In making corrections erase errors COMPLETELY. Make glossy black marks. To arrive at an accurate estimate of your ability and progress, cover the Correct Answers with a sheet of white paper while you are taking this test.

SAMPLE ANSWER SHEET

CORRECT ANSWERS TO SAMPLE QUESTIONS

Now compare your answers with the Correct Answers to Sample Questions. If your answers are not the same as the correct answers shown, go back and study the samples to see where you made a mistake.

1. B	4. C	7. E	10. A	13. B	16. D	19. C
2. A	5. C	8. B	11. D	14. D	17. D	20. C
3. E	6. D	9. E	12. B	15. C	18. A	

TEST II. VOCABULARY: SYNONYMS

TIME: 10 Minutes. 30 Questions.

DIRECTIONS: For each question in this test, select the appropriate letter preceding the word which is most nearly the same in meaning as the italicized word in each sentence.

Correct Answers for this Test are consolidated after the last question.

1. The person who is *diplomatic* in his relations with others is, most nearly
   (A) well dressed (B) very tactful
   (C) somewhat domineering (D) deceitful and tricky
   (E) verbose.

2. Action at this time would be *inopportune*. The word "inopportune" means most nearly
   (A) untimely (B) premeditated
   (C) sporadic (D) commendable
   (E) fortunate.

3. The word *appraise* means most nearly
   (A) consult (B) attribute
   (C) manage (D) honor
   (E) judge.

4. The word *cognizant* means most nearly
   (A) rare (B) reluctant
   (C) aware (D) haphazard
   (E) correlated.

5. *Probity* is an important requirement of many positions. The word "probity" means most nearly
   (A) analytical ability (B) vision
   (C) tried integrity (D) clear insight
   (E) perseverence.

6. The word *denote* means most nearly
   (A) encumber (B) evade
   (C) furnish (D) indicate
   (E) reduce in rank.

7. The competent employee should know that a method of procedure which is *expedient* is most nearly
   (A) unchangeable (B) based upon a false assumption
   (C) unduly harmful (D) difficult to work out
   (E) suitable to the end in view.

8. An incentive which is *potent* is most nearly
   (A) impossible (B) highly effective
   (C) not immediately (D) a remote possibility practicable
   (E) universally applicable.

9. An employer who is *judicious* is most nearly
   (A) domineering (B) argumentative
   (C) sincere (D) arbitrary
   (E) wise.

10. He presented a *controversial* plan. The word "controversial" means most nearly
    (A) subject to debate (B) unreasonable
    (C) complex (D) comparable
    (E) well formulated.

11. To say that the work is *tedious* means, most nearly, that it is
    (A) technical
    (B) interesting
    (C) tiresome
    (D) confidential.

12. A *vivacious* person is one who is
    (A) kind
    (B) talkative
    (C) lively
    (D) well-dressed.

13. An *innocuous* statement is one which is
    (A) forceful
    (B) harmless
    (C) offensive
    (D) brief.

14. To say that the order was *rescinded* means, most nearly, that the order was
    (A) revised
    (B) canceled
    (C) misinterpreted
    (D) confirmed.

15. To say that the administrator *amplified* his remarks means, most nearly, that the remarks were
    (A) shouted
    (B) expanded
    (C) carefully analyzed
    (D) summarized briefly.

16. "Peremptory commands will be resented in any organization." The word *peremptory* means most nearly
    (A) unexpected
    (B) unreasonable
    (C) military
    (D) dictatorial.

17. A person should know the word *sporadic* means, most nearly,
    (A) occurring regularly
    (B) sudden
    (C) scattered
    (D) disturbing.

18. To *oscillate* means, most nearly, to
    (A) lubricate
    (B) waver
    (C) decide
    (D) investigate.

19. A *homogeneous* group of persons is characterized by its
    (A) similarity
    (B) teamwork
    (C) discontent
    (D) differences.

20. A *vindictive* person is one who is
    (A) prejudiced
    (B) unpopular
    (C) petty
    (D) revengeful.

21. "The visitor was *morose*." The word "morose" as used in this sentence means most nearly
    (A) curious
    (B) gloomy
    (C) impatient
    (D) timid.

22. "He was unwilling to *impede* the work of his unit." The word "impede" as used in this sentence means most nearly
    (A) carry out
    (B) criticize
    (C) praise
    (D) hinder.

23. "The *remuneration* was unsatisfactory." The word "remuneration" as used in this sentence means most nearly
    (A) payment
    (B) summary
    (C) explanation
    (D) estimate.

24. A *recurring* problem is one that
    (A) replaces a problem that existed previously
    (B) is unexpected
    (C) has long been overlooked
    (D) comes up from time to time.

25. "His subordinates were aware of this *magnanimous* act." The word "magnanimous" as used in this sentence means most nearly
    (A) insolent
    (B) shrewd
    (C) unselfish
    (D) threatening.

26. "The new employee is a *zealous* worker." The word "zealous" as used in this sentence means most nearly
    (A) awkward
    (B) untrustworthy
    (C) enthusiastic
    (D) skillful.

27. To *impair* means most nearly to
    (A) weaken
    (B) conceal
    (C) improve
    (D) expose.

28. "The unit head was in a *quandary*." The word "quandary" as used in this sentence means most nearly
    (A) violent dispute
    (B) puzzling predicament
    (C) angry mood
    (D) strong position.

29. "His actions were *prudent*." The word "prudent" as used in this sentence means most nearly
    (A) wise
    (B) biased
    (C) final
    (D) limited.

30. "His report contained many *irrelevant* statements." The word "irrelevant" as used in this sentence means most nearly
    (A) unproven
    (B) not pertinent
    (C) hard to understand
    (D) insincere.

END OF TEST

CONSOLIDATE YOUR KEY ANSWERS HERE

Practice using Answer Sheets. Make ONE mark for each answer. Additional and stray marks may be counted as mistakes. In making corrections erase errors COMPLETELY. Make glossy black marks. To arrive at an accurate estimate of your ability and progress, cover the Correct Answers with a sheet of white paper while you are taking this test.

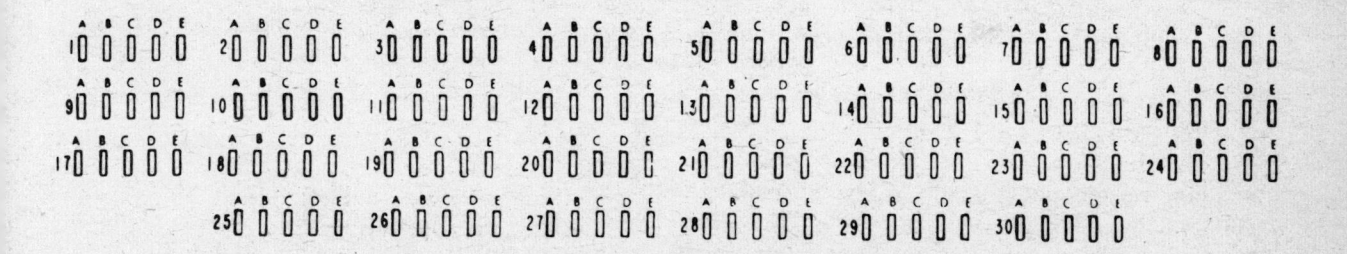

CORRECT ANSWERS TO SAMPLE QUESTIONS

Now compare your answers with the Correct Answers to Sample Questions. If your answers are not the same as the correct answers shown, go back and study the samples to see where you made a mistake.

1. C	5. A	9. B	13. B	17. C	21. B	25. C	29. A
2. B	6. E	10. D	14. B	18. B	22. D	26. C	30. B
3. D	7. C	11. C	15. B	19. A	23. A	27. A	
4. E	8. D	12. C	16. D	20. D	24. D	28. B	

TEST III. VOCABULARY: SYNONYMS

TIME: 10 Minutes. 30 Questions.

DIRECTIONS: *In each of the sentences below, one word is in italics. Following each sentence are four or five lettered words or phrases. For each sentence, choose the letter preceding the word or phrase which most nearly corresponds in meaning with the italicized word.*

Correct Answers for this Test are consolidated after the last question.

1. "He was not present at the *inception* of the program." The word "inception" as used in this sentence means most nearly
   - (A) beginning
   - (B) discussion
   - (C) conclusion
   - (D) rejection
   - (E) finale.

2. The word *solicitude* means most nearly
   - (A) request
   - (B) isolation
   - (C) seriousness
   - (D) concern
   - (E) recluse.

3. A man who performs his work with *discernment* is
   - (A) deliberative
   - (B) constructive
   - (C) unruffled
   - (D) discriminating
   - (E) capricious.

4. Everyone should know that the word *increment* means most nearly
   - (A) improvise
   - (B) account
   - (C) predict
   - (D) specify
   - (E) increase.

5. "The precise method to be employed is immaterial." The word *immaterial* means most nearly
   - (A) unclear
   - (B) unpredictable
   - (C) unimportant
   - (D) not debatable
   - (E) unknown.

6. He felt as though he were *groping* in the dark.
   - (A) lying
   - (B) feeling his way
   - (C) running
   - (D) screaming
   - (E) digging a tunnel

7. "The supervisor *admonished* the clerk for his tardiness." The word "admonished" means most nearly
   - (A) reproved
   - (B) excused
   - (C) transferred
   - (D) punished
   - (E) dismissed.

8. A *homogeneous* group of persons is characterized by its
   - (A) similarity
   - (B) teamwork
   - (C) discontent
   - (D) differences
   - (E) harmony.

9. To *vacillate* means, most nearly, to
   - (A) lubricate
   - (B) waver
   - (C) decide
   - (D) investigate
   - (E) implicate.

10. A clerk should know that the word *sporadic* means, most nearly
    - (A) occurring regularly
    - (B) sudden
    - (C) scattered
    - (D) disturbing
    - (E) invariable.

11. I could plainly hear the *clamor* of the crowd.
    (A) murmur   (B) noise
    (C) questions (D) singing
         (E) arrival

12. The wind blew *incessantly* across the island.
    (A) occasionally (B) disagreeably
    (C) constantly   (D) icily
         (E) noisily

13. They were surprised by the *solidity* of the ice.
    (A) unevenness (B) smoothness
    (C) firmness   (D) clearness
         (E) color

14. The soldiers *repelled* the attackers.
    (A) fled from   (B) surrendered to
    (C) forced back (D) caught sight of
         (E) joined with

15. The *solitude* of the sod hut depressed him.
    (A) loneliness (B) coldness
    (C) crudeness   (D) poverty
         (E) smallness

16. He *declined* our offer of help.
    (A) suspected   (B) misunderstood
    (C) consented to (D) refused
         (E) was annoyed by

17. He tried hard to *avert* the accident.
    (A) describe (B) prevent
    (C) forget   (D) make light of
         (E) pay for

18. They discovered that the doctor was *an impostor*.
    (A) a specialist (B) a foreigner
    (C) an inventor   (D) a pretender
         (E) a magician

19. Many *calamities* can be traced to simple causes.
    (A) joys   (B) disasters
    (C) expenses (D) peaceful moments
         (E) loud noises

20. The knight came upon his *adversary* in the forest.
    (A) servant (B) sweetheart
    (C) leader   (D) enemy
         (E) relative

21. A clerk who is asked to prepare an *abstract* should prepare
    (A) a verbatim record   (B) an original essay
    (C) a translation which is non-technical
    (D) a summary of essential points
    (E) an extensive elaboration.

22. To say that the task assigned to a person is *exacting* means most nearly that the task is
    (A) brief   (B) responsible
    (C) equivocal (D) arithmetical in nature
         (E) severe in its demands.

23. "Contributions to the employee welfare fund shall be prorated." The word *prorated* means most nearly
    (A) on a voluntary basis (B) divided
    (C) compulsory for all   proportionately
    (D) regular in payment   (E) audited.

24. "Complete cooperation by members of the staff is postulated." The word *postulated* means most nearly
    (A) encouraged (B) endangered
    (C) achieved   (D) obviated
         (E) assumed.

25. To say that a person is *dynamic* means most nearly that he is
    (A) careful   (B) stubborn
    (C) energetic (D) insubordinate
         (E) dutiful.

26. To say that someone *misconstrued* directions means most nearly that he has
    (A) followed directions implicitly
    (B) displayed commendable ingenuity
    (C) acted in a supervisory capacity
    (D) interpreted his assignment erroneously
    (E) listened carefully to his instructions.

27. "The supervisor advised his staff that the benefits of the proposed plan are likely to be transitory." The word *transitory* means most nearly
    (A) significant (B) temporary
    (C) obvious   (D) cumulative
         (E) determinate.

28. An action which is *inexplicable* is
    (A) not explicit
    (B) incapable of being explained
    (C) ineffectual
    (D) inexpedient
    (E) inappropriate to the end in view.

29. To say that the circumstances surrounding an act were *extenuating* means most nearly that the circumstances
    (A) were stimulating
    (B) tended to be sustained
    (C) existed for a considerable period before the act
    (D) tended to excuse the act
    (E) were variable and inconsistent.

30. "In presenting his argument, the speaker should be careful lest his argument be specious." The word *specious* means most nearly
    (A) showy
    (B) largely drawn
    (C) too detailed
    (D) inconsiderate
    (E) based on false premises.

CONSOLIDATE YOUR KEY ANSWERS HERE

Practice using Answer Sheets. Make ONE mark for each answer. Additional and stray marks may be counted as mistakes. In making corrections erase errors COMPLETELY. Make glossy black marks. To arrive at an accurate estimate of your ability and progress, cover the Correct Answers with a sheet of white paper while you are taking this test.

SAMPLE ANSWER SHEET

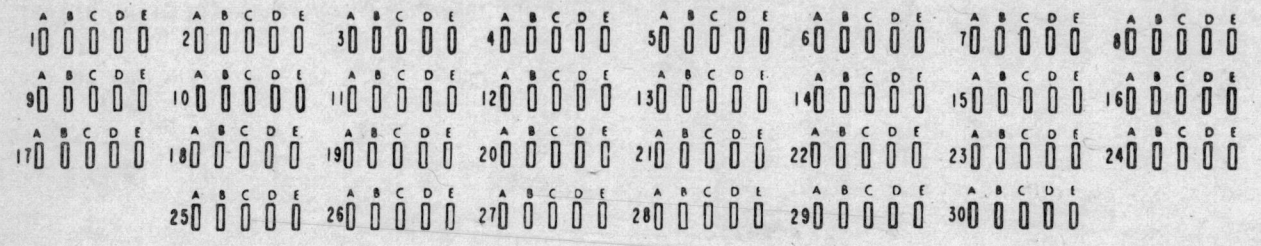

CORRECT ANSWERS TO SAMPLE QUESTIONS

Now compare your answers with the Correct Answers to Sample Questions. If your answers are not the same as the correct answers shown, go back and study the samples to see where you made a mistake.

1. A	5. C	9. B	13. C	17. B	21. D	25. C	29. D
2. D	6. B	10. C	14. C	18. D	22. E	26. D	30. A
3. D	7. A	11. B	15. A	19. B	23. B	27. B	
4. E	8. A	12. C	16. D	20. D	24. E	28. B	

Professional & Administrative Career Exam

ABSTRACT REASONING

Your ability to see the differences between, and the relationship between various abstract symbols is one indication of your ability to learn. It is a measure of your ability to meet new situations and evaluate them. The following practice questions will help to familiarize you with this type of question. As in other analogy problems—verbal analogies and numerical series—the best approach is to translate into words the exact relationship between the key figures. Be sure to avoid the traps of similar figures which do not have the same relationship.

DIRECTIONS: In each of these questions, look at the symbols in the first two boxes. Something about the three symbols in the first box makes them alike; something about the two symbols in the other box with the question mark makes them alike. Look for some characteristic that is common to all symbols in the same box, yet makes them different from the symbols in the other box. Among the five answer choices, find the symbol that can best be substituted for the question mark, because it is like the symbols in the second box, and, for the same reason, different from those in the first box.

TWO TEST QUESTIONS ANALYZED

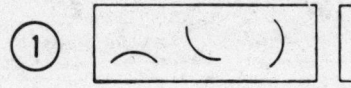

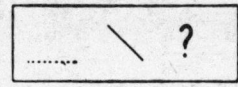

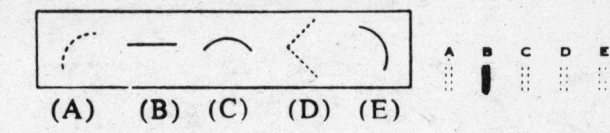

In question 1 all the symbols in the first box are curved, while the symbols in the second box are straight. Of the lettered symbols in the third box, only (B) is straight, so (B) is the correct answer.

(Note that although one symbol in the second box is made of dashes, the other is not. The type of line, therefore, is not the feature that distinguishes this box from the first.)

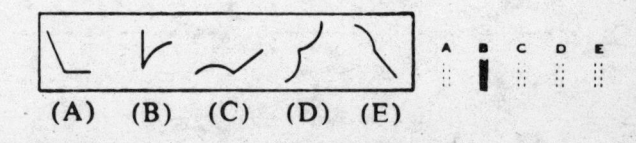

In question 2 the given symbols consist of two lines making an angle. There are curved lines and straight lines in each box; therefore the difference that must be found cannot be the difference between curved and straight. The angles formed in the first box are *obtuse;* those in the second box are *acute.* Now a check of the alternatives shows that only one of them consists of lines making an acute angle; the correct answer is therefore (B).

S 3221

132 / P.A.C.E. Professional-Administrative Career Exam

TEST I. ABSTRACT REASONING

TIME: 20 Minutes. 23 Questions.

DIRECTIONS: In each of these questions, look at the symbols in the first two boxes. Something about the three symbols in the first box makes them alike; something about the two symbols in the other box with the question mark makes them alike. Look for some characteristic that is common to all symbols in the same box, yet makes them different from the symbols in the other box. Among the five answer choices, find the symbol that can best be substituted for the question mark, because it is like the symbols in the second box, and, for the same reason, different from those in the first box.

Correct Answers are consolidated after the last question.

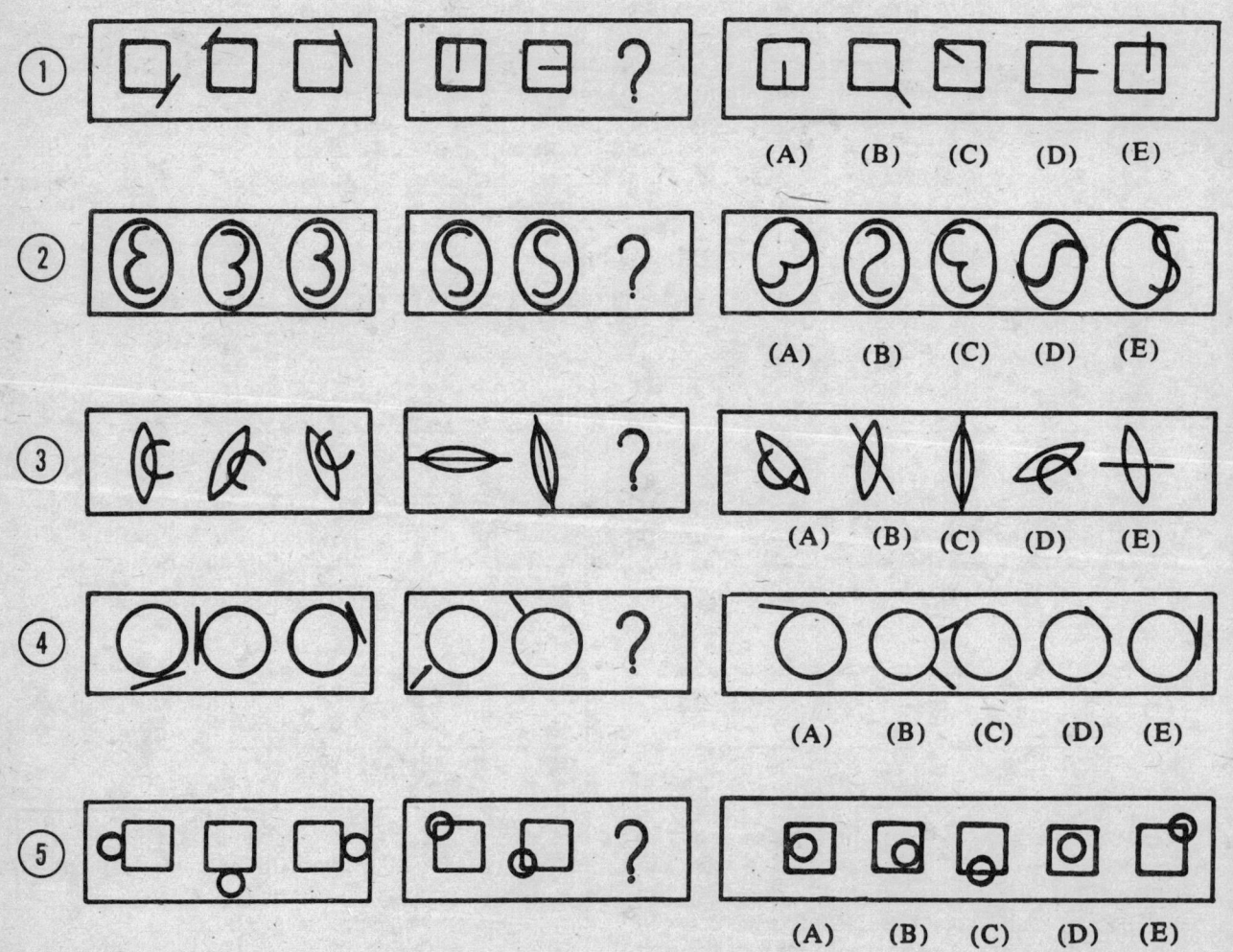

6

(A) (B) (C) (D) (E)

7

(A) (B) (C) (D) (E)

8

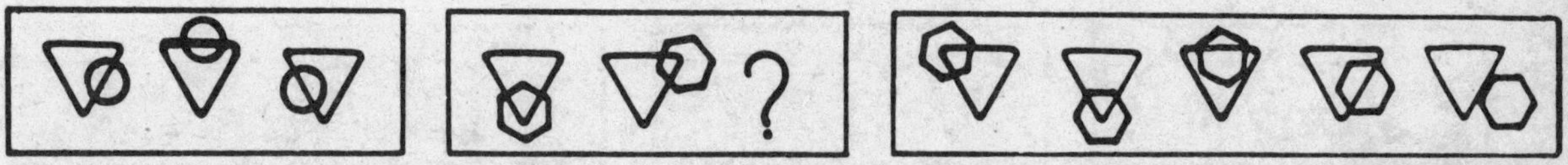

(A) (B) (C) (D) (E)

9

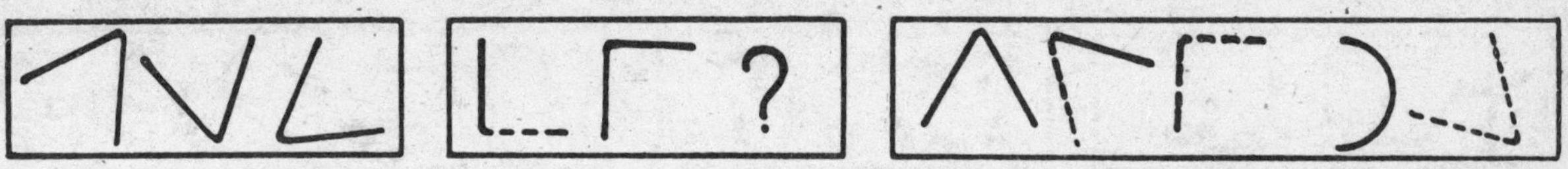

(A) (B) (C) (D) (E)

10

(A) (B) (C) (D) (E)

11

(A) (B) (C) (D) (E)

12

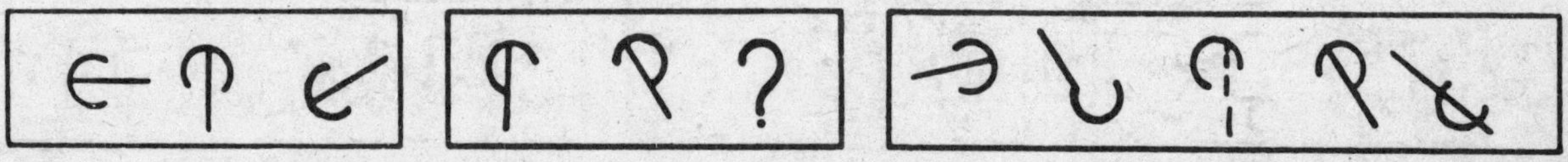

(A) (B) (C) (D) (E)

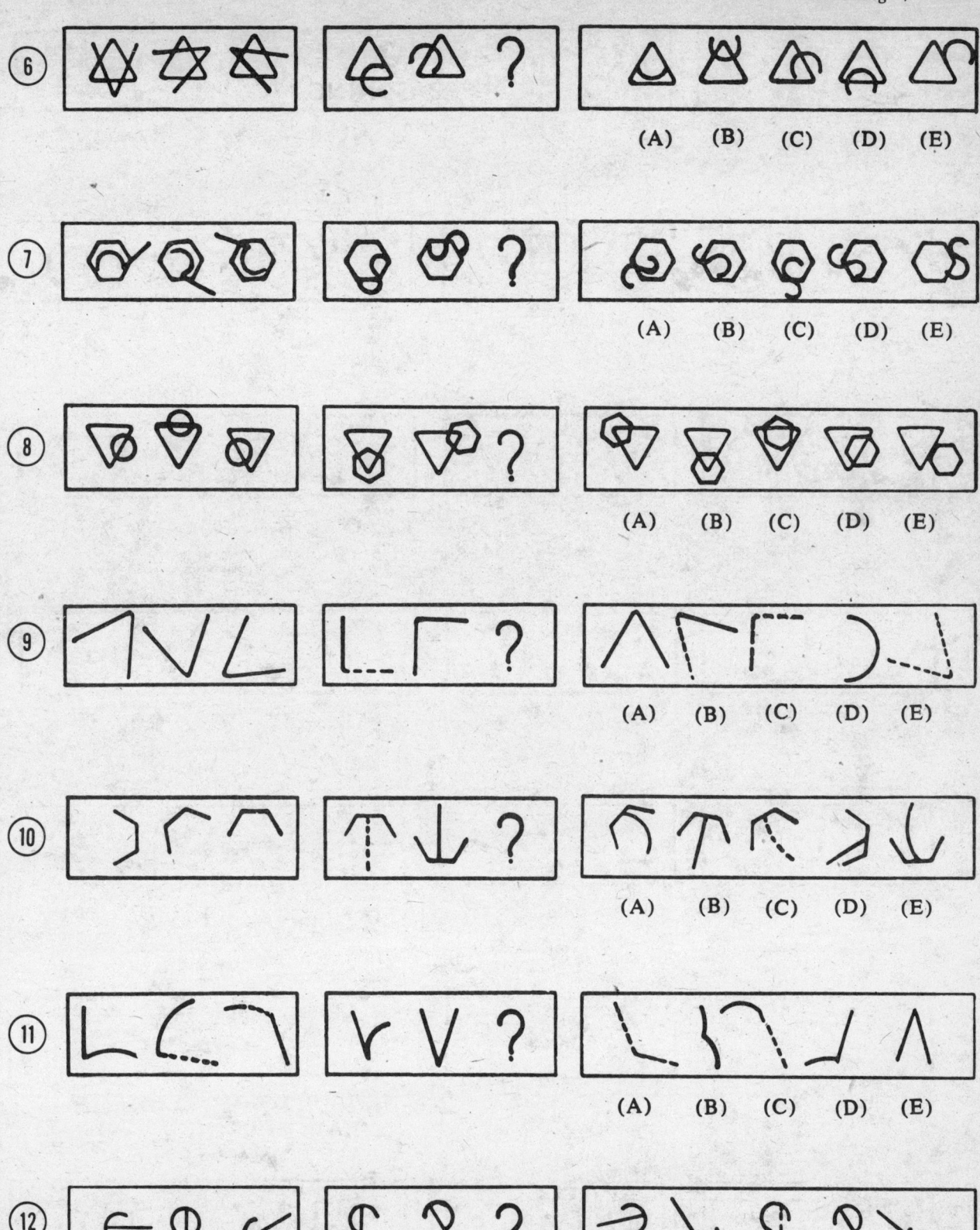

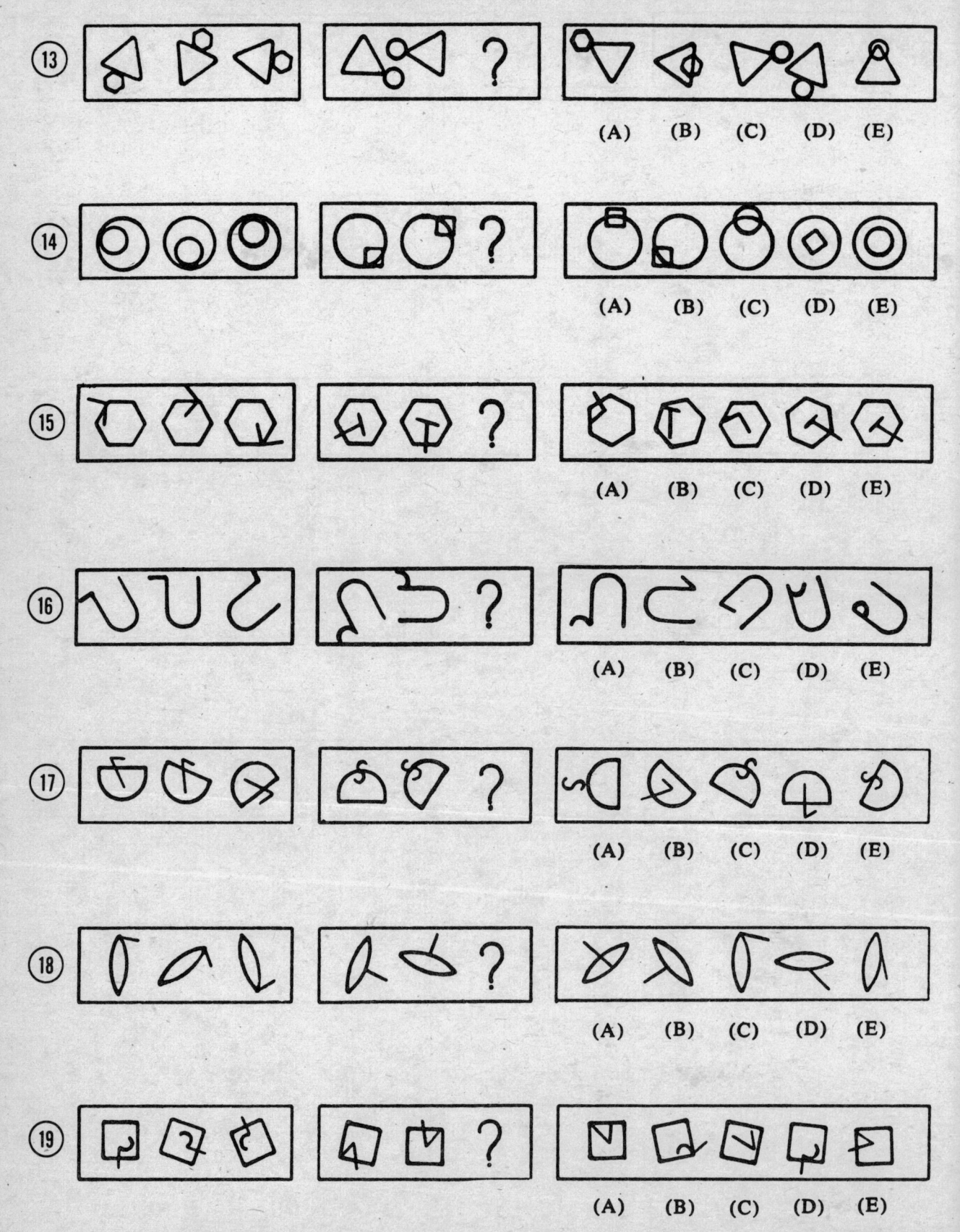

134 / P.A.C.E. Professional-Administrative Career Exam

Abstract Reasoning / 135

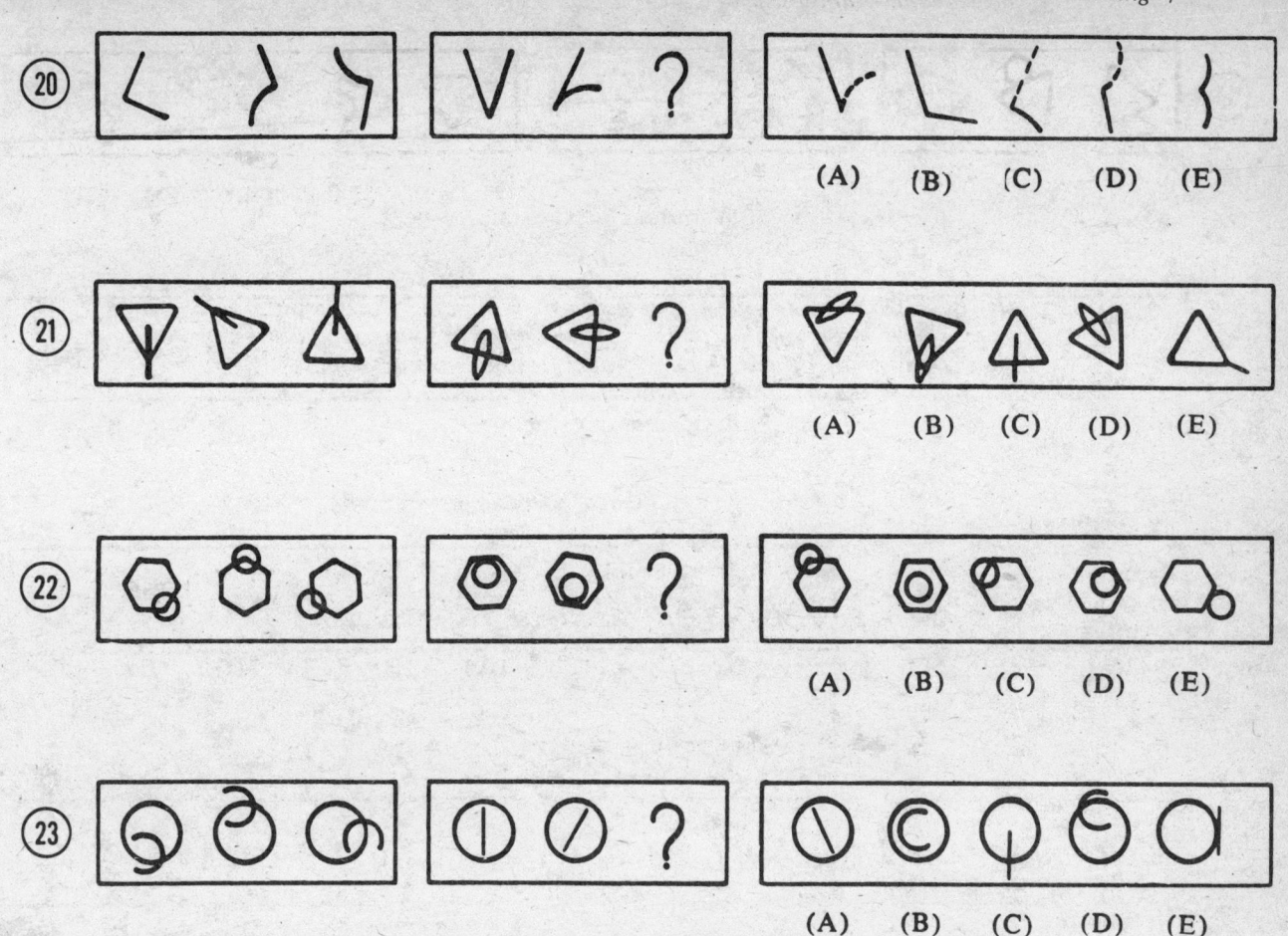

CONSOLIDATE YOUR KEY ANSWERS HERE

Practice using Answer Sheets. Make ONE mark for each answer. Additional and stray marks may be counted as mistakes. In making corrections erase errors COMPLETELY. Make glossy black marks. To arrive at an accurate estimate of your ability and progress cover the Correct Answers with a sheet of white paper while you are taking this test.

CORRECT KEY ANSWERS TO THE PRACTICE QUESTIONS

1. A	4. B	7. D	10. B	13. C	16. A	19. E	22. D
2. B	5. E	8. A	11. E	14. B	17. C	20. A	23. A
3. C	6. C	9. C	12. D	15. E	18. B	21. D	

136 / P.A.C.E. Professional-Administrative Career Exam

TEST II. FIGURE ANALOGIES

TIME: 35 Minutes. 37 Questions.

DIRECTIONS: *In the following questions, the symbols in columns 1 and 2 have a relationship to each other. Select from the symbols in columns A, B, C, and D the symbol which has the same relationship to the symbol in column 3, as the symbol in column 2 has to the symbol in column 1.*

Correct Answers are consolidated after the last question.

TO HELP YOU GET THE HANG OF THINGS...

SAMPLE PROBLEM I: 1 : 2 : : 3 : ?   (A)   (B)   (C)   (D)   (E)

SOLUTION TO SAMPLE PROBLEM I: The correct answer is (D)

Abstract Reasoning / 137

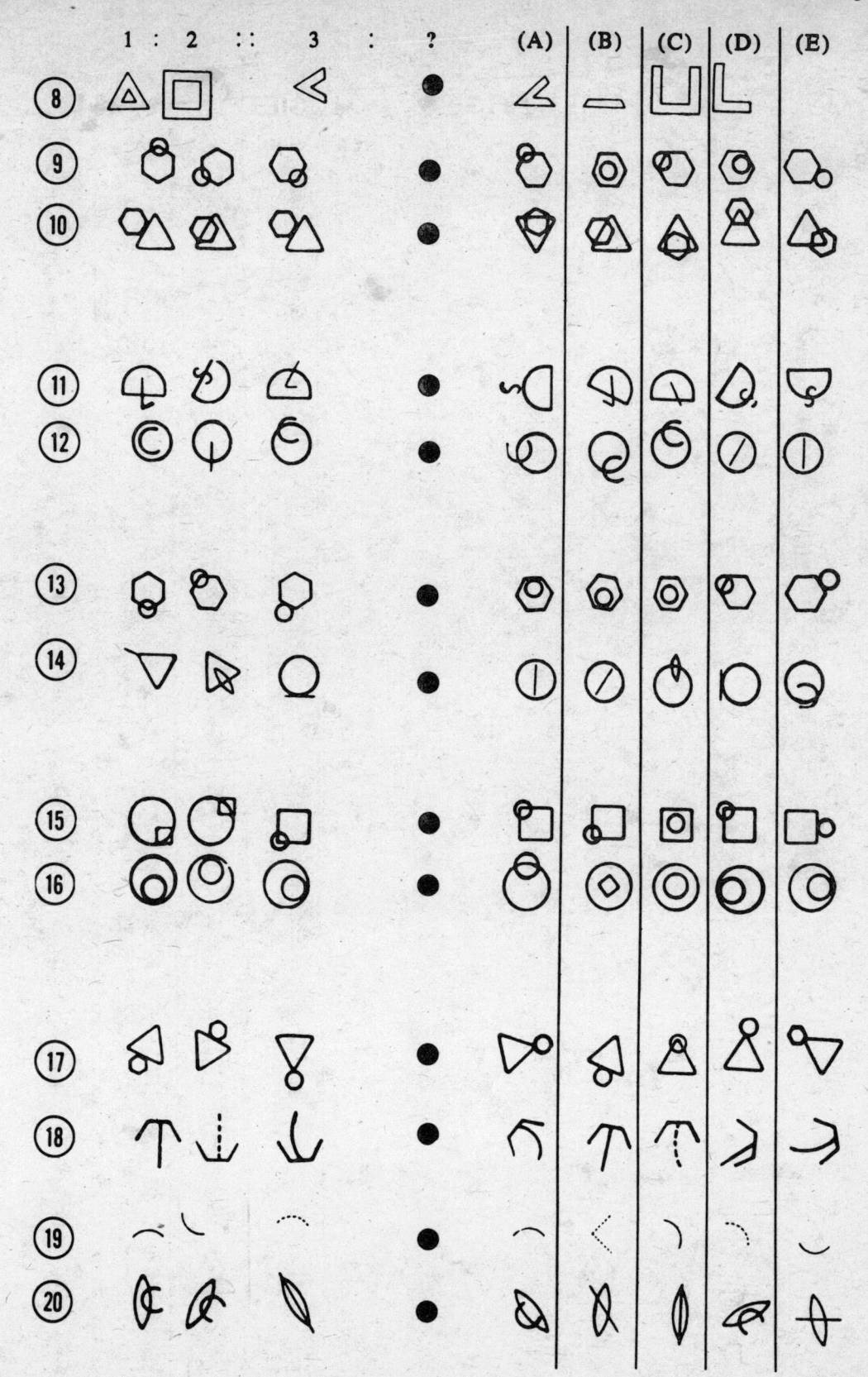

138 / *P.A.C.E. Professional-Administrative Career Exam*

Abstract Reasoning / 139

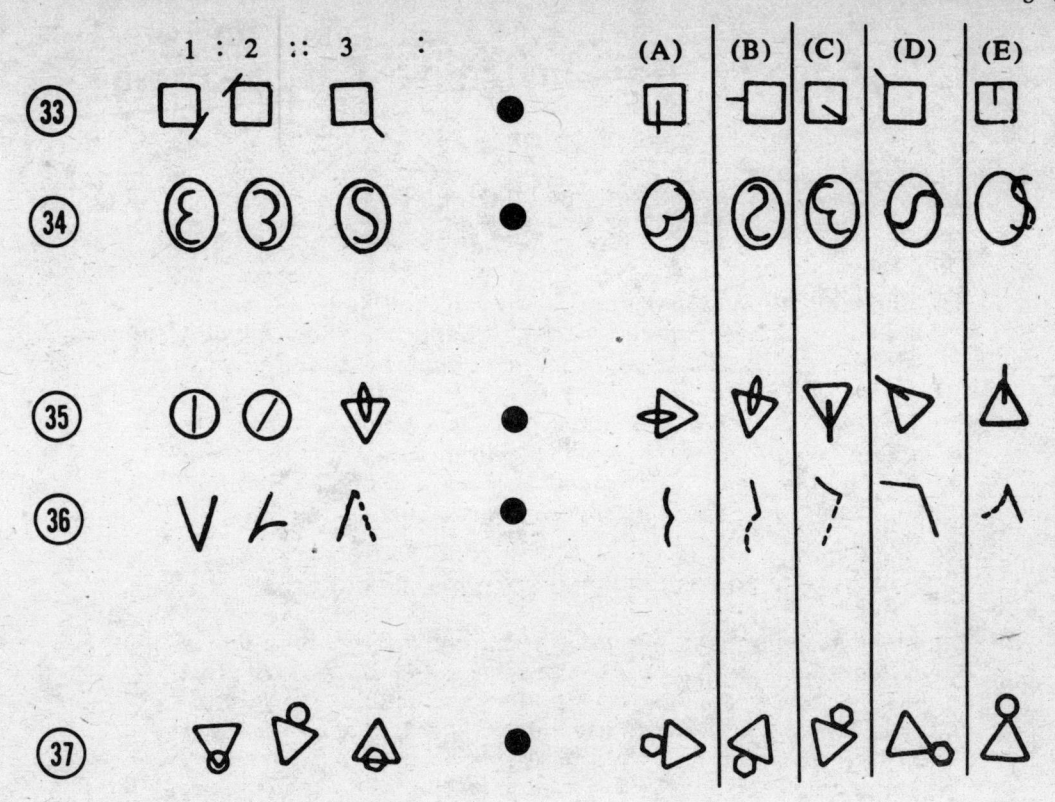

CONSOLIDATE YOUR KEY ANSWERS HERE

Practice using Answer Sheets. Make ONE mark for each answer. Additional and stray marks may be counted as mistakes. In making corrections erase errors COMPLETELY. Make glossy black marks. To arrive at an accurate estimate of your ability and progress cover the Correct Answers with a sheet of white paper while you are taking this test.

CORRECT KEY ANSWERS TO THE PRACTICE QUESTIONS

1. C	6. A	11. D	16. D	21. D	26. E	31. A	36. E
2. B	7. B	12. E	17. D	22. B	27. C	32. A	37. D
3. D	8. C	13. E	18. C	23. B	28. C	33. D	
4. A	9. A	14. D	19. D	24. C	29. A	34. B	
5. A	10. B	15. A	20. C	25. A	30. E	35. B	

Professional & Administrative Career Exam

LETTER SERIES

From sample questions provided by the Civil Service Commission and from our experience with similar tests, we can be fairly certain that you will be asked to answer questions such as those below, which test your ability to see relationship between the elements of a series. These questions are sometimes referred to as series or progressions, and in them you are asked to determine the rule that binds the elements together and then select or arrange the following elements according to that rule.

HOW TO PROFIT FROM THE PRACTICE TESTS

On the following pages you are furnished practice tests consisting of questions like those on the actual exam. The time limit here is just about what you may expect. Take these tests as a series of dress rehearsals strengthening your ability to score high on this type of question. For each test use the Answer Sheet provided to mark down your answers. If the Answer Sheet is separated from the questions, tear it out so you can mark it more easily. As you finish each test, go back and check your answers to find your score, and to determine how well you did. This will help you discover where you need more practice.

DESCRIPTION OF THE TEST AND SAMPLE QUESTIONS

Here are some sample questions for you to do. Mark your answers on the Sample Answer Sheet, making sure to keep your mark inside the correct box. If you want to change an answer, erase the mark you don't want to count. Then mark your new answer. Use a No. 2 (medium) pencil.

Correct Answers are consolidated after the last question.

In each of these questions there is a series of letters which follow some definite order, and at the right there are five sets of two letters each. Look at the letters in the series and determine what the order is; then from the suggested answers at the right, select the set that gives the next two letters in the series in their correct order.

① X C X D X E X
(A) F X   (B) F G
(C) X F   (D) E F
        (E) X G

The series consists of X's alternating with letters in alphabetical order. The next two letters would be F and X; therefore, (A) is the correct answer.

② A B D C E F H
(A) G H   (B) I G
(C) G I   (D) K L
        (E) I H

If you compare this series with the alphabet, you will find that it goes along in pairs, the first pair in their usual order and the next pair in reverse order. The last letter given in the series is the second letter of the pair G—H, which is in reverse order. The first missing letter must, therefore, be G. The next pair of letters would be I—J, in that order; the second of the missing letters is I. The alternative you look for, then, is G I, which is lettered (C).

Series and Progressions / 141

DIRECTIONS: Each question consists of a series of letters or numbers (or both) which follow some definite order. Study each series to determine what the order is. Then look at the answer choices. Select the one answer that will complete the set in accordance with the pattern established.

Suggestions: In solving alphabetic series, it is helpful to write out the alphabet and keep it in front of you as you work. This makes it easier to spot the key to a letter series.

```
A  B  C  D  E  F  G  H  I  J   K   L   M   N   O   P   Q   R   S   T   U   V   W   X   Y   Z
1  2  3  4  5  6  7  8  9  10  11  12  13  14  15  16  17  18  19  20  21  22  23  24  25  26
```

③ a b a b a b a b   (1) a (2) b (3) c (4) d (5) e

For this problem, the series goes: ab ab ab ab. The next letter in the series is <u>a</u>, Choice 1, which has been indicated on the answer sheet as the correct answer.

④ a a b b c c d d   (1) a (2) b (3) c (4) d (5) e

In example ④ above, the series goes like this: aa bb cc dd
The next letter in the series is e, Choice 5, which has been indicated as the correct answer on the answer sheet.

Now do example ⑤ below and indicate the correct answer on the answer sheet.

⑤ c a d a e a f a   (1) d (2) e (3) f (4) g (5) h

In example ⑤, the series goes: ca da ea fa Therefore, the correct answer is <u>g</u>, Choice 4.

Now do example ⑥ and indicate the correct answer on your answer sheet.

⑥ a x b y a x b y a x b   (1) a (2) b (3) c (4) d (5) y

In example ⑥ the series goes like this: axby axby axb. Therefore, the correct answer is y, Choice 5.

CONSOLIDATE YOUR KEY ANSWERS HERE

Practice using Answer Sheets. Make ONE mark for each answer. Additional and stray marks may be counted as mistakes. In making corrections erase errors COMPLETELY. Make glossy black marks. To arrive at an accurate estimate of your ability and progress, cover the Correct Answers with a sheet of white paper while you are taking this test.

SAMPLE ANSWER SHEET

```
    A B C D E      A B C D E    1 2 3 4 5    1 2 3 4 5    1 2 3 4 5    1 2 3 4 5
1 ▯ ▯ ▯ ▯ ▯   2 ▯ ▯ ▯ ▯ ▯   3 ▯ ▯ ▯ ▯ ▯   4 ▯ ▯ ▯ ▯ ▯   5 ▯ ▯ ▯ ▯ ▯   6 ▯ ▯ ▯ ▯ ▯
```

CORRECT ANSWERS TO SAMPLE QUESTIONS

Now compare your answers with the Correct Answers to Sample Questions. If your answers are not the same as the correct answers shown, go back and study the samples to see where you made a mistake.

1. A   2. C   3. 1   4. 5   5. 4   6. 5

TEST I. LETTER SERIES

TIME: 20 Minutes. 25 Questions.

DIRECTIONS: Each question consists of a series of letters or numbers (or both) which follow some definite order. Study each series to determine what the order is. Then look at the answer choices. Select the one answer that will complete the set in accordance with the pattern established.

Suggestions: In solving alphabetic series, it is helpful to write out the alphabet and keep it in front of you as you work. This makes it easier to spot the key to a letter series.

```
A B C D E F G H I J K L M N O P Q R S T U V W X Y Z
1 2 3 4 5 6 7 8 9 10 11 12 13 14 15 16 17 18 19 20 21 22 23 24 25 26
```

Explanations of the key points behind these questions appear with the answers at the end of this test. The explanatory answers provide the kind of background that will enable you to answer test questions with facility and confidence.

		1 2 3 4 5			1 2 3 4 5
1.	a c e g	h i j k l	11.	j c k c	a c e h l
2.	a b d e g	c d h i k	12.	g j e l c	m n o p q
3.	m n p s	t v w x z	13.	c c d f	e f g h i
4.	a z b y c	d g j n x	14.	s g p h m i	j k l m n
5.	z w t	q r s t u	15.	o p n q m	a e n r s
6.	c c d d r	a d e h r	16.	a b d h	b f j l p
7.	a r b s c	d r s t x	17.	s d b t e c u f	a d e r v
8.	n p m o	i j k l m	18.	c d c c e c c c	c d e f g
9.	a b b c c c d d d	b c d e f	19.	q r s r s t	q r s t u
10.	a m c p e	b r s w z	20.	a e i m	a i o q u

		1 2 3 4 5			1 2 3 4 5
21.	c e h l	q s u x y	24.	i i k k	k l m n o
22.	z y w v t	r s t u v	25.	p a h p b i p	a c e j p
23.	g h g f g h g	f g h i j			

CONSOLIDATE YOUR KEY ANSWERS HERE

Practice using Answer Sheets. Make ONE mark for each answer. Additional and stray marks may be counted as mistakes. In making corrections erase errors COMPLETELY. Make glossy black marks. To arrive at an accurate estimate of your ability and progress, cover the Correct Answers with a sheet of white paper while you are taking this test.

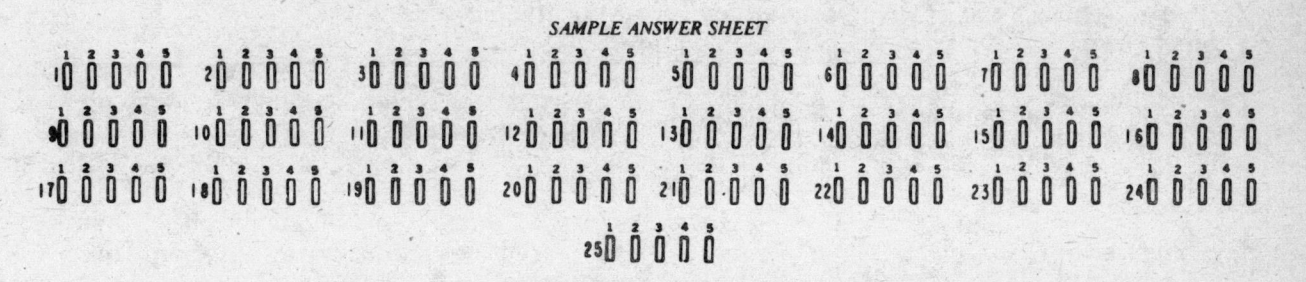

SAMPLE ANSWER SHEET

CORRECT KEY ANSWERS TO THE PRACTICE QUESTIONS

Check our key answers with your own. You'll probably find very few errors. In any case, check your understanding of all questions by studying the following explanatory answers. They illuminate the subject matter. Here you will find concise clarifications of basic points behind the key answers.

1.2	5.1	9.3	13.5	17.2	21.1	25.2
2.3	6.5	10.3	14.1	18.4	22.2	
3.3	7.4	11.5	15.4	19.3	23.1	
4.5	8.4	12.2	16.5	20.4	24.3	

EXPLANATORY ANSWERS CLARIFYING CARDINAL POINTS

Here you have the heart of the Question and Answer Method...getting help when and where you need it. Where one of your Key Answers differs from ours you have a problem which can easily be remedied by reading the explanation. Then, if you have time, you might be able to pick up points on the exam by reading the other explanations, even where you wrote the Key Answers correctly. These explanations stress fundamental facts, ideas, and principles which just might pop up as questions on future exams.

1. **(2)** Add 2 to each letter to get the next letter (*Note*: when we say "add 2," we mean add two to the position of the letter in the alphabet).

2. **(3)** Add 1, add 2; repeat the cycle.

3. **(3)** Add 1; add 2; add 3; etc. (repeat adding 1 to the underlined number each time).

4. **(5)** Odd letters (first, third, etc.): add 1; repeat. Even letters (second, fourth, etc.): subtract 1; repeat.

5. **(1)** Subtract 3; repeat.

6. **(5)** Same letter, different letter; repeat.

7. **(4)** Odd letters: add 1; repeat. Even letters: add 1; repeat.

8. **(4)** Add 2, subtract 3; repeat.

9. **(3)** Letter #1 (a) is repeated once; letter #2 (b) is repeated twice; etc. d is letter number 4, so it is repeated 4 times.

10. **(3)** Odd letters: add 2; repeat. Even letters: add 3; repeat.

11. **(5)** Odd letters: add 1; repeat. Even letters: always c.

12. **(2)** Odd letters: subtract 2; repeat. Even letters; add 2; repeat.

13. **(5)** Add 0; add 1; add 2; etc. (repeat, adding 1 to the underlined number each time).

14. **(1)** Odd letters: subtract 3; repeat. Even letters; add 1; repeat.

15. **(4)** Odd letters: subtract 1; repeat. Even letters; add 1; repeat.

16. **(5)** Multiply by 2; repeat.

17. **(2)** Add 1 to each group of three to get the next group of three.

18. **(4)** The series is d, e, f, etc. but before the first letter is one c, before the second are two c's, etc.

19. **(3)** Add 1, add 1, subtract 1; repeat.

20. **(4)** Add 4; repeat.

21. **(1)** Add 2; add 3; add 4; etc. (repeat, adding 1 to the underlined number each time).

22. **(2)** Subtract 1, subtract 2; repeat.

23. **(1)** The series is simply g h g f, repeated.

24. **(3)** Add 0, add 2; repeat.

25. **(2)** Every third letter beginning with
the first: always p.
the second: add 1; repeat.
the third: add 1; repeat.

TEST II. SERIES AND PROGRESSIONS

TIME: 16 Minutes. 20 Questions.

DIRECTIONS: *Each question consists of a series of letters or numbers (or both) which follow some definite order. Study each series to determine what the order is. Then look at the answer choices. Select the one answer that will complete the set in accordance with the pattern established.*

Suggestions: In solving alphabetic series, it is helpful to write out the alphabet and keep it in front of you as you work. This makes it easier to spot the key to a letter series.

```
A  B  C  D  E  F  G  H  I  J  K  L  M  N  O  P  Q  R  S  T  U  V  W  X  Y  Z
1  2  3  4  5  6  7  8  9 10 11 12 13 14 15 16 17 18 19 20 21 22 23 24 25 26
```

1. 1 D 4 E 9 F
    (A) 10   (B) 12
    (C) G   (D) 16

2. Z 1/25 Y 1/50 X 1/100
    (A) W   (B) T
    (C) 1/10   (D) 1/75

3. 2 3 4 6 7 8 10
    (A) 12   (B) 11
    (C) 9   (D) 5

4. 1 1 2 0 3 −1
    (A) 2   (B) 4
    (C) 6   (D) 8

5. 100 81 64
    (A) 25   (B) 32
    (C) 49   (D) 56

6. 2 6 4 8 6 10
    (A) 6   (B) 8
    (C) 10   (D) 12

7. A Z A Y A X
    (A) A   (B) B
    (C) U   (D) V

8. A B 1 C D 2 E F
    (A) G   (B) D
    (C) 3   (D) 4

9. 2 4 A C 6 8 B
    (A) X   (B) 10
    (C) 3   (D) D

10. 1 3 1 5 1 7 1
    (A) 4   (B) 8
    (C) 1   (D) 9

11. C G K O
    (A) A   (B) Z
    (C) S   (D) T

12. 3 9 27 81
    (A) 243   (B) 500
    (C) 100   (D) 162

146 / *P.A.C.E. Professional-Administrative Career Exam*

13. 1 4 7 10
    (A) 11   (B) 12
    (C) 13   (D) 14

14. A 80 C 60 E 40 G
    (A) 10   (B) 20
    (C) 30   (D) 40

15. 100 98 94 88 80
    (A) 80   (B) 75
    (C) 70   (D) 65

16. 2 6 12 20
    (A) 30   (B) 28
    (C) 26   (D) 24

17. 1 10 3 8 5
    (A) 2   (B) 6
    (C) 12   (D) 14

18. 2 5 10 17
    (A) 19   (B) 23
    (C) 24   (D) 26

19. Z A Y B X
    (A) C   (B) D
    (C) W   (D) V

20. 5 6 4 7 3
    (A) 9   (B) 8
    (C) 7   (D) 6

CONSOLIDATE YOUR KEY ANSWERS HERE

Practice using Answer Sheets. Make ONE mark for each answer. Additional and stray marks may be counted as mistakes. In making corrections erase errors COMPLETELY. Make glossy black marks. To arrive at an accurate estimate of your ability and progress, cover the Correct Answers with a sheet of white paper while you are taking this test.

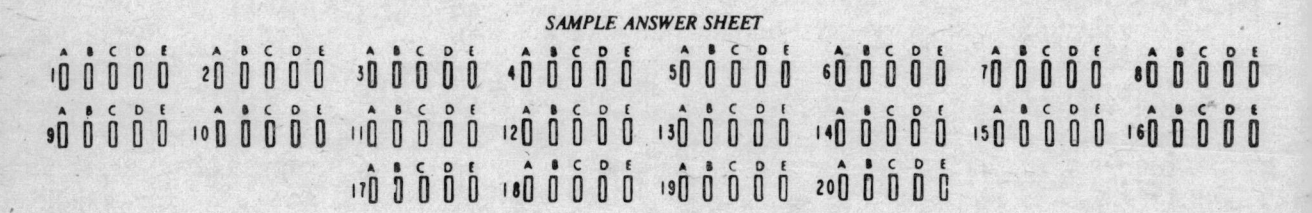

SAMPLE ANSWER SHEET

CORRECT ANSWERS TO THE FOREGOING PRACTICE QUESTIONS

Now compare your answers with these Correct Answers to the Practice Questions. If your answers differ from these, go back and study those questions to see where and how you made your mistakes.

1. D	4. B	7. A	10. D	13. C	16. A	19. A
2. A	5. C	8. C	11. C	14. B	17. B	20. B
3. B	6. B	9. D	12. A	15. C	18. D	

TEST III. SERIES AND PROGRESSIONS

TIME: 8 Minutes. 10 Questions.

DIRECTIONS: For each question read all the choices carefully. Then select that answer which you consider correct or most nearly correct. Blacken the answer space corresponding to your best choice, just as you would do on the actual examination.

Suggestions: In solving alphabetic series, it is helpful to write out the alphabet and keep it in front of you as you work. This makes it easier to spot the key to a letter series.

A B C D E F G H I J K L M N O P Q R S T U V W X Y Z
1 2 3 4 5 6 7 8 9 10 11 12 13 14 15 16 17 18 19 20 21 22 23 24 25 26

Correct Answers are consolidated after the last question.

1. Which is the fifth letter to the right of the letter which is midway between M and Q in the alphabet?
   (A) J   (B) I
   (C) U   (D) T
   (E) S.

2. Which number in this series appears for the second time nearest the beginning? 3 5 6 2 8 7 0 9 5 9 4 4 8 5 3 8 2 0 7 9 1 2
   (A) 9   (B) 8
   (C) 5   (D) 7
   (E) 0.

3. What letter in the sentence you are now reading appears for the fifth time nearest the beginning?
   (A) E   (B) T
   (C) N   (D) A
   (E) H.

4. Find the fourth figure from the end of the next to the largest number and add five to it. 55718 52330 55860 54650 54560 The resulting number will be:
   (A) 10   (B) 11
   (C) 9   (D) 8
   (E) 7.

5. Find the third letter from the end of the word that would come third in this series if the words were arranged alphabetically; classification; detrimental; constitutional; eligibility; barrister.
   (A) I   (B) T
   (C) N   (D) A
   (E) R.

6. Count each S in this Series that is followed by a T next to it if the T is not followed by a Y next to it. How many such S's do you count? S T S Y Q M S T Y M T S T T S Q M S S T Q S T Y T S A M T S T M
   (A) 5   (B) 3
   (C) 4   (D) 2
   (E) 6.

7. Ten five-inch filing boxes are arranged side by side on a shelf. Replace the third box with a six-inch box and add a seven-inch box between the fifth and sixth boxes. Count the inches between the left front corner of the second box and the right front corner of the seventh box as they now stand.
   (A) 38   (B) 29
   (C) 28   (D) 33
   (E) 30.

148 / P.A.C.E. Professional-Administrative Career Exam

8. What would be the tenth letter counting to the right in the word classification, if the first and second letters, the third and fourth letters, the fifth and sixth, etc., were interchanged?
 (A) L (B) A (C) S (D) C (E) T.

9. Find the fourth figure from the beginning of the number that would come fifth if the following code numbers were arranged numerically: S 375.123j4 S 374.23j15 S 375.01j2 S 374.123j4 S 375.4123
 (A) 5 (B) 4 (C) 0 (D) 3 (E) 2.

10. If, according to the compass, you travel south one mile, travel at right angles to the right two miles, travel at right angles to the left three miles, travel at right angles to the left four miles, travel at right angles to the left five miles, in what direction are you traveling the last five miles?
 (A) North
 (B) South
 (C) East
 (D) West
 (E) South-east.

CONSOLIDATE YOUR KEY ANSWERS HERE

Practice using Answer Sheets. Make ONE mark for each answer. Additional and stray marks may be counted as mistakes. In making corrections erase errors COMPLETELY. Make glossy black marks. To arrive at an accurate estimate of your ability and progress, cover the Correct Answers with a sheet of white paper while you are taking this test.

SAMPLE ANSWER SHEET

CORRECT ANSWERS TO THE FOREGOING PRACTICE QUESTIONS

Now compare your answers with these Correct Answers to the Practice Questions. If your answers differ from these, go back and study those questions to see where and how you made your mistakes.

| 1. D | 2. C | 3. B | 4. A | 5. C |
| 6. C | 7. D | 8. D | 9. B | 10. A |

Professional & Administrative Career Exam

NUMERICAL RELATIONS

This is one of the several sections of your test. It's an important section... well worth all the time you can afford. If you apply yourself and employ the correct study methods, this chapter should give you the kind of preparation you need for a high test score. Beginning with the basic operations, it will bring you along step-by-step to the point where you can easily solve the actual test problems. It provides pertinent practice to strengthen abilities you already possess.

THIS type of question tests your knowledge of, and aptitude for, working with numbers—whether as part of arithmetical problems or questions dealing with numbers in general, such as graph interpretation.

Aside from simple math questions such as additions, subtractions, and divisions, Civil Service and other job tests often include specific mathematical problems relating to the position for which the test is given. For example, the position of accountant will include in its test questions and problems on taxes, bookkeeping, interest, etc. Engineers or other professionals will meet questions that pertain to their particular field. For many positions, even on the trainee level, a working knowledge of algebra and geometry is needed, if such knowledge is an integral part of the exam-taker's intended position.

Sometimes the use of a slide rule is permitted in examinations which contain problems that could be worked with its aid. If there is a statement in the announcement of examination, or in the card of admission to the examination room, that the use of a slide rule, protractor, scale, or any other device is permitted, the applicant must furnish the instrument himself if he wishes to use it. If any instrument or device is *required* to be furnished by the applicant, the announcement or admission card will say so. If it is not required but simply permitted, it is up to the applicant to decide whether he will use it or not.

Solutions To Basic Problems

Ten "basic" types of problems are explained and solved in this section. They are followed by previous exam questions which you should be able to solve if you are adequately prepared for the mathematical part of your exam. Each of the ten "basic" problem types are solved in step-by-step fashion. Most of the problems you will face on an actual exam are either like one of these ten types, or a variation of one, since the principles they apply encompass a vast number and variety of problems. Study these example problems which have been solved for you, and then go to the previous exam problems. Your score on these latter problems should be at least 75%.

Profit and Loss

The following terms may be encountered in profit and loss problems:
a. The cost price of an article is the price paid by a person who wishes to sell it again.
b. There may be an allowance or trade discount on the cost price.
c. The list price or marked price is the price at which the article is listed or marked to be sold.
d. There may be a discount or series of discounts on the list price.
e. The selling price or sales price is the price at which the article is finally sold.
f. If the selling price is greater than the cost price, there has been a profit.
g. If the selling price is lower than the cost price, there has been a loss.
h. If the article is sold at the same price as the cost, there has been no loss or profit.
i. Profit or loss may be based either on the cost price or on the selling price.
j. Profit or loss may be stated in terms of dollars and cents, or in terms of per cent.
k. Overhead expenses include such items as rent, salaries, etc. and may be added to the selling price.

---

1. Hammers are bought for $18.00 a dozen. In order to gain 40%, what must the selling price per hammer be?
 (A) $2.10   (B) $2.00
 (C) $2.50   (D) $3.00

SOLUTION: To find the selling price we must multiply the cost by the rate of profit or loss.

In this case the cost is $18.00 divided by 12; $18.00 being the cost of an entire dozen. Since there is a profit of 40% we must multiply the cost by 1.40 or 140%. (If we sold something at 100% of its cost, we should be getting what we paid for it.)

$$\frac{18}{12} \times 1.40 = \begin{array}{r} 18 \\ \times\ 1.40 \\ \hline 720 \\ 18 \\ \hline 25.20 \end{array}$$

$$\begin{array}{r} 2.10 \\ 12\overline{)25.20} \end{array}$$ **Answer**

2. Hammers are bought for $30.00 a dozen and sold at $3.50 each. The rate of profit on the transaction is:
 (A) 30%   (B) 40%
 (C) 50%   (D) 45%

SOLUTION: To find the rate of profit or loss, we first find the actual profit or loss and then find what percent of the COST this is.

Multiplying $3.50 by 12 to find the cost of a dozen hammers:

$$\$3.50 \times 12 = \$42.00$$

Subtracting the cost from the selling price to find the actual profit:

$$\begin{array}{r} \$42.00 \\ -\ 30.00 \\ \hline \$12.00 \end{array}$$

Finding what percent of the cost the profit is involves converting a fraction into a percent.

We multiply the fraction by 100 and perform the indicated divisions:

$$\frac{\$12}{\$30} \times 100 = \begin{array}{r} 40\% \\ 30\overline{)1200} \end{array}$$ **Answer**

Addition of Fractions

3. If we add 8-1/5, 45-5/8, 2-17/20, 14-1/2, and 1-21/40 the answer will be
  (A) 70-8/10   (B) 72-7/10
  (C) 72-1/5   (D) 70-7/10.

SOLUTION: In adding mixed numbers like these, we perform three additions: The addition of the whole numbers, the addition of the fractions, and combination of the added whole numbers and fractions. Adding the whole numbers presents no difficulty. Our sum is 70.

$$8 + 45 + 2 + 14 + 1 = 70$$

To add the fractions we must first find the least common denominator. In this case it is 40.

Then for each separate fraction we divide the denominator into the common denominator and multiply the resulting quotient by the numerator.

We add all these products and divide by the common denominator. Here are the actual calculations:

$$
\begin{array}{rr}
 & 40 \\
8\text{-}1/5 & 8 \\
45\text{-}5/8 & 25 \\
2\text{-}17/20 & 34 \\
14\text{-}1/2 & 20 \\
1\text{-}21/40 & 21 \\
\hline
 & \dfrac{108}{40} = 2\dfrac{28}{40} = 2\dfrac{7}{10}
\end{array}
$$

$$
\begin{array}{r}
70 \\
+\ 2\dfrac{7}{10} \\
\hline
72\dfrac{7}{10}
\end{array}
$$ **Answer**

Interest

4. $1,850 is invested for 50 days at a rate of 5%. The interest return is
  (A) $12.00   (B) $10.00
  (C) $12.67   (D) $13.00.

SOLUTION: While there are many short cuts used by banks and commercial houses in computing interest, the best plan for the candidate is to understand thoroughly all the steps involved in this computation and to use them all intelligently.

Expressed as a formula, interest may be computed thus: $P \times R \times T = I$. If we are given interest, principal and time, and asked to find the Rate, the operation may be expressed thus:

$$R = \frac{I}{P \times T}$$

And if we are given R, T, and I, and asked to find the Principal, this is the formula:

$$P = \frac{I}{R \times T}$$

If we multiply the principal by the rate of interest, and the length of time the money draws interest, we have the amount of interest due.

If the money were to bear interest for a year we would only have to multiply $1,850 by 5% (5/100) in this example. However, the money only bears interest for 50 days or 50/365 of a year. The rest is done by simple cancellation.

$$\frac{\$1850 \times 5 \times 50}{100 \times 365} = \frac{925}{73} = \$12.67$$ **Answer**

152 / *P.A.C.E. Professional-Administrative Career Exam*

5. What amount of money yields $40.00 per month if invested at an annual rate of 5%
    (A) $9,000   (B) $9,500
    (C) $9,600   (D) $9,400.

SOLUTION: To find the principal we must divide interest by rate by time.

If we multiply $40.00 per month by twelve we find the interest yield for a year. $40 × 12 = $480.00. The Time factor in this problem is now one year.

For the rest we have only to follow out our formula:

$$P = \frac{I}{R \times T} = P = \frac{\$480}{\frac{5}{100} \times 1}$$

DIVISION OF FRACTIONS: At this point an interesting difficulty presents itself: The division of fractions. To divide $80 by 5/100 we have simply to invert the fraction and multiply thus:

$$\$480 \div \frac{5}{100} = \$480 \times \frac{100}{5} = \$9,600 \quad \textbf{Answer}$$

6. A woman invested $4,000 in a speculative venture for 9 months. A second woman invested $6,000 in the same business for 6 months. The net gain was $720.00. What was the second woman's return on her investment if all the profits were divided between the two women?
    (A) $360   (B) $700
    (C) $400   (D) $350.

SOLUTION: So far as regards dividends, the investment of $6,000 for 6 months is the same as the investment of $36,000 for 1 month. The same statement can be made regarding $4,000 for 9 months.

First Woman — $4,000 for 9 months = $36,000 for 1 month.

Second Woman — $6,000 for 6 months = $36,000 for 1 month.

Both $72,000 for 1 month.

It is a coincidence that the shares of the two women in this example are the same. However, the procedure here is exactly the same as though they had different shares.

We find what part the second woman's share bears to the total. We then take this proportion of the total income and our result is the second woman's share.

$$\frac{36,000}{72,000} \times 720 = \$360 \quad \textbf{Answer}$$

7. The rate of interest on a principal of $10,000 that will yield $80.00 in 65 days is
    (A) 4%   (B) 5.5%
    (C) 4.49%   (D) 6%.

SOLUTION: The formula here is

$$R = \frac{I}{P \times T}$$

Substituting, we have:

$$R = \frac{\$80}{10,000 \times \frac{65}{365}} = \frac{\$80}{\frac{650,000}{365}} =$$

$$\$80 \times \frac{365}{650,000} = \frac{29,200}{650,000}$$

CONVERTING A FRACTION INTO A PERCENT: This is a simple operation if the proper steps be known and taken. We must convert the fraction $\frac{29,200}{650,000}$ into a percent so that we may properly express the rate of interest.

To change a fraction into a percent we must multiply the fraction by 100 and then carry through the indicated division.

$$\frac{29,200}{650,000} \times 100 = \frac{2,920,000}{650,000} =$$

$$650,000 \overline{)2,920,000} \quad 4.49\% \quad \textbf{Answer}$$

Assessment

8. If a piece of property is assessed at $45,700 and the tax rate on real property is $2.40 per $1,000, the amount of tax that must be paid on this property is
(A) $110
(B) $112
(C) $109.68
(D) $109.

SOLUTION: Since the tax rate is $2.40 per $1,000, we must determine how many thousands of dollars are involved. To do this, we divide $45,700 by $1,000. And the result is 45.7.

$$45,700 \div 1,000 = 45.7$$

When we multiply 45.7 by $2.40, we learn the amount of the tax—

$$45.7 \times \$2.40 = \$109.68 \text{ Answer}$$

9. $60,000 worth of land is assessed at 120% of its value. If the tax rate is $2.56 per 1,000 the amount of tax to be paid is
(A) $190
(B) $195
(C) $184.32
(D) $180.

SOLUTION: To find how much the land has been assessed:

$$60,000 \times \frac{12\cancel{0}}{10\cancel{0}} =$$

$$\frac{720,00\cancel{0}}{1\cancel{0}} = \$72,000$$

If tax is $2.56 per $1,000, multiply:

$$\begin{array}{r} 2.56 \\ \times\ 72 \\ \hline 512 \\ 1792\ \\ \hline \$184.32 \end{array} \text{ Answer}$$

Cubic Volume

10. A bin measures 14 feet by 9 feet by 7½ feet. Allowing 4/5 bushel of grain per cubic foot, how many bushels will the bin hold?

SOLUTION:

Length × Width × Height = Cubic Area.

L × W × H = Cubic Area

$$14 \times 9 \times 7\tfrac{1}{2} = \cancel{14}^{7} \times 9 \times \frac{15}{\cancel{2}} = 945 \text{ cubic ft.}$$

Since each cubic foot of space holds 4/5 bushel of grain:

$$\cancel{945}^{189} \times \frac{4}{\cancel{5}} = 756 \text{ Bushels.} \text{ Answer}$$

Literal Problems

11. If L explosions occur during a given month and result in Q dollars of loss, the average loss per explosion in dollars is:

(A) L × Q
(B) Q/L
(C) L/A
(D) 12K/2P
(E) none.

SOLUTION: This is a simple problem in determining an average. The presence of letters rather than numbers makes it slightly more difficult by imposing upon us the burden of using fundamental principles rather than habitual modes of action.

The average loss per explosion is the total loss divided by the number of explosions, or the average loss per explosion equals

$$\frac{\text{Total amount of loss}}{\text{Number of explosions}}$$

Since the total loss in a given month is Q and the number of explosions is L we may say that the average loss per explosion is $\frac{Q}{L}$ **Answer**

12. If there is a total of J garbage trucks in operation in New York City, covering a total street mileage of N miles at an average speed of E miles per hour, we can find the average street mileage per truck from the above data, without considering

(A) the number of cars
(B) the total street mileage
(C) the average speed
(D) any of these values
(E) any further data besides the above.

SOLUTION: The average street mileage per truck is the total street mileage divided by the total number of trucks, that is, the average street mileage per truck = $\frac{\text{Total street mileage}}{\text{Total No. of trucks}}$

(if we had 20 trucks covering a total street mileage of 300 miles then the average mileage covered by each truck is 15 miles or

$$\frac{300}{20} = 15 \text{ miles.})$$

From this it is clear that the average speed of the trucks does not come into the consideration of the average mileage per truck and therefore (C) is correct. **Answer**

13. During 1964, T families took out insurance policies, representing an increase of M families over the number taking them in 1962. In 1963, however, the number taking out insurance was P less than in 1962. If there were R insurance agents in each of these 3 years, the average number of policies written per insurance agent in 1963 was:

(A) $\frac{T - M}{P \quad R}$ (B) $\frac{T - M - P}{R}$

(C) $\frac{M + T - R}{R}$ (D) $\frac{T + M + P}{R}$

SOLUTION: We must first determine how many people took out insurance in 1963 and get this quantity in terms of T, M, and P.

in 1964—T families took out insurance.

in 1962—T − M families took out insurance. (since 1964 is an increase of M over 1962.)

in 1963—(no. in 1962) − P (since it was P less than 1962) = T − M − P = Total number of Policies in 1937.

Now the average number of policies per insurance agent:

$$\frac{\text{Total number of policies in 1963}}{\text{Total number of insurance agents in 1963}} = \frac{T - M - P}{R}$$ **Answer**

Numerical Relations / 155

14. Clerk A sorts B letters per hour, clerk C sorts D letters per hour. The D letters which clerk C sorts exceed those which clerk A sorts by 10 letters per hour. Measured in number sorted per 8-hour day, clerk C exceeds A by:

(A) $D - B \times 10$ (B) $(D - B) \times 8$
(C) $D + C - A + B$ (D) $C + D - A + B$

SOLUTION: The D letters sorted per hour by clerk C exceeds (is greater than) the B letters sorted per hour by clerk A, by an amount of 10 letters per hour, or D is 10 more than B. In symbols: $D = B + 10$.

In 8 hours, clerk C will have sorted 8 D letters while clerk A will have sorted 8 B letters and since the difference in one hour is 10 letters, in 8 hours, the difference will be 8×10. $8D = 8B + 80$ or bringing 8 B to the other side: $8D - 8B = 80$ or factoring out the 8 on the left.

We have $8(D - B) = 80$ which is the amount of letters by which clerk C's output exceeds clerk A's output and hence answer (B) above is correct. **Answer**

15. The annual salary of a machinist is R dollars more than that of his assistant. His assistant earns V dollars annually. The amount in monthly salary, by which the machinist exceeds his assistant is given by:

(A) $\dfrac{V - R}{13}$ (B) $\dfrac{RV}{12}$
(C) $R - V$ (D) $12V - R$
(E) $\dfrac{R}{12}$

SOLUTION: The annual salary of the machinist is $V + R$ dollars. The annual salary of his assistant is V dollars. The monthly salary of the machinist is $\dfrac{V}{12} + \dfrac{R}{12}$ dollars. (Since in a year the machinist receives 12 times as much as he receives in a month, we divide the yearly salary by 12 to find the amount earned in one month.) Similarly, the monthly salary of his assistants is $\dfrac{V}{12}$ dollars. Therefore the machinist's monthly salary exceeds his assistant's salary, monthly, by $\dfrac{R}{12}$ dollars. **Answer (E) is correct.**

16. A family of 5 has two employed members earning L dollars a month. The family receives a total semi-monthly relief allowance of M dollars. If the rent allowance is N dollars, and the amount spent for food is twice that for rent, the amount spent monthly for all items other than food and rent is:

(A) $L + 2M - 3N$

(B) $N + L + M$

(C) $L + M - 2N$

SOLUTION: The amount spent monthly for all items other than food and rent is the total income for one month minus the total expenditure for food and rent.

Total income $= L + 2M$ (since M is a semi-monthly allowance, the monthly allowance is 2M or M multiplied by 2.)

Total exp. for food and rent $= N$ (for rent) $+ 2N$ (food)—since the amount spent for other items $= L + 2M - N - 2N = L + 2M - 3N$. **Answer**

17. If psychological studies of college students show K per cent to be emotionally unstable, the number of college students not emotionally unstable per one hundred college students is:

(A) 100 minus K

(B) 100 times (K minus)

(C) K minus 1

SOLUTION: Since K percent $= \dfrac{K}{100}$ in 100 students, K% of 100 are emotionally unstable then $\dfrac{K}{100} \times 100 = K$ students are unstable.

Therefore the remaining students are emotionally stable and they number $100 - K$.

Answer (A) is correct.

Rate, Time, and Distance Problems

In all these problems the formula to be followed is very simple:

Rate (speed) X Time = Distance.

If you are given the RATE and DISTANCE and are asked to find time then you simply make the obvious modification in the formula:

$$\text{Time} = \frac{\text{Distance}}{\text{Rate}}$$

To find rate given distance and time:

$$\frac{\text{Distance}}{\text{Time}} = \text{Rate}$$

There are many complications that can be introduced but if these fundamental ideas can be kept clearly in view few difficulties will be encountered.

---

18. Two hikers start walking from the city line at different times. The second hiker whose speed is 4 miles per hour starts 2 hours after the first hiker whose speed is 3 miles per hour. Determine the amount of time and distance that will be consumed before the second hiker catches up with the first.

SOLUTION: Since the first man has a 2 hour headstart and is walking at the rate of 3 miles per hour he is 6 miles from the city line when the second hiker starts.

Rate X Time = Distance.

Subtracting 3 miles per hour from 4 miles per hour gives us 1 mile per hour or the difference in the rates of speed of the two men. In other words, the second hiker gains one mile on the first hiker in every hour.

Since there is a 6 mile difference to cut down and it is cut down one mile every hour, it is clear that the second hiker will need 6 hours to overtake his companion.

In this time he will have traveled $4 \times 6 = 24$ or 24 miles. The first hiker will have been walking 8 hours since he had a 2 hour headstart $8 \times 3 = 24$.

Time = 6 hours
Distance = 24 miles   **Answer**

19. The same two hikers start walking toward each other along a road connecting two cities which are 60 miles apart. Their speeds are the same as in the preceding problem, 3 and 4 miles per hour. How much time will elapse before they meet?

SOLUTION: In each hour of travel toward each other the men will cut down a distance equal to the sum of their speeds. $3 + 4 = 7$ miles per hour. To meet they must cut down 60 miles, and at 7 miles per hour this would be

$$\frac{D}{R} = T \quad \frac{60}{7} = 8\frac{4}{7} \text{ hours.} \quad \textbf{Answer}$$

20. The problem might also have asked: "How much distance must the slower man cover before the two hikers meet?" In such case we should have gone through the same steps plus one additional step:

The time consumed before meeting was $8\frac{4}{7}$ hours. To find the distance covered by the slower hiker we merely multiply his rate by the time elapsed.

$$R \times T = D \quad 3 \times 8\frac{4}{7} = 25\frac{5}{7} \quad \textbf{Answer}$$

Time and Work Problems

21. If A does a job in 6 days, and B does the same job in 3 days, how long will it take the two of them, working together, to do the job?

SOLUTION: Almost any problem of this type can be solved quite simply by fractions, without resorting to higher mathematics.

A. If A does the whole job in 6 days, he will do 1/6 of the job in one day.
If B does the whole job in 3 days, he will do 1/3 of the job in one day.

B. 1/3 + 1/6 = 1/2

C. 1/2 of the job will be finished in one day if the two men work together.

D. The whole job will be finished in two days.
Answer

EXPLANATION OF SOLUTION:

A. If you are given the time that a job takes you have merely to find the reciprocal of that time in order to find how much of the work would be done in one day. Finding the reciprocal simply means inverting the figure.

If you do a job in 2 1/2 days, you would do 2/5 of the job in one day.

2 1/2 = 5/2

Finding the reciprocal or inverting:

5/2 = 2/5

Another way of looking at the same operation:

All of the work is done in 5/2 days. In other words it takes 5 half days to finish the job. In one half day 1/5 of the job would be completed, and consequently in one day (2/2) 2/5 of the job would be completed.

CAUTION: If the total time for the job is given in HOURS you will, by getting the reciprocal, find what fraction of the work is done in one HOUR. The procedure for the rest of the problem, of course, is the same as above, except that the answer is in hours.

B. The total time must be reduced to a fraction of the total job because it would not do to simply add the time consumed by each man. 3 days and 6 days added together yield nine days, which is merely TIME and tells us nothing of the AMOUNT OF WORK. But 1/3 and 1/6 do represent amounts of work.

C. Adding these two fractions together we discover the part of the job that would be completed in one day.

D. If we are told that a certain fraction represents the amount of work done in one day and if we wish to find how long the entire job would take, we find the reciprocal of the fraction.

1/2 in 1 day   2/2 (or all) in 2/1 days.

Two principles should be kept in mind.

1. To find the part, invert the time.
2. To find the time, invert the part.

22. A and B working together do a job in 4½ days. B, working alone, is able to do the job in 10 days. How long would it take A, working alone, to do the job?

SOLUTION: All of the job in 9/2 days. $\frac{2}{9}$ of the job in 1 day.

If B takes 10 days to do the job alone he will do 1/10 of the job in one day.

To find the work done by A in one day we subtract B's work from the amount of work done by the two men together in one day.

$$2/9 - 1/10 = \frac{20-9}{90} = \frac{11}{90}$$

11/90 represents the portion of the total job done by A in one day.

Inverting, we found how long it would take him to do the entire job.

$$\frac{90}{11} = 8\frac{2}{11} \text{ Days.} \quad \textbf{Answer}$$

23. If A can do a job in 6 days which B can do in 5-1/2 days, and C can do in 2-1/5 days, how long would the job take if A, B, and C were working together?

SOLUTION:

A Does the job in 6 days: 1/6 of the job in 1 day.
B Does the job in 5-1/2 days: 2/11 of the job in 1 day.
C Does the job in 2-1/5 days: 5/11 of the job in 1 day.

Adding the work done by A, B, and C in one day to find the work done by all three in one day.

$$\frac{1}{6} + \frac{2}{11} + \frac{5}{11} = \frac{11 + 12 + 30}{66} = \frac{53}{66}$$

Finding the reciprocal of $\frac{53}{66}$ in order to find how long the total job would take:

$$\frac{66}{53} = 1\frac{13}{53} \text{ Days.} \quad \textbf{Answer}$$

24. One pipe fills a pool in 20 minutes, a second can fill the pool in 30 minutes, and a third can fill it in 10 minutes. How long would it take the three together to fill the pool?

SOLUTION: First pipe—fills in 20 minutes—fills 1/20 of pool in 1 minute.
Second pipe—fills in 30 minutes—fills 1/30 of pool in 1 minute.
Third pipe—fills in 10 minutes—fills 1/10 of pool in 1 minute.

Adding three fractions together to determine what part of the pool will be filled in one minute when the three pipes are working together.

$$1/20 + 1/30 + 1/10 = \frac{3 + 2 + 6}{60} = \frac{11}{60}$$

If 11/60 of the pool is filled in one minute the reciprocal of the fraction will tell us how many minutes will be required to fill the whole pool.

$$\frac{60}{11} = 5\frac{5}{11} \text{ Minutes.} \quad \textbf{Answer}.$$

Numerical Relations / 159

Problems in Proportions

25. If 5 men can build 6 miles of railroad track in 40 days, how many miles of track can be built by 3 men in 15 days?

SOLUTION: One of the best methods of solving such problems is by directly making the necessary cancellations, divisions, and multiplications.

In this example, we wish to find how many miles of track will be built if both the number of workers and the working time are reduced. It is easily seen that the amount of track constructed will be less than under the old conditions. But how much less?

Since we now have 3 men where before there were 5, we may assume that so far as manpower is concerned, production will be 3/5 as high as when 5 men were working. Consequently:

$$6 \times \frac{3}{5} = \frac{18}{5} = 3\frac{3}{5} \text{ Miles of track.}$$

Thus we know that if 3 men worked 40 days they would build 3-3/5 miles of track.

But another factor serves to lessen production. And that is the decrease in time. Only 15 days are expended, or 15/40 of the time that was expended before. Consequently:

$$3\frac{3}{5} + \frac{15}{40} = \frac{18}{5} \times \frac{15}{40}$$
$$= \frac{270}{200} = 1\frac{7}{20} \text{ Miles of track.}$$

The two arithmetical operations just shown can, of course, be combined into one. Thus:

$$6 \times \frac{3}{5} \times \frac{15}{40} = 1\frac{7}{20} \text{ Miles of track.}$$
Answer.

26. If 5 men build 6 miles of railroad track in 40 days, how many miles of track can be built by 8 men working 90 days?

SOLUTION: Here we have a problem which is similar to the previous one, with this exception: more men are working a longer period of time and consequently the answer will yield not a reduced but an increased number of miles of track.

If we multiply a number by a fraction whose value is less than one, we are reducing the value of that number. If, however, we multiply the number by a fraction whose value is more than one, we are increasing the value of that number. In solving this problem, then, we would not multiply $6 \times \frac{40}{90} \times \frac{5}{8}$. That would produce a number less than 6 and we know that our answer should be more than 6 since we have more men working a longer time than were required to produce 6 miles of track. The proper way of expressing the facts given in the example is:

$$6 \times \frac{90}{40} \times \frac{8}{5} = \frac{4320}{200} = 21\frac{12}{20} \text{ Miles of track.}$$
Answer

Some examples indicate an increase in one factor and a decrease in another.

27. If 10 men earn $500 in 12 days, how much will 6 men earn in 15 days?

SOLUTION: The number of men involved decreases and consequently the fraction will be less than one. The smaller number will therefore be the numerator.

$$\$500 \times \frac{6}{10}$$

The number of days worked increases and so the fraction will be more than one. The larger number will therefore be the numerator.

$$\$500 \times \frac{6}{10} \times \frac{15}{12} = \frac{45,000}{120} = \$375$$
Answer

Mixture Problems

28. A wine merchant has 32 gallons of wine worth $1.50 a gallon. If he wishes to reduce the price to $1.20 a gallon, how many gallons of water must he add?
    (A) 10
    (B) 9
    (C) 8
    (D) 7.

SOLUTION: First let us find the cost of the 32 gallons of undiluted wine at the old price.
32 × $1.50 = $48.00.

$48, then, is the value of the wine that is ultimately to be mixed with water. By the conditions of the problem, $48 will be the price realized from the sale of the wine at the new price of $1.20.

To find how many gallons of wine we shall have at the new price let us divide $48 by $1.20, the new price. The answer, of course, is 40. We see then that we must have 40 gallons of the $1.20 wine.

This is 8 gallons more than the undiluted wine. And that difference of 8 gallons is made up by water.

    Answer (C) is correct.

29. A bakery shop sold 3 kinds of cake. The prices of these three kinds were 25¢, 30¢, and 35¢ per pound. The income from these sales was $36. If the number of pounds of each kind of cake sold was the same, how many pounds were sold?

SOLUTION: To buy all three kinds of cake would cost 25¢ + 30¢ + 35¢ = 90¢.

If we divide $36, the total income, by 90¢, the total price of the three kinds of cake, we will know how many times each kind of cake was sold in order to realize the $36. $\frac{\$36.00}{\$.90} = 40$.

Since there were just as many of each kind of cake sold, the total number of pounds sold = 40 × 3 = 120. **Answer**

30. The number of dimes in a cash register was equal to the number of quarters. There were five times as many nickels as quarters. All these coins together totalled $120. How many of each were there?

SOLUTION: Let us again make groups, this time of coins. A group will consist of five nickels + 1 quarter + 1 dime which equals 60¢. If we divide $120 by 60¢ we find that there are 200 such 60¢ groups contained in $120. Since there are 5 nickels in every one of the 200 groups we multiply 200 by 5 to find the number of nickels—1,000.
There are 200 dimes, 200 quarters and 1,000 nickels. **Answer**

TEST I. MATHEMATICS

TIME: 110 Minutes. 95 Questions.

DIRECTIONS: For each of the following questions, select the choice that best answers the question or completes the statement. Do this before looking at the answers we provide. Key answers, together with concise explanations of the main points behind each question, are consolidated at the end of the test.

1. Assuming that the series will continue in the same pattern, the next number in the series 3, 5, 11, 29 . . . is:
   (A) 41   (B) 47   (C) 65   (D) 83

2. DCCXLIX in Roman numerals represents the number:
   (A) 749   (B) 764   (C) 1249   (D) 1264

3. If the total area of a picture measuring 10 inches by 12 inches plus a matting of uniform width surrounding the picture is 224 square inches, the width of the matting is:
   (A) 2 inches   (B) 2 $4/11$ inches
   (C) 3 inches   (D) 4 inches

4. The net price of a $25 item after successive discounts of 20% and 30% is:
   (A) $11.00   (B) $12.50
   (C) $14.00   (D) $19.00

5. The cost of 63 inches of ribbon at $.12 per yard is:
   (A) $.20   (B) $.21   (C) $.22   (D) $.23

6. If 1½ cups of cereal are used with 4½ cups of water, the amount of water needed with ¾ of a cup of cereal is:
   (A) 2 cups   (B) 2⅛ cups
   (C) 2¼ cups   (D) 2½ cups

7. Under certain conditions, sound travels at about 1100 ft. per second. If 88 ft. per second is approximately equivalent to 60 miles per hour, the speed of sound, under the above conditions, is, of the following, closest to:
   (A) 730 miles per hour
   (B) 740 miles per hour
   (C) 750 miles per hour
   (D) 760 miles per hour

8. If one angle of a triangle is three times a second angle and the third angle is 20 degrees more than the second angle, the second angle is (in degrees):
   (A) 32   (B) 34   (C) 40   (D) 50

9. Assuming that on a blueprint ¼ inch equals 12 inches, the actual length in feet of a steel bar represented on the blueprint by a line 3⅜ inches long is:
   (A) 3⅜   (B) 6¾   (C) 12½   (D) 13½

10. If Mrs. Jones bought 3¾ yards of dacron at $1.16 per yard and 4⅔ yards of velvet at $3.87 per yard, the amount of change she receives from $25 is:
    (A) $2.12   (B) $2.28
    (C) $2.59   (D) $2.63

11. The water level of a swimming pool, 75 feet by 42 feet, is to be raised four inches. The number of gallons of water needed for this is:
    (A) 140   (B) 7,854.5
    (C) 31,500   (D) 94,500

12. If shipping charges to a certain point are 62 cents for the first five ounces and 8 cents for each additional ounce, the weight of a package for which the charges are $1.66 is:
    (A) 13 ounces   (B) 1⅛ pounds
    (C) 1¼ pounds   (D) 1½ pounds

13. If 15 cans of food are needed for seven men for two days, the number of cans needed for four men for seven days is:
    (A) 15   (B) 20   (C) 25   (D) 30

14. The total saving in purchasing 30 13-cent ice cream pops for a class party at a reduced rate of $1.38 per dozen is:
    (A) $.35   (B) $.40   (C) $.45   (D) $.50

15. A candy recipe calls for, among other things, 1½ cups of sugar and ¾ of a cup of boiling water. Mary wants to use this recipe, but has only one cup of sugar. How much boiling water should she use?
(A) ¼ cup (B) ⅓ cup
(C) ½ cup (D) ⅝ cup

16. In a 3-hour examination of 350 questions, there are 50 mathematics problems. If twice as much time should be allowed for each problem as for each of the other questions, how many minutes should be spent on the mathematical problems?
(A) 45 minutes (B) 52 minutes
(C) 60 minutes (D) 72 minutes

17. A rectangular picture measures 4½″ by 6¾″. If the picture is proportionally enlarged so that the shorter side is 7½″, what will be the length of the longer side?
(A) 9¾″ (B) 11¼″
(C) 13½″ (D) 20¼″

18. A typewriter was listed at $120.00 and was bought for $96.00. What was the rate of discount?
(A) 16⅔% (B) 20%
(C) 24% (D) 25%

19. In two hours, the minute hand of a clock rotates through an angle of
(A) 90° (B) 180°
(C) 360° (D) 720°

20. Assuming that the following series will continue in the same pattern, the next number in the series 2, 6, 14, 30, 62, ... is
(A) 96 (B) 126
(C) 186 (D) 216

21. An individual intelligence test is administered to John A when he is 10 years 8 months old. His recorded M.A. is 160 months. What I.Q. should be recorded?
(A) 80 (B) 125
(C) 128 (D) 160

22. When it is noon at prime meridian on the equator, what time is it at 75° north latitude on this meridian?
(A) 12 N. (B) 3 P.M.
(C) 5 P.M. (D) 7 A.M.

23. A carpenter needs boards for 4 shelves, each 2′9″ long, and ½″ thick. How many feet of board should he buy?
(A) 11 (B) 11⅛
(C) 13 (D) 15½

24. CMXLIX in Roman numerals is the equivalent of
(A) 449 (B) 949
(C) 969 (D) 1149

25. If you subtract —1 from +1 the result will be
(A) —2 (B) 0
(C) 1 (D) 2

26. Of the following, the one which is the equivalent of 2⅕ is
(A) ⅕ of 2 (C) ⅖ of 1
(B) 2 and ⅕ of 1 (D) 2 and ⅕ of 2

27. A man bought a TV set that was listed at $160. He was given successive discounts of 20% and 10% The price he paid was
(A) $112.00 (C) $119.60
(B) $115.20 (D) $129.60

28. The total length of fencing needed to enclose a rectangular area 46 feet by 34 feet is
(A) 26 yards 1 foot (C) 52 yards 2 feet
(B) 26⅔ yards (D) 53⅓ yards

29. Mr. Jones' income for a year is $15,000. He pays $2250 for income taxes. The percent of his income that he pays for income taxes is
(A) 9 (C) 15
(B) 12 (D) 22

30. Of the following, the one that is NOT a meaning of ⅔ is
(A) 1 of the 3 equal parts of 2
(B) 2 of the 3 equal parts of 1
(C) 2 divided by 3
(D) a ratio of 3 to 2

31. If the average weight of boys of John's age and height is 105 lbs. and if John weighs 110% of average, then John weighs
(A) 110 lbs. (C) 115½ lbs.
(B) 110.5 lbs. (D) 126 lbs.

32. On a house plan on which 2 inches represents 5 feet, the length of a room measures 7½ inches. The actual length of the room is
    (A) 12½ feet   (C) 17½ feet
    (B) 15¾ feet   (D) 18¾ feet

33. If pencils are bought at 35 cents per dozen and sold at 3 for 10 cents, the total profit on 5½ dozen is
    (A) 25 cents   (C) 28½ cents
    (B) 27½ cents   (D) 31½ cents

34. It costs 31 cents a square foot to lay linoleum. To lay 20 square yards of linoleum it will cost
    (A) $16.20   (C) $55.80
    (B) $18.60   (D) $62.00

35. The total number of eighths in two wholes and three-fourths is
    (A) 11   (C) 19
    (B) 14   (D) 22

36. The difference between one hundred five thousand eighty-four and ninety-three thousand seven hundred nine is
    (A) 11,375   (C) 56,294
    (B) 12,131   (D) 56,375

37. If a recipe for a cake calls for 2½ cups of flour and you wish to make three such cakes, the number of cups of flour you would have to use is
    (A) 6½   (C) 9
    (B) 7½   (D) 9½

38. A piece of wood 35 feet, 6 inches long was used to make 4 shelves of equal length. The length of each shelf was
    (A) 8.9 inches   (C) 8 feet, 9½ in.
    (B) 8 feet, 9 inches (D) 8 feet, 10½ in.

39. If n and m are both positive integers greater than one, the largest fraction in the following group would be
    (A) $\dfrac{2n}{m}$ (C) $\dfrac{2n+1}{m-1}$
    (B) $\dfrac{2n}{m+1}$ (D) $\dfrac{2n+1}{2(n-1)}{m}$

40. John's father received a bonus of $450, which was 5% of his annual salary. His annual salary was
    (A) $9500   (C) $800
    (B) $9000   (D) $7500

41. The ratio of ¼ to ⅗ is
    (A) 1 to 3   (C) 5 to 12
    (B) 3 to 20   (D) 3 to 4

42. Of the following, the fraction that is equal to ⅚ is
    (A) $\dfrac{5+2}{6+2}$ (C) $\dfrac{5\times5}{6\times6}$
    (B) $\dfrac{5\times2}{6\times2}$ (D) $\dfrac{5-2}{6-2}$

43. Jane has two pieces of ribbon. One piece is 2¾ yards; the other, 2⅔ yards. To make the two pieces equal she must cut off from the longer piece
    (A) 9 inches   (C) 6 inches
    (B) 8 inches   (D) 3 inches

44. The Mayflower sailed from Plymouth, England to Plymouth Rock, a distance of approximately 2800 miles, in 63 days. The average speed in miles per hour was closest to which one of the following?
    (A) ½   (C) 2
    (B) 1   (D) 3

45. Dividing the numerator of a fraction by 2 always
    (A) leaves the value of the fraction unchanged
    (B) makes the value of the fraction twice as great
    (C) makes the value of the fraction half as great
    (D) makes the denominator equal to the numerator

46. The scholarship board of a certain college loaned a student $200 at an annual rate of 6% from September 30 until December 15. To repay the loan and accumulated interest the student must give the college an amount closest to which one of the following?
    (A) $202.50   (C) $203.50
    (B) $203   (D) $212

47. Pren and Wright invested $8000 and $6000, respectively, in a hardware business. At the end of the year, the profits were $3800. Each partner received 6% on his investment and the remainder was shared equally. What was the total that Pren received?
    (A) $2380
    (B) $2260
    (C) $1960
    (D) $1840

48. Assuming that 2.54 centimeters = 1 inch, a metal rod that measures 1½ feet would most nearly equal which one of the following?
    (A) 380 centimeters
    (B) 46 centimeters
    (C) 30 centimeters
    (D) none of these

49. Of the following, the number whose value is 1½% is
    (A) .0015
    (B) .012
    (C) .0150
    (D) .105

50. The regular price of a TV set that sold for $118.80 at a 20% reduction sale is
    (A) $148.50
    (B) $142.60
    (C) $138.84
    (D) $95.04

51. Of the following, the number which is nearest in value to 5 is
    (A) 4.985
    (B) 5.005
    (C) 5.01
    (D) 5.1

52. Successive discounts of 10% and 10% are equivalent to a single discount of
    (A) 15%
    (B) 18%
    (C) 19%
    (D) 20%

53. A governmental agency made 768 investigations in 1958, 960 investigations in 1959, and 1200 investigations in 1960. If the rate of increase remains the same, how many investigations will be made in 1961?
    (A) 1600
    (B) 1500
    (C) 1440
    (D) 1416

54. The present size of a dollar bill in the United States is 2.61 inches by 6.14 inches. The number of square inches of paper used for one bill is closest to which one of the following?
    (A) 160 square inches
    (B) 17.8 square inches
    (C) 16.0 square inches
    (D) 1.78 square inches

55. To represent 10½% on a chart of 100 equal squares, one must
    (A) fill in ten squares and one-half of an eleventh
    (B) fill in nine squares and one-half of a tenth
    (C) fill in fifteen squares
    (D) show ten squares each half filled in

56. If .098 is subtracted from 3, the remainder is
    (A) 2.002
    (B) 2.098
    (C) 2.902
    (D) 2.92

57. Assuming that on a blueprint ⅛ inch equals 12 inches of actual length, the actual length (in feet) of a steel bar represented on the blueprint by a line 3¾ inches long is
    (A) 3¾
    (B) 30
    (C) 45
    (D) 360

58. In a circle graph a segment of 108 degrees is shaded to indicate the overhead in doing $150,000 gross business. The overhead amounts to
    (A) $1,200
    (B) $4,500
    (C) $12,000
    (D) $45,000

59. In a song with $\frac{4}{4}$ time signatures, one may find within a bar any one of the following combinations of notes *except*
    (A) two quarter notes, two eighth notes, four sixteenth notes
    (B) two quarter notes, one eighth note, six sixteenth notes
    (C) two quarter notes, two eighth notes, two sixteenth notes
    (D) two quarter notes, three eighth notes, two sixteenth notes

60. The Baltimore Colts won 8 games and lost 3. The ratio of games won to games played is
    (A) 8 : 11   (B) 3 : 11   (C) 8 : 3   (D) 3 : 8

61. Of the following, an expression whose value decreases as x increases to 10 is
(A) $\dfrac{2x+1}{3}$
(B) $\dfrac{4}{15-x}$
(C) $\dfrac{2x-1}{3}$
(D) $\dfrac{6}{2x-1}$

62. The relationship between .01% and .1 is
(A) 1 to 10 (B) 1 to 100 (C) 1 to 1000
(D) 1 to 10,000

63. When the fractions 2/3, 5/7, 8/11 and 9/13 are arranged in ascending order of size, the result is
(A) 8/11, 5/7, 9/13, 2/3
(B) 5/7, 8/11, 2/3, 9/13
(C) 2/3, 8/11, 5/7, 9/13
(D) 2/3, 9/13, 5/7, 8/11

64. If the outer diameter of a metal pipe is 2.84 inches and the inner diameter is 1.94 inches, the thickness of the metal is
(A) .45 of an inch (B) .90 of an inch
(C) 1.94 inches (D) 2.39 inches

65. An office manager employs 3 typists at $45 per week, 2 general clerks at $40 per week, and a messenger at $32 per week. The average weekly wage of these employees is
(A) $37.25
(C) $41.17
(B) $39.00
(D) none of these

66. If x is less than 10, and y is less than 5, it follows that
(A) x is greater than y
(B) x—y=5
(C) x = 2 y
(D) x + y is less than 15

67. A rectangular bin 4 feet long, 3 feet wide, and 2 feet high is solidly packed with bricks whose dimensions are 8 inches, 4 inches, and 2 inches. The number of bricks in the bin is
(A) 54   (B) 648
(C) 1,296 (D) none of these

68. A dealer sells an article at a loss of 50% of the cost. Based on the selling price, the loss is
(A) 25%
(B) 50%
(C) 100%
(D) none of these

69. An autoist drives 60 miles to his destination at an average speed of 40 miles per hour and makes the return trip at an average rate of 30 miles per hour. His average speed per hour for the entire trip is (A) 35 miles (B) 34-2/7 miles (C) 43-1/3 miles (D) none of these

70. In the Fahrenheit scale, the temperature that is equivalent to 50° Centigrade is (A) 122° (B) 90° (C) 106° (D) none of these

71. If the base of a rectangle is increased by 30% and the altitude is decreased by 20% the area is increased by (A) 25% (B) 10% (C) 5% (D) 4%

72. Of the following sets of fractions, the set which is arranged in increasing order is
(A) 7/12, 6/11, 3/5, 5/8 (B) 6/11, 7/12, 5/8, 3/5 (C) 6/11, 7/12, 3/5, 5/8
(D) none of these

73. If the price of an automobile, including a 3% sales tax, is $2729.50, the amount of the sales tax is (A) $79.50 (B) $129.50 (C) $81.89 (D) none of these

74. If the sum of the edges of a cube is 48 inches, the volume of the cube is (A) 512 inches (B) 96 cubic inches (C) 64 cubic inches (D) none of these

75. A rectangular flower bed whose dimensions are 16 yards by 12 yards is surrounded by a walk 3 yards wide. The area of the walk is (A) 93 square yards (B) 96 square yards (C) 204 square yards (D) none of these

76. If the radius of a circle is diminished by 20%, the area is diminished by (A) 20% (B) 400% (C) 40% (D) 36%

77. If a distance estimated at 150 feet is really 140 feet, the per cent of error in this estimate is (A) 6-2/3% (B) 7-1/7% (C) 10% (D) none of these

78. If an airplane flies 550 yards in 3 seconds, the speed of the airplane, expressed in miles per hour, is (A) 125 (B) 375 (C) 300 (D) none of these

79. If the numerator and the denominator of a fraction are increased by the same quantity, the resulting fraction is (A) always greater than the original fraction (B) always less than the original fraction (C) always equal to the original fraction (D) none of these

80. A merchant sold two radios for $120. each. One was sold at a loss of 25% of the cost and the other was sold at a gain of 25% of the cost. On both transactions combined the merchant lost (A) $64 (B) $36 (C) $16 (D) none of these

81. The number missing in the series 2, 6, 12, 20, ?, 42, 56, 72 is (A) 30 (B) 40 (C) 36 (D) none of these

82. If two angles of a triangle are acute angles, the third angle (A) is less than the sum of the two given angles (B) is an acute angle (C) is the largest angle of the triangle (D) may be an obtuse angle

83. If an automobile travels 80 miles at the rate of 20 miles per hour and then returns over the same route at the rate of 40 miles per hour, the average speed per hour for the entire trip (going and return) is (A) 30 miles (B) 26⅔ miles (C) 60 miles (D) 33⅓ miles

84. The difference between one-tenth of 2000 and one-tenth per cent of 2000 is (A) 0 (B) 18 (C) 180 (D) 198

85. If the radius of a circle is decreased by 5 inches, the resulting decrease in its circumference is (A) 10π inches (B) 5 inches (C) 12 inches (D) 16 inches

86. If one acute angle of a right triangle is 5 times the other, the number of degrees in the smallest angle of the triangle is (A) 18° (B) 30° (C) 75° (D) 15°

87. The single commercial discount which is equivalent to successive discounts of 10% and 10% is (A) 20% (B) 19% (C) 17% (D) 15%

88. The price of an article has been reduced 25%. In order to restore the original price the new price must be increased by (A) 20% (B) 25% (C) 33-1/3% (D) 40%

89. A mortgage on a house in the amount of $4000 provides for quarterly payments of $200 plus interest on the unpaid balance at 4½%. The total second payment to be made is (A) $371.00 (B) $285.50 (C) $242.75 (D) $240.00

90. If four triangles are constructed with sides of the length indicated below, the triangle which will not be a right triangle is (A) 5, 12, 13 (B) 3, 4, 5 (C) 8, 15, 17 (D) 12, 15, 18

91. The number of hours it takes the sun to move from a point 60° N latitude, 30° E longitude, to a point 30° N latitude, 120° W longitude, is (A) 10 (B) 14 (C) 6 (D) 2

92. A piece of cardboard in the shape of a 15-inch square is rolled so as to form a cylindrical surface, without overlapping. The number of inches in the diameter of the cylinder is approximately (A) 45 (B) 23 (C) 5 (D) 2.5

93. A stationer buys blankbooks at $.75 per dozen and sells them at 25 cents apiece. The gross profit based on the cost is (A) 50% (B) 300% (C) 200% (D) 100%

94. A room 27 feet by 32 feet is to be carpeted. The width of the carpet is 27 inches. The length, in yards, of the carpet needed for this floor is (A) 1188 (B) 648 (C) 384 (D) 128

95. A bird flying 400 miles covers the first 100 at the rate of 100 miles an hour, the second 100 at the rate of 200 miles an hour, the third 100 at the rate of 300 miles an hour, and the last 100 at the rate of 400 miles an hour. The average speed was (in miles per hour) (A) 192 (B) 212 (C) 250 (D) 150

Numerical Relations / 167

CONSOLIDATE YOUR KEY ANSWERS HERE

Practice using Answer Sheets. Make ONE mark for each answer. Additional and stray marks may be counted as mistakes. In making corrections erase errors COMPLETELY. Make glossy black marks. To arrive at an accurate estimate of your ability and progress, cover the Correct Answers with a sheet of white paper while you are taking this test.

CORRECT KEY ANSWERS TO THE PRACTICE QUESTIONS

Now compare your answers with these Correct Key Answers. If your answers differ from these, go back and study the Practice Questions to see where and how you made your mistakes. In doing this, the following Explanatory Answers should prove helpful. They provide concise clarifications of the basic points behind the Key Answers. Even where your Key Answers are the same as ours, go over the explanations carefully because they may be quite useful in helping you pick up extra points on the exam.

1.D	13.D	25.D	37.B	49.C	61.D	73.A	85.A
2.A	14.C	26.B	38.D	50.A	62.C	74.C	86.D
3.A	15.C	27.B	39.C	51.B	63.D	75.C	87.B
4.C	16.A	28.D	40.B	52.C	64.A	76.D	88.C
5.B	17.B	29.C	41.C	53.B	65.C	77.B	89.C
6.C	18.B	30.D	42.B	54.C	66.D	78.B	90.D
7.C	19.D	31.C	43.D	55.A	67.B	79.A	91.A
8.A	20.B	32.D	44.C	56.C	68.C	80.C	92.C
9.D	21.B	33.B	45.C	57.B	69.B	81.A	93.B
10.C	22.A	34.C	46.A	58.D	70.A	82.D	94.D
11.B	23.A	35.D	47.C	59.C	71.D	83.B	95.A
12.B	24.B	36.A	48.B	60.A	72.C	84.D	

168 / P.A.C.E. Professional-Administrative Career Exam

EXPLANATORY ANSWERS CLARIFYING CARDINAL POINTS

Here you have the heart of the Question and Answer Method...getting help when and where you need it. Where one of your Key Answers differs from ours you have a problem which can easily be remedied by reading the explanation.

1. SOLUTION:
   1) Series: 3, 5, 11, 29, —
   Triple the difference between the two preceding terms in the series and then add this tripled difference to get the next term in the series.
   EXAMPLE
   Term of series: 1st 2nd 3rd 4th 5th
   Number in series: 3 5 11 29 **83**
   Difference   2 6 18 54

   ANSWER: 83   (D)

2. SOLUTION: The following principles apply for the Roman numeration system.

   (1) Repetition: If two adjacent symbols are alike, each symbol names the same number and the numbers named are to be added.

   (2) Addition: If two numerals are not alike, one must name a smaller number than the other. If the numeral for the smaller number is written to the right of the other numeral, the smaller number is to be added.

   (3) Subtraction: If the numeral for the smaller number of a pair of numerals appears to the left of the other numeral, the smaller number is to be subtracted.

   DCCXLIX = 749   (A)

   $$\begin{array}{r}\text{PROOF}\\\hline D = 500\\ CC = 200\\ XL = 40\\ IX = 9\\\hline 749\end{array}$$

3. SOLUTION:
   $12'' \times 10'' = 120''$
   224 sq. in. − 120 sq. in. = 104 sq. in.
   $2(10 \cdot x) + 2(12 \cdot x) + 4x^2 = 104$
   $20x + 24x + 4x^2 = 104$
   $4x^2 + 44x − 104 = 0$ (divide by 4)
   $x^2 + 11x − 26 = 0$ (quadratic equation factoring) $(x + 13)(x − 2) = 0$ (a)

   ANSWER: x = 2   (A)

   Explanation of factoring in Example 3
   If the product of two factors = 0, then at least one of the factors must be zero.

ILLUSTRATION

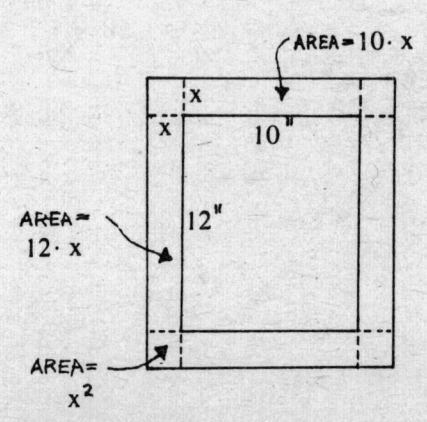

[Figure: rectangle 10" × 12" with border of width x; AREA = 10·x (top), AREA = 12·x (side), AREA = x² (corner)]

EXAMPLE
If $a \cdot b = 0$, then either $a = 0$, or $b = 0$ or both. The two factors above, $x + 13$ and $x − 2$, are like the a and b above.
If $x − 2 = 0$, then $x = 2$ (answer)
If $x + 13 = 0$, then $x = −13$.
The second solution must be discarded (being negative) since it doesn't fit the conditions of the problem.

4. SOLUTION:
   $25 \times .20 = 5.00$ first discount
   $25 − 5 = 20.00$
   $20 \times .30 = 6.00$ second discount
   $20 − 6 = 14.00$ Net Price

   ANSWER: $14   (C)

5. SOLUTION:
   36 inches = 1 yard
   63 inches ÷ 36 = 1¾ yards
   $\$.12 \times 1¾ = \$.12 \times \dfrac{7}{4} = \dfrac{.84}{4} = \$.21$ Cost of ribbon

   ANSWER: $.21   (B)

6. **SOLUTION:**
$1\frac{1}{2}c : 4\frac{1}{2}c :: \frac{3}{4}c : x$

$$\frac{3}{2}x = \frac{9}{2} \cdot \frac{3}{4}$$

$$x = \frac{9}{2} \cdot \frac{3}{4} \cdot \frac{2}{3}$$

$$x = \frac{9}{4} \text{ or } 2\frac{1}{4} \text{ cups water}$$

ANSWER: 2¼ (C)

7. **SOLUTION:**
Sound travels 1100 ft. per sec.
88 ft. per sec. = 60 mi. per hr.

$$\frac{1100 \text{ ft./sec.}}{88 \text{ ft./sec.}} = \frac{x \text{ mi./hr.}}{60 \text{ mi./hr.}}$$

$$x = \frac{\cancel{88}^{15} \cdot \cancel{1100}^{50}}{\cancel{88}_{22}} = 750 \text{ mi./hr.}$$

ANSWER: 750 (C)

8. **SOLUTION:**
$x = $ angle 2
$3x = $ angle 1
$x + 20 = $ angle 3
$x + 3x + x + 20° = 180°$
$5x = 180° - 20°$
$5x = 160°$
$x = 32°$

ANSWER: 32 (A)

9. **SOLUTION:**
On blueprint ¼ in. = 12 in. or 1 ft.

$$3\frac{3}{8} \div \frac{1}{4} = \frac{27}{8} \div \frac{1}{4}$$

$$\frac{27}{\cancel{8}_2} \times \frac{\cancel{4}^1}{1} = \frac{27}{2} = 13\frac{1}{2} \text{ length in feet}$$

ANSWER: 13½ (D)

10. **SOLUTION:**
$\$1.16 \times 3\frac{3}{4} = \$1.16 \times \frac{15}{4} = \$ 4.35$ cost—dacron
$\$3.87 \times 4\frac{2}{3} = \$3.87 \times \frac{14}{3} = \$18.06$ cost—velvet
$\$ 4.35 + \$18.06 = \$22.41$
$\$25.00 - \$22.41 = \$2.59$ change

ANSWER: $2.59 (C)

11. **SOLUTION:**
The volume of water to be added (4 in. = ⅓ ft.)

$$75 \times \cancel{42}^{14} \times \frac{1}{\cancel{3}_1} = 1050 \text{ cu. ft.}$$

Since there are 7.4805 gal. in a cu. ft. then
$1050 \times 7.4805 = 7854.5$ gal.

ANSWER: 7854.5 (B)

12. **SOLUTION:**
$\$1.66 - \$.62 = \$1.04$ charge for additional weight over 5 ozs.
$\$1.04 \div \$.08 = 13$ ounces additional
$13 \text{ oz.} + 5 \text{ oz.} = 18 \text{ oz.}$
$16 \text{ oz.} = 1 \text{ pound}$
$18 \text{ oz.} \div 16 \text{ oz.} = 1\frac{1}{8}$ pounds

ANSWER: 1⅛ pounds (B)

13. **SOLUTION:**
First find number of cans each man needs for one day.
$\frac{15}{7} = $ no. of cans each man needs for 2 days.
$\frac{15}{7} \times \frac{1}{2} = \frac{15}{14}$ no. of cans each man needs for 1 day.
Then, the no. of cans needed by 4 men for 7 days
$\frac{15}{14} \times 7 \times 4 = 30$ cans

ANSWER: 30 (D)

14. **SOLUTION:**
$30 \times \$.13 = \$3.90$ cost for 30 pops
$30 \div 12 = 2\frac{1}{2}$ doz.
$\$1.38 \times 2\frac{1}{2} = \$3.45$ cost by doz.
$\$3.90 - \$3.45 = \$.45$ saving

ANSWER: $.45 (C)

15. **SOLUTION:**
1½ cups sugar   ¾ cup boiling water
Has only 1 cup sugar
Let $x = $ boiling water $\frac{3}{4}c : x :: 1\frac{1}{2}c : 1$

$$\frac{3/4}{1\frac{1}{2}} = \frac{x}{1}$$

$\frac{3}{2}x = \frac{3}{4}$
$x = \frac{3}{4} \cdot \frac{2}{3} = \frac{1}{2}$ cup

ANSWER: ½ cup (C)

16. **SOLUTION:** Let x = number of minutes on each non-math question
    50 math questions   3 hr. = 180 min.
    350 ques. − 50 math. = 300 other ques.
    $$2(50x) + 300x = 180 \text{ min.}$$
    $$100x + 300x = 180 \text{ min.}$$
    $$400x = 180 \text{ min.}$$
    $$x = \frac{180}{400} = \frac{9}{20} \text{ min. on each non-math problem}$$
    Each math. problem takes $2 \cdot (9/20) = 9/10$ min.
    $50 \cdot 9/10$ min. = 45 min.

    ANSWER: 45 min.   (A)

17. **SOLUTION:**
    Let x = longer side
    4½ in. : 7½ in. :: 6¾ in. : x
    $$\frac{4½}{7½} = \frac{6¾}{x}$$
    $$\frac{9}{2}x = \frac{15}{2} \cdot \frac{27}{4}$$
    $$x = \frac{15}{2} \cdot \frac{27}{4} \cdot \frac{2}{9} = \frac{45}{4} = 11¼$$

    ILLUSTRATIONS

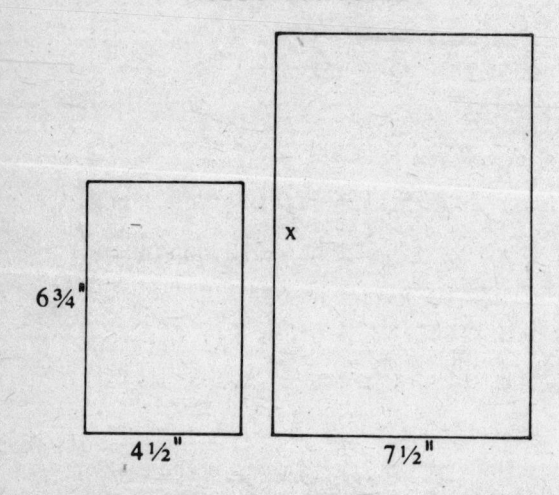

    [Diagram: two rectangles, smaller 4½" × 6¾", larger 7½" × x]

    ANSWER: 11¼   (B)

18. **SOLUTION:**
    $120 − $96 = $24 discount
    $$\frac{\$24}{\$120} = \frac{4}{20} = \frac{1}{5} = 20\% \text{ Rate of discount}$$

    ANSWER: 20%   (B)

19. **SOLUTION:**
    1 hr. = 360°   360° = clock circle
    2 hr. = 2 × 360° = 720° minute hand rotates.

    ANSWER: 720°   (D)

20. **SOLUTION:**
    Series 2, 6, 14, 30, 62,—
    Double the difference found by subtracting first term from second term; add this doubled difference to get the next term in the series.
    Terms of series: 1st 2nd 3rd 4th 5th 6th
    Numbers in series: 2, 6, 14, 30, 62 **126**
    Difference: 4   8   16 32 64

    ANSWER: 126   (B)

21. **SOLUTION:**
    Mental Age = MA = 160 mo.
    Chronological Age = CA = 10 yr. 8 mo.
    10 yr. 8 mo. = 128 mo. CA
    $$\frac{160 \text{ mo.}}{128 \text{ mo.}} = 1.25 \quad 1.25 \times 100 = 125 \text{ I.Q.}$$
    (Mult. by 100 because I.Q. is like a %)

    ANSWER: 125   (B)

22. **SOLUTION:**
    Same time anywhere on the same meridian, therefore it would be noon at 75° N. latitude when it is noon at prime meridian on the equator.

    ANSWER: 12M or noon   (A)

23. **SOLUTION:**
    2'9" long = 2 9/12 = 2¾ ft.
    4 × 2¾ ft. = 4/1 × 11/4 = 44/4 = 11 ft.

    ANSWER: 11 ft.   (A)

24. **SOLUTION:**
    CMXLIX
    See page xx for explanation of Roman numerals.

    1000 − 100 = 900
    50 − 10 = 40
    10 − 1 = 9
    ―――
    949

    ANSWER: 949   (B)

25. **SOLUTION:**
    Subtract −1 from +1
    +1
    −1(+1) change signs
    +2

    Think: what number must be added to −1 to give +1?

    ANSWER: 2   (D)

Numerical Relations / 171

26. SOLUTION:
 A) $\frac{1}{5}$ of 2 = $\frac{2}{5}$ B) 2 and $\frac{1}{5}$ of 1 = $2\frac{1}{5}$
 C) $\frac{2}{5}$ of 1 = $\frac{2}{5}$ D) 2 and $\frac{1}{5}$ of 2 = $2\frac{2}{5}$

 ANSWER: 2 and $\frac{1}{5}$ of 1 (B)

27. SOLUTION:
 $160 List Price   Successive disc.
                of 20% and 10%
 $160 × 20% = $160 × $\frac{1}{5}$ = $32 1st disc.
 $160 − $32 = $128
 $128 × 10% = $128 × $\frac{1}{10}$ = $12.80 2nd disc.
 $128 − $12.80 = $115.20 Cost Price

 ANSWER: $115.20 (B)

28. SOLUTION:
 Find Perimeter
 2 equal sides 2 × 46' = 92'   2 sides
 2 equal sides 2 × 34' = 68'   2 sides
                      ———
                      160' perimeter
 160' ÷ 3 = $53\frac{1}{3}$ yards

ILLUSTRATION

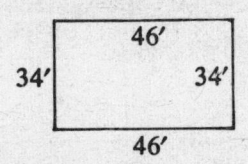

```
       46'
    ┌───────┐
34' │       │ 34'
    └───────┘
       46'
```

 ANSWER: $53\frac{1}{3}$ yards (D)

29. SOLUTION
 Find % of income
 $15,000 = yearly income
 $ 2250 = income taxes (yearly)
 $\frac{2250}{15000}$ = $\frac{3}{20}$ = 15% of income for income taxes

 ANSWER: 15% (C)

30. SOLUTION:
 A = 1 of the 3 equal parts of 2 = $\frac{2}{3}$
 B = 2 of the 3 equal parts of 1 = $\frac{2}{3}$
 C = 2 divided by 3 = $\frac{2}{3}$
 D = a ratio of 3 to 2 = $\frac{3}{2}$ = $1\frac{1}{2}$ Answer
        because it is not $\frac{2}{3}$

 ANSWER: A ratio of 3 to 2 (D)

31. SOLUTION:
 105 lb. average weight
 105 lb. × 110% = 105 lb. × 1.10 = 115.50 or $115\frac{1}{2}$ lbs. (John's weight)

 ANSWER: $115\frac{1}{2}$ lbs. (C)

32. SOLUTION:
 2 in. on house plan represents 5 ft.; room measured $7\frac{1}{2}$ in.
 One inch represents $\frac{5}{2}$ ft.
 $\frac{5}{2}$ × $7\frac{1}{2}$ = $\frac{5}{2}$ × $\frac{15}{2}$ = $\frac{75}{4}$ = $18\frac{3}{4}$ ft. length of room

 ANSWER: $18\frac{3}{4}$ feet (D)

33. SOLUTION:
 Pencils sell for 3 for 10¢
 Pencils bought for 35¢ a doz.
 Profit on $5\frac{1}{2}$ dozen = ?
 3 Pencils = $\frac{3}{12}$ = $\frac{1}{4}$ doz. 1 doz. = 40¢
 40¢ − 35¢ = 5¢ profit per dozen
 $5\frac{1}{2}$ doz. × 5¢ = $27\frac{1}{2}$¢ profit

 ANSWER: $27\frac{1}{2}$ cents (B)

34. SOLUTION:
 20 sq. yds. = 20 × 9 sq. ft. = 180 sq. ft.
 $ .31 cost of 1 sq. ft.
 180 sq. ft. × $.31 = $55.80 cost of 20 sq. yd.

 ANSWER: $55.80 (C)

35. SOLUTION:
 Total number of eighths in $2\frac{3}{4}$
 $2\frac{3}{4}$ = $2\frac{6}{8}$ = $\frac{22}{8}$ = 22 eighths

 ANSWER: 22 (D)

36. SOLUTION
 Find difference
  105084
   93709
  ―――――
   11375 difference

 ANSWER: 11,375 (A)

37. SOLUTION:
 To make 3 cakes
 3 × $2\frac{1}{2}$ cups flour
 3 × $\frac{5}{2}$ = $\frac{15}{2}$c = $7\frac{1}{2}$ cups flour

 ANSWER: $7\frac{1}{2}$ (B)

38. SOLUTION:
 35 ft. 6 in. long = piece of wood
 35' 6" = $35\frac{1}{2}$ ft.
 $35\frac{1}{2}$ ft. ÷ 4 = $\frac{71}{2}$ × $\frac{1}{4}$ = $\frac{71}{8}$ = $8\frac{7}{8}$ ft.
 $\frac{7}{8}$ ft. = $\frac{7}{8}$ × 12 = $\frac{21}{2}$ = $10\frac{1}{2}$ in.

 ANSWER: 8 ft. $10\frac{1}{2}$ in. (D)

39. SOLUTION:
 Notice that if the denominator of a fraction remains the same while the numerator increases, the value of the fraction gets larger and larger, as in the following examples:
 $\frac{2}{3}$, $\frac{3}{3}$, $\frac{5}{3}$, $\frac{10}{3}$, $\frac{25}{3}$, $\frac{100}{3}$

172 / P.A.C.E. Professional-Administrative Career Exam

Also, if the numerator of a fraction remains the same while the denominator increases, the value of the fraction gets smaller and smaller, as in the following:
$\frac{2}{3}, \frac{2}{5}, \frac{2}{9}, \frac{2}{25}, \frac{2}{100}, \frac{2}{3000}$

Then comparing (A) and (D): both have the same denominator, m, but the numerator of (A) is 2n, which is larger than that of (D), which is $2n-2$; therefore (A) is larger than (D).

Comparing (A) and (B): both have the same numerator, 2n, but the denominator of (B) is larger; therefore (A) is larger than (B).

Comparing (A) and (C): the numerator of (C) is larger than that of (A) while the denominator of (C) is smaller than that of (A). Therefore (C) is larger than (A) and is the largest of the four fractions.

ANSWER: $\frac{2n+1}{m-1}$ (C)

40. SOLUTION:
Find annual salary
Bonus = 5% = $450
$450 \div 5\% = \$450 \times \frac{100}{5} = \$9000$ annual salary

ANSWER: $9000 (B)

41. SOLUTION:
Ratio of ¼ to ⅗
$\frac{1}{4} \div \frac{3}{5} = \frac{1}{4} \times \frac{5}{3} = \frac{5}{12}$, ratio of 5 to 12

ANSWER: 5 to 12 (C)

42. SOLUTION:
Find fraction equal to ⅚
A) $= \frac{5+2}{6+2} = \frac{7}{8}$
B) $= \frac{5 \times 2}{6 \times 2} = \frac{5}{6}$ ans.
C) $= \frac{5 \times 5}{6 \times 6} = \frac{25}{36}$
D) $= \frac{5-2}{6-2} = \frac{3}{4}$

ANSWER: $\frac{5 \times 2}{6 \times 2} = \frac{5}{6}$ (B)

43. SOLUTION:
$2\frac{3}{4} = 2\frac{9}{12}$ 36 in. = 1 yd.
$-2\frac{2}{3} = 2\frac{8}{12}$ $\frac{1}{12} \times \frac{36}{1} = 3$ in.
$\frac{1}{12}$ yd. longer

ANSWER: 3 inches (D)

44. SOLUTION:
2800 mi. in 63 days
$2800.00 \div 63 = 44.44$ mi. per day
24 hrs. = 1 day
$44.44 \div 24 = 1.85 \frac{1}{6}$ or 2 mi. per hr.

ANSWER: 2 (C)

45. SOLUTION:
Consider the fraction $\frac{4}{9}$
If we divide numerator by 2, the fraction is $\frac{2}{9}$ which equals
$\frac{1}{2} \times \frac{4}{9} = \frac{2}{9}$
Therefore dividing the numerator of a fraction by 2 always makes the value of the fraction half as great.

ANSWER: makes the value of the fraction half as great (C)

46. SOLUTION:
Sept. 30 until Dec. 15 = 2½ months
Annual rate = 6%
Fraction of year on which to compute interest
$\frac{2\frac{1}{2}}{12} = \frac{\frac{5}{2}}{12} = \frac{5}{24}$

$\$200 \times \frac{6}{100} \times \frac{5}{24} = \frac{10}{4} = \$2\frac{1}{2}$ or $2.50 in interest

$200.00 + $2.50 = $202.50 repays to college

ANSWER: $202.50 (A)

47. SOLUTION:
       Pren
$8000 invested
$\times .06$
$480.00 investment received

       Wright
$6000
$\times .06$
$360.00 investment received

$480 + $360 = $840 interest received

Numerical Relations / 173

$3800 profit for year
−840 received as interest
─────────
$2960 profit to divide evenly

$$\frac{\$2960}{2} = \$1480 \text{ profit for each}$$

$480 + $1480 = $1960 Pren received

ANSWER: $1960   (C)

48. **SOLUTION:**
Assume 2.54 centimeters = 1 in.

$1\frac{1}{2}$ ft. $= \frac{3}{2} \times \frac{12}{1} = 18$ in.

2.54 × 18 in. = 45.72 = 46 centimeters

ANSWER: 46 centimeters   (B)

49. **SOLUTION**

$1\frac{1}{2}\% = \frac{1\frac{1}{2}}{100} = \frac{3}{2} \times \frac{1}{100} = \frac{3}{200} = .015$

ANSWER: .0150   (C)

50. **SOLUTION:**
20% reduction = 80% Selling Price
$118.80 ÷ 80% = Cost
$118.80 ÷ .80 = $148.50 Cost

ANSWER: $148.50   (A)

51. **SOLUTION:**
A = 4.985   5.000−4.985=.015 difference
B = 5.005   5.005−5.000=.005 difference
C = 5.01   5.010−5.000=.010 difference
D = 5.1   5.100−5.000=.100 difference
Smallest difference is for 5.005

ANSWER: 5.005   (B)

52. **SOLUTION:**
Successive discounts of 10% and 10% is equivalent to single discount of 19%
100% − 10% = 90%
90% × 90% = 81%
100% − 81% = 19% single discount

ANSWER: 19%   (C)

53. **SOLUTION:**
768 investigations in 1958
960 investigations in 1959
1200 investigations in 1960
Find rate of increase from 1958 to 1959.

$\frac{960}{768} = \frac{5}{4}$ rate for 1959 compared to 1958.

Also find rate of increase from 1959 to 1960.

$\frac{1200}{960} = \frac{5}{4}$ rate for 1960 compared to 1959.

Therefore, we have a geometric series of constant ratio $\frac{5}{4}$.

$1200 \times \frac{5}{4} = 1500$ investigations in 1961

ANSWER: 1500   (B)

54. **SOLUTION:**
```
    2.61 in.
  × 6.14 in.
  ─────────
    1044
   2610
  156600
  ─────────
  16.0254 sq. in. = number sq. in. for $1 bill
```

ANSWER 16.0 sq. in.   (C)

55. **SOLUTION:**
10½% of 100 equal squares

$10\frac{1}{2}\% = \frac{10.5}{100} = \frac{21}{200}$

$100 \times \frac{21}{200} = \frac{2100}{200} = 10\frac{1}{2}$ squares

ANSWER: fill in ten squares and ½ of an eleventh   (A)

56. **SOLUTION:**
Subtract .098 from 3
```
  3.000
 − .098
 ──────
  2.902 = difference
```

ANSWER: 2.902   (C)

57. **SOLUTION:**
Assume $\frac{1}{8}$ in. represents 12 in. = 1 ft.

$3\frac{3}{4}$ in. $= \frac{15}{4}$ in. long

$\frac{15}{4} \div \frac{1}{8} = \frac{15}{4} \times \frac{8}{1} = 30$ ft. long

ANSWER: 30   (B)

58. SOLUTION:
In circle graph a segment = 108°
circle = 360°

$$\frac{108° \times \$150,000}{360°} = \$45,000 \text{ overhead}$$

ANSWER: $45,000 (D)

59. SOLUTION:

Bar of song with $\frac{4}{4}$ time signature

$A = \frac{2}{4} + \frac{2}{8} + \frac{4}{16} = \frac{8+4+4}{16} = \frac{16}{16}$

$B = \frac{2}{4} + \frac{1}{8} + \frac{6}{16} = \frac{8+2+6}{16} = \frac{16}{16}$

$C = \frac{2}{4} + \frac{2}{8} + \frac{2}{16} = \frac{8+4+2}{16} = \frac{14}{16}$ less than 1

$D = \frac{2}{4} + \frac{3}{8} + \frac{2}{16} = \frac{8+6+2}{16} = \frac{16}{16}$

ANSWER: two quarter notes, two eighth notes, two sixteenth notes (C)

60. SOLUTION:
Won 8 games and lost 3   Games played = 11
Ratio of games won to games played 8:11

ANSWER: 8:11 (A)

61. SOLUTION:
See explanation in problem 39 just past.
In (A) and (C) x is in the numerator, and positive, so those fractions increase as x increases (denominator remains constant).
In (B), x is in denom., subtracted from 15; so as x increases to 10 the denominator gets smaller and the fraction increases (numerator constant).
In (D) the denominator increases with x, while the numerator is constant, so the value of the fraction decreases.

ANSWER: $\frac{6}{2x-1}$ (D)

62. SOLUTION:
Relationship between .01% and .1

.01% = .0001 $\frac{.0001}{.1} = \frac{1}{1000}$

Relationship 1 to 1000

ANSWER: 1 to 1000 (C)

63. SOLUTION:
Arrange these fractions in ascending order $\frac{2}{3}, \frac{5}{7}, \frac{8}{11}, \frac{9}{13}$

L.C.D. = 3 × 7 × 11 × 13 = 3003

$\frac{2}{3} = \frac{2002}{3003}$ (1)

$\frac{5}{7} = \frac{2145}{3003}$ (3)

$\frac{8}{11} = \frac{2184}{3003}$ (4)

$\frac{9}{13} = \frac{2079}{3003}$ (2)

ANSWER: $\frac{2}{3}, \frac{9}{13}, \frac{5}{7}, \frac{8}{11}$ (D)

64. SOLUTION:
2.84 inches outer diameter
−1.94 inches inner diameter
  .90 difference in diameter

$\frac{.90}{2} = .45$ inch thickness

ILLUSTRATION

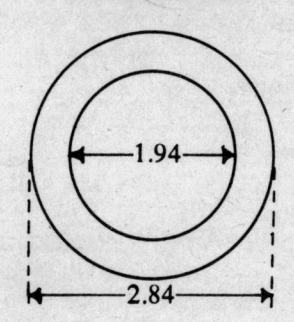

(circle with inner diameter 1.94 and outer diameter 2.84)

ANSWER: .45 of an inch (A)

65. SOLUTION:
6 workers employed:
3 typists @ $45 per wk.
2 clerks @ $40 per wk.
1 messenger @ $32 per wk.

$135—3 typists
$ 80—2 clerks
$ 32—1 messenger
$247—received by all

6) $247.000
$ 41.166 or $41.17 average weekly wage

ANSWER: $41.17 (C)

Numerical Relations / 175

66. SOLUTION:
$$x < 10 \text{ (read "x is less than 10")}$$
$$y < 5$$
$$\overline{x + y < 15}$$
Inequalities like those above, can be added, much like equations, provided both inequality signs are in the same direction (either both are < meaning "less than" or both are >, meaning "more than") The results are unequal in the same direction.

ANSWER: $x + y$ is less than 15   (D)

67. SOLUTION:
4 ft. × 3 ft. × 2 ft.   change to inches
$$\frac{48 \text{ in.} \times 36 \text{ in.} \times 24 \text{ in.}}{8 \text{ in.} \times 4 \text{ in.} \times 2 \text{ in.}} = 648 \text{ bricks}$$

ANSWER: 648   (B)

68. SOLUTION:
Selling Price = loss of 50% of cost
100% = cost
$$\frac{50\% \text{ (loss)}}{50\% \text{ (Sell. P.)}} = \frac{.50}{.50} = 100\% \text{ is the loss}$$

ANSWER: 100%   (C)

69. SOLUTION:
60 mi. ÷ 40 mi. = 1½ hr.
60 mi. ÷ 30 mi. = 2 hr.   120 mi. in 3½ hr.
1½ hr. + 2 hr. = 3½ hr.
$$120 \text{ mi.} \div 3\frac{1}{2} = 120 \times \frac{2}{7} = \frac{240}{7} =$$
34²⁄₇ mi. per hr.

ANSWER: 34²⁄₇ mi.   (B)

70. SOLUTION:
The formula for changing Centigrade to Fahrenheit is given as:
$$\frac{9}{5}(C) + 32 = F$$
$$\frac{9}{5}(50) + 32 = 122 \text{ F}$$

ANSWER: 122   (A)

71. SOLUTION:
Reg. area = 100% = 1.00
Base of rectangle increased 30% = 1.30
Width decreased by 20% = .80 times original length
1.30 × .80 = 1.04 new area compared to original
1.04 − 1.00 = .04 increase, or 4%

ANSWER: 4%   (D)

72. SOLUTION:
⁷⁄₁₂, ⁶⁄₁₁, ³⁄₅, ⁵⁄₈   L.C.D. = 1320
$$\frac{7}{12} = \frac{770}{1320} \qquad \frac{3}{5} = \frac{792}{1320}$$
$$\frac{6}{11} = \frac{720}{1320} \qquad \frac{5}{8} = \frac{825}{1320}$$

ANSWER: ⁶⁄₁₁, ⁷⁄₁₂, ³⁄₅, ⁵⁄₈   (C)

73. SOLUTION:
Find sales tax
Price of auto including 3% sales tax = $2729.50
$2729.50 ÷ 1.03 = cost price = $2650 cost (cost price = cost without tax)
$2729.50 S.P. − $2650.00 cost = $79.50 sales
$2729.50 S.P. − 2650.00 cost = $79.50 sales tax

ANSWER: $79.50   (A)

74. SOLUTION:
12 edges in a cube
48 inches ÷ 12 = 4″ edge
Volume of a cube = 4^3 in. = 64 cu. in.

ILLUSTRATION

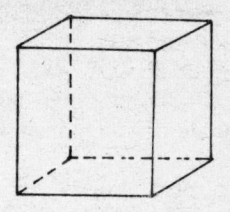

ANSWER: 64 cubic inches   (C)

75. SOLUTION:
Dimensions of large rectangle are:
   22 yd. × 18 yd.
Area of large rectangle is:
   22 yd. × 18 yd. = 396 sq. yd.
Area of small rectangle is:
   16 yd. × 12 yd. = 192 sq. yd.
Area of path is difference or
   396 sq. yd. − 192 sq. yd. = 204 sq. yd.

ILLUSTRATION

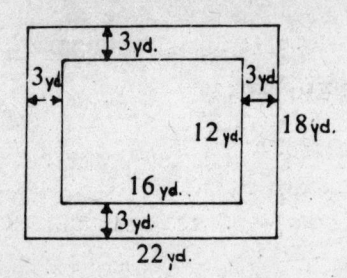

```
        3 yd.
   ┌──────────┐
3yd│          │3yd
   │   12 yd. │    18 yd.
   │  16 yd.  │
   └──────────┘
        3 yd.
       22 yd.
```

ANSWER: 204 sq. yd.   (C)

76. **SOLUTION:**
    πr^2 = are of a circle; $20\% = \frac{1}{5}$ diminished
    $\pi(r - \frac{1}{5} r)^2 =$
    $\pi(\frac{4}{5} r)^2 = \pi \frac{16}{25} r^2$
    $\pi r^2 = \frac{25}{25} \pi r^2 - \frac{16}{25} \pi r^2 = \frac{9}{25} \pi r^2$ Area diminished
    $\frac{9}{25} \pi r^2 \div \pi r^2 = \frac{9}{25} = 36\%$

    ANSWER: 36%   (D)

77. **SOLUTION:**
    distance estimated = 150 ft.
    real distance   = 140 ft.
    150 ft. — 140 ft. = 10 ft.
    10 ft. ÷ 140 ft. = $.07 \frac{20}{140} = .07\frac{1}{7}$
    % of error $7\frac{1}{7}$

    ANSWER: $7\frac{1}{7}\%$ (B)

78. **SOLUTION:**
    An airplane flies 550 yd. in 3 sec.
    1 mile = 1760 yd.
    Fraction of mile traveled in 3 sec. is:
    $\frac{550}{1760} = \frac{5}{16}$ mi.
    In an hour there are 60×60 or 3600 sec.
    $3600 \div 3$ sec. = 1200
    $1200 \times \frac{5}{16} = 375$ mi. per hr.

    ANSWER: 375   (B)

79. **SOLUTION:**
    We assume we have a proper fraction with numerator smaller than denominator. If both are increased by the same amount the percentage increase is larger in the numerator and the value of the resulting fraction is larger. Consider these examples:

$\frac{2}{5} = .4$

Adding one to both numerator and denominator:

$\frac{2+1}{5+1} = \frac{3}{6} = .5$

Adding two more to numerator and denominator:

$\frac{3+2}{6+2} = \frac{5}{8} = .625$

Adding five more to numerator and denominator:

$\frac{5+5}{8+5} = \frac{10}{13} = .769$

ANSWER: always greater than the original fraction.   (A)

80. **SOLUTION:**
    Loss of ¼ or 25% of cost
    Gain of ¼ or 25% of cost
    ¾ = $120 Selling Price
    $120 = Selling Price
    ¼ = Cost
    ¼ + ¼ = 5/4   5/4 = $120
    ¼ = $40 loss   ¼ = $24 gain
    $40 — $24 = $16 loss on both transactions

    ANSWER: $16   (C)

81. **SOLUTION:**
    Series 2, 6, 12, 20, __, 42, 56, 72.
    Subtract the first term from the second term to find the difference; each succesive difference between terms thereafter will be increased by 2.

    Terms of series: 1st 2nd 3rd 4th 5th
    Number in series: 2   6   12   20   30
    Difference: 4   6   8   10

    T   6th 7th 8th
    N   42   56   72
    D   12   14   16

    ANSWER: 30   (A)

82. **SOLUTION**
    If two angles of a triangle are acute angles, the third may be an obtuse angle.

ILLUSTRATION

ANSWER: may be an obtuse angle   (D)

Numerical Relations / 177

83. SOLUTION:
80 miles at 20 miles per hour = 4 hrs. traveled
Return 80 miles at 40 mi. per hour = 2 hrs. traveled
4 hr. + 2 hr. = 6 hr. total time for traveling
80 mi. + 80 mi. = 160 mi. going and coming
160 mi. ÷ 6 hrs. = 26 4/6 mi. = 26 2/3 mi. average speed

ANSWER: 26 2/3 miles   (B)

84. SOLUTION:
1/10 of 2000 = 200
1/10% of 2000 = 1/10 × 1/100 × 2000 = 2
200 − 2 = 198

ANSWER: 198   (D)

85. SOLUTION:
d = 2r
radius decreased by 5, or circumference by 10
πd = circumference before decreased
π(d − 10) = πd − 10π, circumference after decrease
difference is πd − (πd − 10π) =
πd − πd + 10π = 10π inches

ANSWER: 10π inches   (A)

86. SOLUTION:
x + 5x = 90°
6x = 90°
x = 15° smallest
5x = 75° larger acute angle

ILLUSTRATION

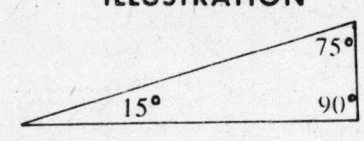

75°
15°   90°

ANSWER: 15°   (D)

87. SOLUTION:
100% − 10% = 90% = .90
.90 × .90 = .81 = 81%
100% − 81% = 19%

ANSWER: 19%   (B)

88. SOLUTION:
25% reduction = 1/4
Selling Price = 3/4 of original price
Must add 1/4 of original price. Based on reduced price this percentage is:
1/4 ÷ 3/4 = 1/4 × 4/3 = 1/3 = 33 1/3%

ANSWER: 33 1/3%   (C)

89. SOLUTION:
$4000 mortgage
$200 + int. 4 1/2 % of unpaid bal.
$4000 − $200 = $3800 prin. after 1st payment
Since payments are made quarterly, interest is computed for 1/4 of a year.

$$4\tfrac{1}{2}\% = \frac{9\%}{2} = \frac{9}{200}$$

$$\$3800 \times \frac{1}{4}\left(\frac{9}{200}\right) =$$

$$\$\cancel{3800}^{19} \times \frac{9}{\cancel{800}_{4}} = \frac{\$171}{4} = \$42.75 \text{ int.}$$

$200 + $42.75 = $242.75 second payment.

ANSWER: $242.75   (C)

90. SOLUTION:
Check each triangle to see for which ones the Pythagorean Theorem holds: that the sum of the squares of the legs equals the square of the hypotenuse. (The hypotenuse would always be the longest side.)

$A^2 = 13^2 = 169$ $5^2 + 12^2 =$
                         $25 + 144 = 169$
$B^2 = 5^2 = 25$ $3^2 + 4^2 =$
                         $9 + 16 = 25$
$C^2 = 17^2 = 289$ $8^2 + 15^2 =$
                         $64 + 225 = 289$
$D^2 = 18^2 = 324$ $12^2 + 15^2 =$
                         $144 + 225 = 369$

Therefore 12, 15, 18 is not a right triangle

ANSWER: 12, 15, 18   (D)

91. SOLUTION:
Need to work only with longitude because there are 360° around the globe, and it takes one day or 24 hours to make a complete revolution.
360° ÷ 24 = 15° of longitude = 1 hr. of time
E   W
30° + 120° = 150°
150° ÷ 15° = 10 hours

ANSWER: 10   (A)

92. **SOLUTION:**
Circumference = 15"   find d
$$c = \pi d$$
$$\frac{15''}{\frac{22}{7}} = d$$
$$15 \div \frac{22}{7} = 15 \times \frac{7}{22} = \frac{105}{22} = 4\frac{17}{22}$$
or approx. 5"

ANSWER: 5   (C)

93. **SOLUTION:**
Cost = $.75 doz.
Selling Price = 12 × $.25 = $3.00
$3.00 − $.75 = $2.25 profit 1 dozen
$$\frac{\$2.25}{\$.75} = 3 \text{ or } 300\%$$

ANSWER: 300%   (B)

94. **SOLUTION:**
Area of room = 27' × 32' = 864 sq. ft.
Width of carpet = 27" = 2¼ ft.
$$864 \div 9/4 =$$
$$\cancel{864}^{96} \times \frac{4}{\cancel{9}_1} = 384 \text{ ft. carpeting}$$

3 ft. = 1 yard
384 ÷ 3 = 128 yd.

ANSWER: 128   (D)

95. **SOLUTION:**
400 miles bird flew in all

first 100 mi. at 100 m.p.h. = 1 hr. = $\frac{12}{12}$

second 100 mi. at 200 m.p.h. = ½ hr. = $\frac{6}{12}$

third 100 mi. at 300 m.p.h. = ⅓ hr. = $\frac{4}{12}$

fourth 100 mi. at 400 m.p.h. = ¼ hr. = $\frac{3}{12}$

$$\frac{12}{12} + \frac{6}{12} + \frac{4}{12} + \frac{3}{12} = \frac{25}{12} = 2\frac{1}{12} \text{ hr.}$$

400 miles ÷ $\frac{25}{12}$ =

$$\cancel{400}^{16} \text{ mi.} \times \frac{12}{\cancel{25}_1} = 192 \text{ mi. per hr.}$$

ANSWER: 192   (A)

Professional & Administrative Career Exam

PART FOUR

Final Exam and Advice

4

Professional & Administrative Career Exam

FINAL SAMPLE EXAM FOR PRACTICE

This professionally-constructed Sample Examination is patterned on the actual exam, although it is not a copy of the forthcoming exam, nor of previous exams. The actual exams are closely guarded and may not be duplicated. The exam you'll take may have more difficult questions in some areas than you'll encounter on this Sample Examination. On the other hand, some questions may be easier, but don't bank on it. We mean to give you confidence...not over-confidence.

The time allowed for the entire examination is 3½ hours.

ANALYSIS AND FORECAST: SAMPLE EXAM FOR PRACTICE	
Since the number of questions for each test may vary on different forms of the actual examination, the time allotments below are flexible.	
SUBJECT TESTED	*Time Allowed*

UNDERSTANDING AND USING WRITTEN LANGUAGE
  Read and Deduce
  Synonyms
	35 Min. as follows:
	20 Minutes
	15 Minutes

DERIVING GENERAL PRINCIPLES FROM PARTICULAR DATA
  Letter Series
  Abstract Reasoning
	35 Min. as follows:
	20 Minutes
	15 Minutes

DERIVING CONCLUSIONS FROM GIVEN DATA
  Read and Infer
  Logical Sequence
	35 Min. as follows:
	20 Minutes
	15 Minutes

QUANTITATIVE ABILITY	35 Minutes
CHART AND TABLE INTERPRETATION	35 Minutes
DERIVING CONCLUSIONS FROM INCOMPLETE DATA PLUS GENERAL KNOWLEDGE	35 Minutes

Correct key answers to all these test questions will be found at the end of the test.

DIRECTIONS FOR ANSWERING QUESTIONS

For each question read all the lettered choices carefully. Then select that answer which you consider correct or most nearly correct and complete. Blacken the lettered space on your answer sheet corresponding to your best selection, just as you would have to do on the actual examination.

FOR THE SAMPLE QUESTION that follows, select the appropriate letter preceding the word which is most nearly the same in meaning as the capitalized word:

1. DISSENT: (A) approve   (B) depart
                          (C) disagree   (D) enjoy

DISSENT is most nearly the same as (C), disagree, so that the acceptable answer is shown thus on your answer sheet:

     A   B   C   D
     ∥   ∥   ▮   ∥

A NOTE ABOUT TEST TIMES.

The time allotted for each Test in each Examination in this book is based on a careful analysis of all the information now available. The time we allot for each test, therefore, merely suggests in a general way approximately how much time you should expend on each subject when you take the actual Exam. We have not, in every case, provided precisely the number of questions you will actually get on the examination. It's just not possible to know what the examiners will finally decide to do for every Test in the Examination. It might be a good idea to jot down your "running" time for each Test, and make comparisons later on. If you find that you're working faster, you may assume you're making progress. Remember, we have timed each Test uniformly. If you follow all our directions, your scores will all be comparable.

ANSWER SHEET FOR SAMPLE EXAMINATION II.

Consolidate your key answers here just as you would do on the actual exam. Using this type of Answer Sheet will provide valuable practice. Tear it out along the indicated lines and mark it up correctly. Use a No. 2 (medium) pencil. Make only ONE mark for each answer. Additional and stray marks may be counted as mistakes. In making corrections erase errors COMPLETELY. Make glossy black marks.

TEST I. READ AND DEDUCE

TEST II. SYNONYMS

TEST III. LETTER SERIES

TEST IV. ABSTRACT REASONING

TEST V. READ AND INFER

TEST VI. LOGICAL SEQUENCE

184 / *P.A.C.E. Professional-Administrative Career Exam*

TEST VII. MATHEMATICS

TEST VIII. ARITHMETIC COMPUTATIONS

TEST IX. DATA INTERPRETATION

TEST X. APPLYING GENERAL KNOWLEDGE

Understanding and Using Written Language

TEST I. READ AND DEDUCE

TIME: 20 Minutes. 15 Questions.

DIRECTIONS: Below each of the following passages, you will find questions or incomplete statements about the passage. Each statement or question is followed by lettered words or expressions. Select the word or expression that most satisfactorily completes each statement or answers each question in accordance with the meaning of the passage. Write the letter of that word or expression on your answer paper.

1. "A city directory, where available, interleaved with suitable blank leaves and subdivided into a number of volumes equal to the maximum number of employees assigned to directory work at one time, shall be used to give directory service. Where a city directory is not published, a telephone directory, if available, may be used. Dual use of a city directory and a telephone directory shall be confined to firm, insured, c.o.d., special handling, and special delivery mail."

   The paragraph best supports the statement that the use of a city directory
   A) at times may be supplemented by the use of a telephone directory
   B) is of little value unless postal directory service is kept current
   C) is less productive than is the use of a telephone directory
   D) is to be confined to insured, c.o.d., and special delivery mail
   E) provides more accurate information than does the use of a telephone directory

2. "Taxes are deducted each pay period from the amount of salaries or wages, including payments for overtime and night differential, paid to employees of the postal service in excess of the withholding exemptions allowed under the Internal Revenue Act. The amount of tax to be withheld from each payment of wages to any employee, except fourth-class postmasters, will be determined from the current official table of pay and withholding exemptions published by the Post Office Department."

   The paragraph best supports the statement that the salaries of most postal employees
   A) are paid in amounts depending upon the exemptions fixed by the Department
   B) do not include overtime or night differential payments
   C) are determined by provisions of the Internal Revenue Act
   D) include taxable overtime or night differential payments that are due each pay period
   E) are subject to tax deductions if the salaries are greater than exemptions

3. "Telegrams should be clear, concise, and brief. Omit all unnecessary words. The parts of speech most often used in telegrams are nouns, verbs, adjectives, and adverbs. If possible, do without pronouns, prepositions, articles, and copulative verbs. Use simple sentences, rather than complex and compound."

   The paragraph best supports the statement that in writing telegrams one should always use
   A) common and simple words
   B) only nouns, verbs, adjectives, and adverbs
   C) incomplete sentences
   D) only words essential to the meaning
   E) the present tense of verbs

4. "The Suggestion System is conducted to give thorough and understanding study to ideas presented by postal employees for promoting the welfare of postal personnel and for improving mail handling and other postal business; and to encourage and reward postal employees who think out, develop, and present acceptable ideas and plans. Through this system the talent and ability of postal employees are to be used for improving postal service and reducing expenses."

   The paragraph best supports the statement that one purpose of the Suggestion System is to
   A) maintain a unit of experienced employees to plan and develop improvements

B) obtain ideas that will help postal employees improve their work
C) offer promotions to postal employees who suggest useful changes in service
D) provide pay raises for employees who increase their output
E) reduce postal operating expenses by limiting postal service

5. "Metered mail must bear the correct date of mailing in the meter impression. When metered mail bearing the wrong date or time is presented for mailing, it shall be run through the canceling machine or otherwise postmarked to show the proper date and time, and then dispatched. The irregularity shall be called to the attention of the mailer. If the irregularity is repeated, the mail may be refused."

The paragraph best supports the statement that, if a first mailing of metered mail bears a wrong date or time,
A) no action shall be taken by the postal service
B) the mailing privileges of the sender may be canceled
C) the mailer will not be permitted to submit additional improperly prepared mail
D) the mailer will be notified of the error before the mail is dispatched
E) the postal service accepts the responsibility for correction

6. "Through advertising, manufacturers exercise a high degree of control over consumers' desires. However, the manufacturer assumes enormous risks in attempting to predict what consumers will want and in producing goods in quantity and distributing them in advance of final selection by the consumers."

The paragraph best supports the statement that manufacturers
A) can eliminate the risk of overproduction by advertising
B) completely control buyers' needs and desires
C) must depend upon the final consumers for the success of their undertakings
D) distribute goods directly to the consumers
E) can predict with great accuracy the success of any product they put on the market

7. "In the business districts of cities, collections from street letter boxes are made at stated hours, and collectors are required to observe these hours exactly. Any businessman using these boxes can rely with certainty upon the time of the next collection."

The paragraph best supports the statement that
A) mail collections are both efficient and inexpensive
B) mail collections in business districts are more frequent during the day than at night
C) mail collectors are required to observe safety regulations exactly
D) mail collections are made often in business districts
E) mail is collected in business districts on a regular schedule

8. "The function of business is to increase the wealth of the country and the value and happiness of life. It does this by supplying the material needs of men and women. When the nation's business is successfully carried on, it renders public service of the highest value."

The paragraph best supports the statement that
A) all businesses which render public service are successful
B) human happiness is enhanced only by the increase of material wants
C) the value of life is increased only by the increase of wealth
D) the material needs of men and women are supplied by well-conducted business
E) business is the only field of activity which increases happiness

9. "In almost every community, fortunately, there are certain men and women known to be public-spirited. Others, however, may be selfish and act only as their private interests seem to require."

The paragraph best supports the statement that those citizens who disregard others are
A) fortunate
B) needed
C) found only in small communities
D) not known
E) not public-spirited

10. "Whenever two groups of people whose interests at the moment conflict meet to discuss a solution of that conflict, there is laid a basis for an interchange of facts and ideas which increases the total range of knowledge of both parties and tends to break down the barrier which their restricted field of information has helped to create."

The paragraph best supports the statement that conflicts between two parties may be brought closer to a settlement through
A) frank acknowledgement of error
B) the exchange of accusations
C) gaining a wider knowledge of facts
D) submitting the dispute to an impartial judge
E) limiting discussion to plans acceptable to both groups

11. "Formerly it was only unskilled labor which was shifted from place to place in the wake of industrial booms. Since so many business concerns have become nationwide in the fields they cover, the white-collar workers have been in a similar state of flux."

The paragraph best supports the statement that the growth of big business has resulted in
A) a shifting supply of unskilled labor
B) an increased tendency toward movement of workers
C) an increased proportion of white-collar jobs
D) the stabilization of industrial booms
E) the use of fewer workers to do equal work

12. "In accordance with the ancient principle that a sovereign state may not be sued without its consent, a special Court of Claims has been established in each of several States of the United States. In this court, claims may be brought against the State. However, the State legislature must make the necessary appropriation before the claim awarded by the court can be paid."

The paragraph best supports the statement that a
A) sovereign state cannot be sued by its citizens
B) claim against a State can only be brought with the approval of the State legislature
C) sovereign state can only be sued by a Court of Claims
D) Court of Claims does not have the authority to enforce payment of approved claims
E) resident or business firm of any State has the right to bring suit against that State

13. "What constitutes skill in any line of work is not always easy to determine; economy of time must be carefully distinguished from economy of energy, as the quickest method may require the greatest expenditure of muscular effort, and may not be essential or at all desirable."

The paragraph best supports the statement that
A) the most efficiently executed task is not always the one done in the shortest time
B) energy and time cannot both be conserved in performing a single task
C) if a task requires muscular energy it is not being performed economically
D) skill in performing a task should not be acquired at the expense of time
E) a task is well done when it is performed in the shortest time

14. "All undeliverable first-class mail, except first-class parcels and parcel post paid with first-class postage, which cannot be returned to the sender, is sent to a dead-letter branch. Undeliverable matter of the third- and fourth-classes of obvious value for which the sender does not furnish return postage and undeliverable first-class parcels and parcel-post matter bearing postage of the first-class, which cannot be returned, is sent to a dead parcel-post branch."

The paragraph best supports the statement that matter that is sent to a dead parcel-post branch includes all undeliverable
A) mail, except first-class letter mail, that appears to be valuable
B) mail, except that of the first-class, on which the sender failed to prepay the original mailing costs
C) parcels on which the mailer prepaid the first-class rate of postage
D) third- and fourth-class matter on which the required return postage has not been paid
E) parcels on which first-class postage has been prepaid, when the sender's address is not known

15. "Civilization started to move rapidly when man freed himself of the shackles that restricted his search for truth."
The paragraph best supports the statement that the progress of civilization
A) came as a result of man's dislike for obstacles
B) did not begin until restrictions on learning were removed
C) has been aided by man's efforts to find the truth
D) is based on continually increasing efforts
E) continues at a constantly increasing rate

END OF TEST

Go on to do the following Test in this Examination, just as you would be expected to do on the actual exam.

TEST II. SYNONYMS

TIME: 15 Minutes. 30 Questions.

DIRECTIONS: Each of the numbered words given below is followed by four lettered words. For each numbered word, select the lettered word which most nearly defines it.

Correct answers for these questions appear at the end of this examination, together with the answers to all other tests.

1. ANATHEMA
   - (A) curse
   - (B) blessing
   - (C) hymn
   - (D) benison.

2. VULNERABLE
   - (A) sacred
   - (B) dangling
   - (C) vaulting
   - (D) weak.

3. ACCENTUATE
   - (A) emphasize
   - (B) abbreviate
   - (C) acclaim
   - (D) assess.

4. ZEALOUS
   - (A) lazy
   - (B) enthusiastic
   - (C) envious
   - (D) careless.

5. VESTIGE
   - (A) design
   - (B) strap
   - (C) trace
   - (D) bar.

6. YEARN
   - (A) crave
   - (B) gape
   - (C) feel sleepy
   - (D) feel bored.

7. VETERINARY
   - (A) retired soldier
   - (B) civil servant
   - (C) hospital
   - (D) animal doctor.

8. STUPEFY
   - (A) subjugate
   - (B) stun
   - (C) resect
   - (D) imprecate.

9. WAXY
   - (A) large
   - (B) serious
   - (C) cereus
   - (D) seric.

10. TRYST
    - (A) meeting
    - (B) trick
    - (C) drama
    - (D) trifle.

11. FUNDAMENTAL
    - (A) adequate
    - (B) essential
    - (C) official
    - (D) truthful.

12. SUPPLANT
    - (A) approve
    - (B) displace
    - (C) satisfy
    - (D) vary.

13. OBLITERATE
    - (A) erase
    - (B) demonstrate
    - (C) review
    - (D) detect.

14. ANTICIPATE
    - (A) foresee
    - (B) approve
    - (C) annul
    - (D) conceal.

15. EXORBITANT
    - (A) priceless
    - (B) extensive
    - (C) worthless
    - (D) excessive.

16. RELUCTANT
    - (A) anxious
    - (B) constant
    - (C) drastic
    - (D) hesitant.

17. PREVALENT
    - (A) current
    - (B) permanent
    - (C) durable
    - (D) temporary.

18. AUGMENT
    - (A) conclude
    - (B) suggest
    - (C) increase
    - (D) unite.

19. FRUGAL
    - (A) friendly
    - (B) thoughtful
    - (C) hostile
    - (D) economical.

20. AUSTERITY
    - (A) priority
    - (B) severity
    - (C) anxiety
    - (D) solitude.

21. PLAINT
    - (A) retribution
    - (B) easily bent
    - (C) lament
    - (D) fish.

22. IMPETUS
    - (A) excitable
    - (B) impulse
    - (C) vigor
    - (D) prevention.

23. DISSENT
    - (A) approve
    - (B) depart
    - (C) disagree
    - (D) protest.

24. FACILITY
    - (A) happiness
    - (B) willingness
    - (C) ease
    - (D) desirability.

25. LAUDABLE
    - (A) opium
    - (B) distasteful
    - (C) praiseworthy
    - (D) salable.

26. RECUMBENT
    - (A) cumbersome
    - (B) recurrent
    - (C) reclining
    - (D) occupant.

27. RAZE
    - (A) clear
    - (B) scrape
    - (C) demolish
    - (D) erect.

28. HALLOW
    - (A) consecrate
    - (B) scoop out
    - (C) buy
    - (D) call.

29. PLAUSIBLE
    - (A) stop
    - (B) true
    - (C) spacious
    - (D) specious.

30. PARTISAN
    - (A) soldier
    - (B) adherent
    - (C) mechanic
    - (D) division.

END OF TEST

Go on to do the following Test in this Examination, just as you would be expected to do on the actual exam.

Deriving General Principles from Particular Data

TEST III. SERIES

TIME: 20 Minutes. 20 Questions.

DIRECTIONS: *Each question consists of a series of letters or numbers (or both) which follow some definite order. Study each series to determine what the order is. Then look at the answer choices. Select the one answer that will complete the set in accordance with the pattern established.*

Suggestions: *In solving alphabetic series, it is helpful to write out the alphabet and keep it in front of you as you work. This makes it easier to spot the key to a letter series.*

Correct answers for these questions appear at the end of this examination, together with the answers to all other tests.

```
A  B  C  D  E  F  G  H  I  J  K  L  M  N  O  P  Q  R  S  T  U  V  W  X  Y  Z
1  2  3  4  5  6  7  8  9 10 11 12 13 14 15 16 17 18 19 20 21 22 23 24 25 26
```

1. A B D G K
   - (A) X
   - (B) P
   - (C) Q
   - (D) Y

2. 2 1 6 2 18 3
   - (A) 20
   - (B) 54
   - (C) 50
   - (D) 60

3. 8 13 23 38 58
   - (A) 100
   - (B) 90
   - (C) 83
   - (D) 72

4. A D G J
   - (A) M
   - (B) N
   - (C) O
   - (D) P

5. 2 5 4 3 6 1 5
   - (A) 8
   - (B) 7
   - (C) 3
   - (D) 2

6. A 3 C 5 E
   - (A) G
   - (B) 7
   - (C) H
   - (D) 5

7. 2 3 3 4 3 3 6 3
   - (A) 5
   - (B) 4
   - (C) 3
   - (D) 2

8. B C Z B C Z
   - (A) D
   - (B) B
   - (C) X
   - (D) Y

9. 32 16 8 4
   - (A) 10
   - (B) 30
   - (C) 6
   - (D) 2

10. 1 2 2 4 3 8
    - (A) 5
    - (B) 10
    - (C) 6
    - (D) 4

190

11. A 5 I 13 Q 21 Y
    (A) 7   (B) 29
    (C) 31   (D) 15

12. 49 F 25 D 9 B
    (A) 1   (B) 3
    (C) 5   (D) G

13. 3 3 7 0 11 −3
    (A) −15   (B) 4
    (C) 15   (D) −7

14. 2 12 21 29 36
    (A) 42   (B) 52
    (C) 62   (D) 72

15. 4 8 25 50 36 72 40
    (A) 54   (B) 64
    (C) 76   (D) 80

16. 1 3 6 10
    (A) 6   (B) 12
    (C) 15   (D) 9

17. 1 2 2 4 3 6
    (A) 2   (B) 4
    (C) 6   (D) 8

18. 10 11 9 12 8 13
    (A) 5   (B) 7
    (C) 9   (D) 11

19. 26 A 24 C 22 E
    (A) 14   (B) 16
    (C) 18   (D) 20

20. 1 A 2 E 3 I 4 O 5
    (A) 6   (B) 7
    (C) U   (D) V

END OF TEST

Go on to do the following Test in this Examination, just as you would be expected to do on the actual exam.

192 / *P.A.C.E. Professional-Administrative Career Exam*

TEST IV. ABSTRACT REASONING

TIME: 15 Minutes. 16 Questions.

DIRECTIONS: In each of these questions, look at the symbols in the first two boxes. Something about the three symbols in the first box makes them alike; something about the two symbols in the other box with the question mark makes them alike. Look for some characteristic that is common to all symbols in the same box, yet makes them different from the symbols in the other box. Among the five answer choices, find the symbol that can best be substituted for the question mark, because it is like the symbols in the second box, and, for the same reason, different from those in the first box.

Correct answers for these questions appear at the end of this examination, together with the answers to all other tests.

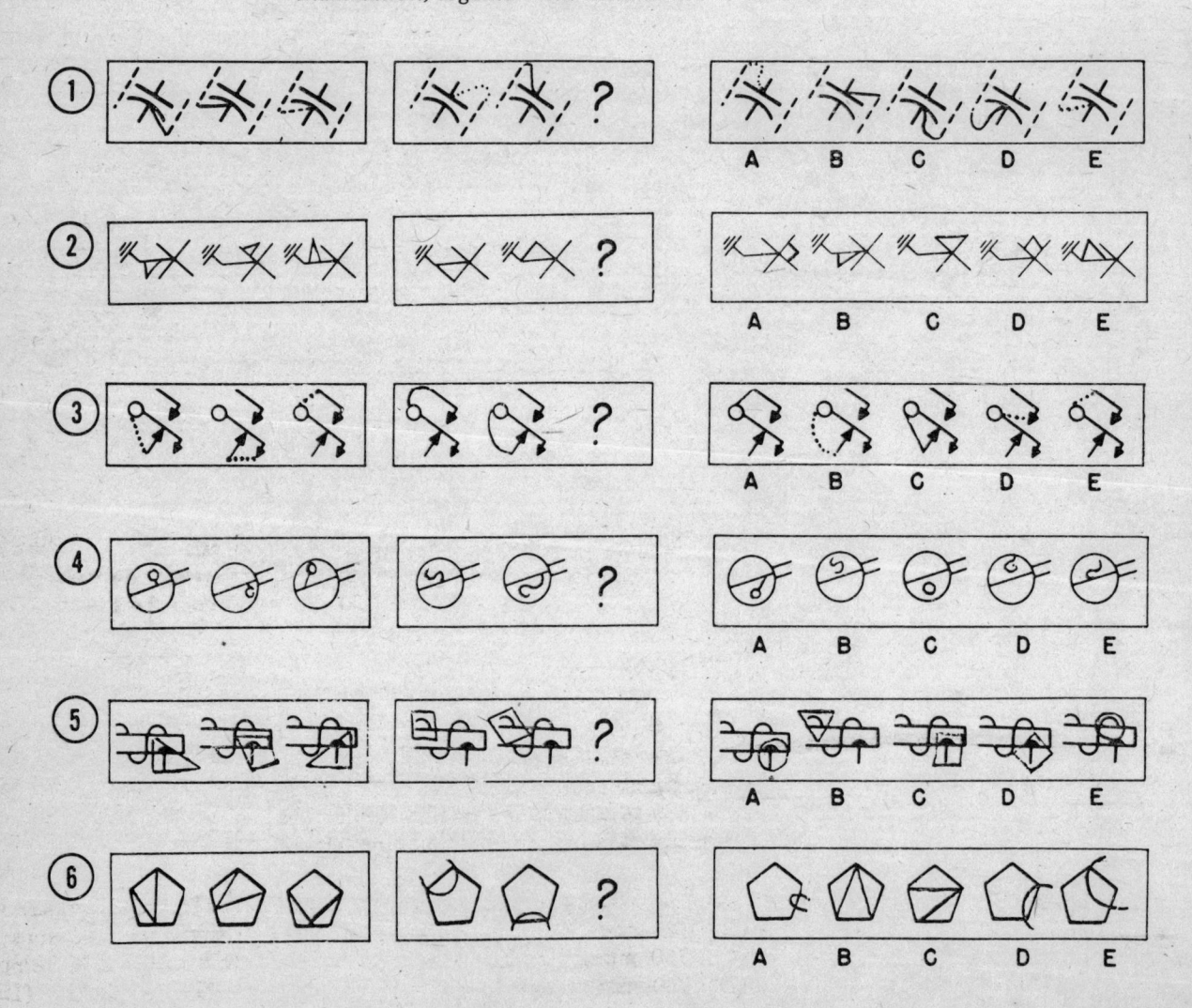

Second Sample Exam For Practice / 193

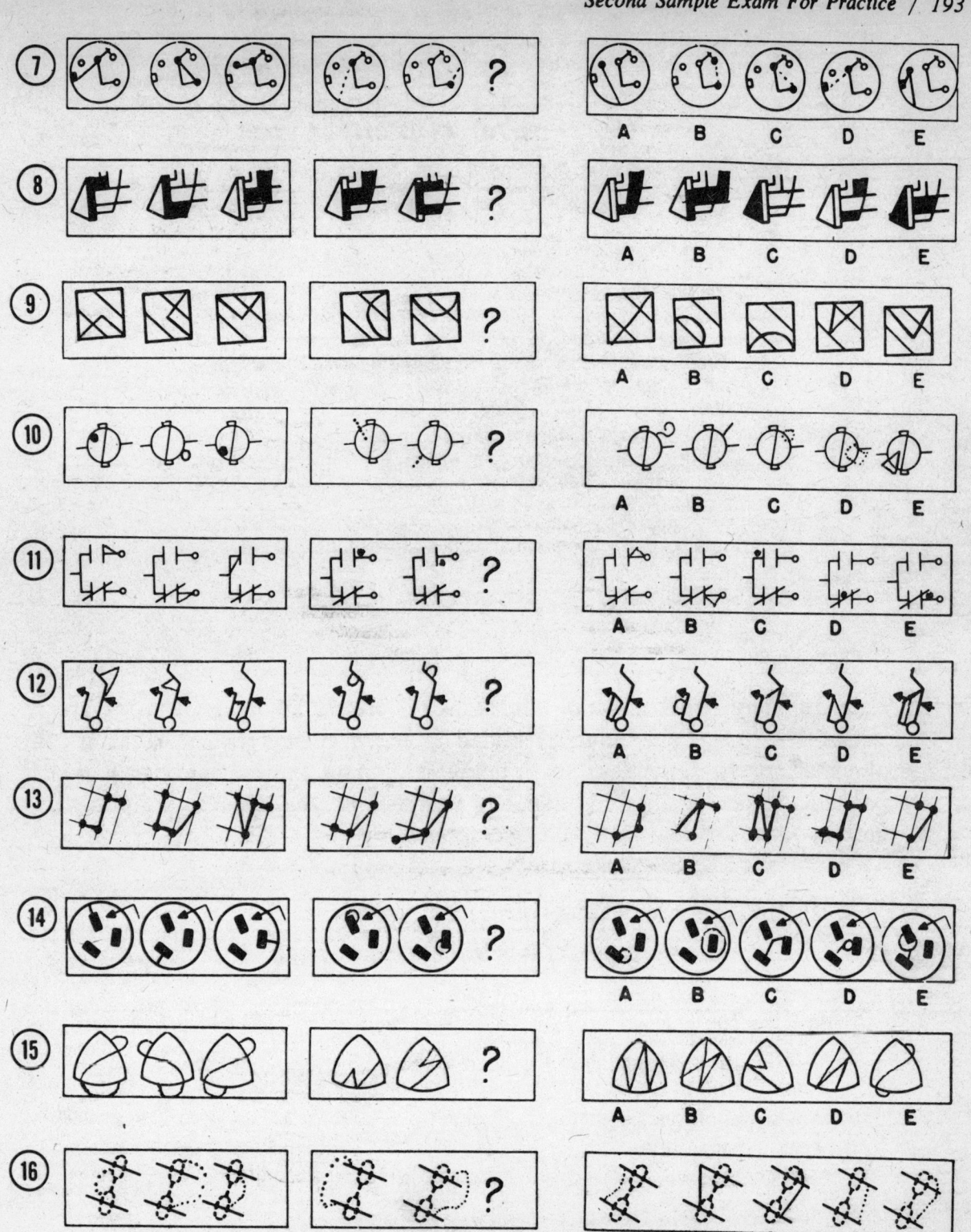

END OF TEST

Go on to do the following Test in this Examination, just as you would be expected to do on the actual exam.

Deriving Conclusions from Given Data

TEST V. READ AND INFER

TIME: 20 Minutes. 16 Questions.

This reading comprehension test consists of a number of different passages. One or more questions are based on each passage. The questions are composed of incomplete statements about the passage. Each incomplete statement is followed by five choices lettered (A) (B) (C) (D) (E). Mark your answer sheet with the letter of that choice which best completes the statement, and which best conveys the meaning of the passage.

Correct answers for these questions appear at the end of this examination, together with the answers to all other tests.

Reading Passage

Unfortunately, specialization in industry creates workers who lack versatility. When a laborer is trained to perform only one task, he is almost entirely dependent for employment upon the demand for that particular skill. If anything happens to interrupt that demand he is unemployed.

1. This paragraph indicates that
    (A) the unemployment problem is a direct result of specialization in industry
    (B) the demand for labor of a particular type is constantly changing
    (C) the average laborer is not capable of learning more than one task at a time
    (D) some cases of unemployment are due to laborers' lack of versatility
    (E) too much specialization is as dangerous as too little

Reading Passage

Good management is needed now more than ever. The essential characteristic of management is organization. An organization must be capable of handling responsibility and authority. It must also be able to maintain the balance and perspective necessary to make the weighty decisions thrust upon it today.

2. The above paragraph is a plea for

(A) better business
(B) adequately controlled responsibility
(C) well-regulated authority
(D) better management through organization
(E) less perspective and more balance

Reading Passage

The increasing size of business organizations has resulted in less personal contact between superior and subordinate. Consequently, business executives today depend more upon records and reports to secure information and exercise control over the operations of various departments.

3. According to this paragraph, the increasing size of business organizations

(A) has caused a complete cleavage between employer and employee
(B) has resulted in less personal contact between superior and subordinate
(C) has tended toward class distinctions in large organizations
(D) has resulted in a more direct means of controlling the operations of various departments
(E) has made evaluation of the work of the employee more objective

Reading Passage

Lacking a flair for positive administration, the mediocre executive attempts to insure efficiency by implanting job anxiety in his subordinates. This safe, unimaginative method secures the barest minimum of efficiency.

4. Of the following, the most accurate statement according to this quotation is that

   (A) implanting anxiety about job retention is a method usually employed by the mediocre executive to improve the efficiency of his organization
   (B) an organization will operate with at least some efficiency if employees realize that unsatisfactory work performance may subject them to dismissal
   (C) successful executives with a flair for positive administration relieve their subordinates of any concern for their job security
   (D) the implantation of anxiety about job security in subordinates should not be used as a method of improving efficiency
   (E) anxiety in executives tends to make them think that it is present in employees also

Reading Passage

In large organizations some standardized, simple, inexpensive method of giving employees information about company policies and rules, as well as specific instructions regarding their duties, is practically essential. This is the purpose of all office manuals of whatever type.

5. The above selection notes that office manuals

   (A) are all about the same
   (B) should be simple enough for the average employee to understand
   (C) are necessary to large organizations
   (D) act as constant reminders to the employee of his duties
   (E) are the only means by which the executive of a large organization can reach his subordinates

Reading Passage

The ability to do a particular job and performance on the job do not always go hand in hand. People with great potential abilities sometimes fall down on the job because of laziness or lack of interest, while people with mediocre talents achieve excellent results through industry and loyalty to the interests of their employers. The final test of any employee is his performance on the job.

6. The most accurate of the following statements, on the basis of the above paragraph, is that

(A) employees who lack ability are usually not industrious
(B) an employee's attitudes are more important than his abilities
(C) mediocre employees who are interested in their work are preferable to employees who possess great ability
(D) superior capacity for performance should be supplemented with proper attitudes

7. On the basis of the above paragraph, the employee of most value to his employer is *not* necessarily the one who

(A) best understands the significance of his duties
(B) achieves excellent results
(C) possesses the greatest talents
(D) produces the greatest amount of work

8. According to the above paragraph, an employee's efficiency is best determined by an

(A) appraisal of his interest in his work
(B) evaluation of the work performed by him
(C) appraisal of his loyalty to his employer
(D) evaluation of his potential ability to perform his work

Reading Passage

Interest is essentially an attitude of continuing attentiveness, found where activity is satisfactorily self-expressive. Whenever work is so circumscribed that the chance for self-expression or development is denied, monotony is present.

9. On the basis of this selection, it is most accurate to state that

(A) tasks which are repetitive in nature do not permit self-expression and therefore create monotony
(B) interest in one's work is increased by financial and non-financial incentives
(C) jobs which are monotonous can be made self-expressive by substituting satisfactory working conditions
(D) workers whose tasks afford them no opportunity for self-expression find such tasks to be monotonous
(E) work is monotonous unless there is activity which satisfies the worker

Reading Passage

During the past few years business has made rapid strides in applying to the field of office management the same fundamental principles of procedure and method that have been in successful use for years in production work. Present-day competition, resulting in smaller margins of profit, has made it essential to give careful attention to the efficient organization and management of internal administrative affairs so that individual productivity may be increased and unit costs reduced.

10. According to the above paragraph

   (A) office management always lags behind production work
   (B) present day competition has increased individual productivity
   (C) efficient office management seeks to reduce gross costs
   (D) the margin of profits widens as individual productivity is increased
   (E) similar principles have met with equal success in the fields of office management and production work

Reading Passage

Direct lighting is the least satisfactory lighting arrangement. The desk or ceiling light with a reflector which diffuses all the rays downward is sure to cause glare on the working surface.

11. The above paragraph indicates that direct lighting is least satisfactory as a method of lighting chiefly because

   (A) the light is diffused causing eye strain
   (B) the shade on the individual desk lamp is not constructed along scientific lines
   (C) the working surface is usually obscured by the glare
   (D) the ordinary reflector causes the rays to fall perpendicularly
   (E) direct lighting is injurious to the eyes

Reading Passage

The principal advantage of wood over steel office equipment lies, surprisingly, in the greater safety afforded papers in a fire. While the wooden exterior of a file cabinet may burn somewhat, the papers will not be charred as quickly as they would in a steel cabinet. This is because wood burns slowly and does not transmit heat, while steel, although it does not burn, is a conductor of heat. So, under similar circumstances, papers would be charred more quickly in a steel cabinet.

12. Judging from this information alone, the principal advantage of wood over steel office equipment is

   (A) in case of fire, papers will not be destroyed in a wooden cabinet
   (B) wooden equipment is cheaper to replace
   (C) steel does not resist fire as well as wood
   (D) steel equipment is heavy and cannot be moved about very easily
   (E) wood is a poor conductor of heat

Reading Passage

Forms are printed sheets of paper on which information is to be entered. While what is printed on the form is most important, the kind of paper used in making the form is also important. The kind of paper should be selected with regard to the use to which the form will be subjected. Printing a form on an unnecessarily expensive grade of paper is wasteful. On the other hand, using too cheap or flimsy a form can materially interfere with satisfactory performance of the work the form is being planned to do. Thus a form printed on both sides normally requires a heavier paper than a form printed only on one side. Forms to be used as permanent records, or which are expected to have a very long life in files, require a quality of paper which will not disintegrate or discolor with age. A form which will go through a great deal of handling requires a strong tough paper, while thinness is a necessary qualification where the making of several carbon copies of a form will be required.

13. According to this paragraph, the type of paper used for making forms

   (A) should be chosen in accordance with the use to which the form will be put
   (B) should be chosen before the type of printing to be used has been decided upon
   (C) is as important as the information which is printed on it
   (D) should be strong enough to be used for any purpose

14. According to this paragraph, forms that are

    (A) printed on both sides are usually economical and desirable
    (B) to be filed permanently should not deteriorate as time goes on
    (C) expected to last for a long time should be handled carefully
    (D) to be filed should not be printed on inexpensive paper

Reading Passage

The equipment in a mail room may include a mail metering machine. This machine simultaneously stamps, postmarks, seals, and counts letters as fast as the operator can feed them. It can also print the proper postage directly on a gummed strip to be affixed to bulky items. It is equipped with a meter which is removed from the machine and sent to the post office to be set for a given number of stampings of any denomination. The setting of the meter must be paid for in advance. One of the advantages of metered mail is that it by-passes the cancellation operation and thereby facilitates handling by the post office. Mail metering also makes the pilfering of stamps impossible, but does not prevent the passage of personal mail in company envelopes through the meters unless there is established a rigid control or censorship over outgoing mail.

15. According to this selection, the post office

    (A) is responsible for training new clerks in the use of mail metering machines
    (B) usually recommends that both large and small firms adopt the use of mail metering machines
    (C) is responsible for setting the meter to print a fixed number of stampings
    (D) examines the mail metering machines to see that they are properly installed in the mail room

16. According to the above, the use of mail metering machines

    (A) requires the employment of more clerks in a mail room than does the use of postage stamps
    (B) interferes with the handling of large quantities of outgoing mail
    (C) does not prevent employees from sending their personal letters at company expense
    (D) usually involves smaller expenditures for mail room equipment than does the use of postage stamps

END OF TEST

TEST VI. LOGICAL SEQUENCE

TIME: 15 Minutes. 15 Questions.

Directions: Arrange each group of five sentences in logical order so that each group makes up a well-organized paragraph. Then answer the questions that follow each group of five sentences.

PARAGRAPH 1

1. I learned this in my forty years in China from many friends, who, though illiterate, were wise and sophisticated.

2. I contend that this is a myth: that since most Chinese are illiterate they are, therefore, ignorant.

3. It all adds up to this—knowing how to read does not mean that one reads or thinks.

4. Actually there is surprisingly little connection between illiteracy and ignorance.

5. I learned it again in my own country, where I have found literacy and ignorance in frequent combination.

1. It the five sentences above were arranged in logical order, Sentence 1 would be
   (A) first
   (B) directly after Sentence 2
   (C) directly after Sentence 3
   (D) directly after Sentence 4
   (E) directly after Sentence 5

2. Sentence 2 would be
   (A) first
   (B) directly after Sentence 1
   (C) directly after Sentence 3
   (D) directly after Sentence 4
   (E) directly after Sentence 5

3. Sentence 3 would be
   (A) first
   (B) directly after Sentence 1
   (C) directly after Sentence 2
   (D) directly after Sentence 4
   (E) directly after Sentence 5

4. Sentence 4 would be
   (A) first
   (B) directly after Sentence 1
   (C) directly after Sentence 2
   (D) directly after Sentence 3
   (E) directly after Sentence 5

5. Sentence 5 would be
   (A) first
   (B) directly after Sentence 1
   (C) directly after Sentence 2
   (D) directly after Sentence 3
   (E) directly after Sentence 4

PARAGRAPH 2

1. The actors are the only unashamed artists in the theatre.
2. A surprising number of *great* plays—and I fear this means *old* plays—has been seen on Broadway.
3. Not that they are sheer idealists—it so happens that the great roles are in the great plays.
4. Since neither the public nor the critics nor the producers can be said to have demanded them, one must give credit to the handful of star actors who insisted on playing in them.
5. The obstacles in the path of, say, a Shakespeare production would never be overcome but for the zeal of an Olivier, a Gielgud, a Katherine Cornell, or a Maurice Evans.

6. If the five sentences above were arranged in logical order, Sentence 1 would be
   (A) first
   (B) directly after Sentence 2
   (C) directly after Sentence 3
   (D) directly after Sentence 4
   (E) directly after Sentence 5.

7. Sentence 2 would be
   (A) first
   (B) directly after Sentence 1
   (C) directly after Sentence 3
   (D) directly after Sentence 4
   (E) directly after Sentence 5.

8. Sentence 3 would be
   (A) first
   (B) directly after Sentence 1
   (C) directly after Sentence 2
   (D) directly after Sentence 4
   (E) directly after Sentence 5.

9. Sentence 4 would be
   (A) first
   (B) directly after Sentence 1
   (C) directly after Sentence 2
   (D) directly after Sentence 3
   (E) directly after Sentence 5.

10. Sentence 5 would be
    (A) first
    (B) directly after Sentence 1
    (C) directly after Sentence 2
    (D) directly after Sentence 3
    (E) directly after Sentence 4.

PARAGRAPH 3

1. Death is caused by another importation, Dutch elm disease, a fungus infection which the beetles carry from tree to tree.
2. During the past fourteen years, thousands of top-lofty United States elms have been marked for death by the activities of the tiny European elm bark beetle.
3. Every household and village that prizes an elm-shaded lawn or commons must now watch for this disease.
4. The beetles, however, do not do fatal damage.
5. Since there is yet no cure for it, the infected trees must be pruned or felled, and the wood must be burned in order to protect other healthy trees.

11. If the five sentences above were arranged in logical order, Sentence 1 would be
    (A) first
    (B) directly after Sentence 2
    (C) directly after Sentence 3
    (D) directly after Sentence 4
    (E) directly after Sentence 5.

12. Sentence 2 would be
    (A) first
    (B) directly after Sentence 1
    (C) directly after Sentence 3
    (D) directly after Sentence 4
    (E) directly after Sentence 5.

13. Sentence 3 would be
    (A) first
    (B) directly after Sentence 1
    (C) directly after Sentence 2
    (D) directly after Sentence 4
    (E) directly after Sentence 5.

14. Sentence 4 would be
    (A) first
    (B) directly after Sentence 1
    (C) directly after Sentence 2
    (D) directly after Sentence 3
    (E) directly after Sentence 5.

15. Sentence 5 would be
    (A) first
    (B) directly after Sentence 1
    (C) directly after Sentence 2
    (D) directly after Sentence 3
    (E) directly after Sentence 4.

END OF TEST

Go on to do the following Test in this Examination, just as you would be expected to do on the actual exam.

Quantitative Ability

TEST VII. MATHEMATICS

TIME: 35 Minutes. 25 Questions.

Each question in this test has four or five suggested answers numbered (1), (2), (3), (4) or (5). On your answer sheet, blacken the numbered space that is the same as the answer you have selected for each question.

1. Find the sum: 1/2+1/3+3/5+7/10.

   1) 12/20
   2) 1-5/30
   3) 2-2/15
   4) 3-1/5
   5) 4-1/2

2. X dollars invested at 4% simple interest for 2 years will yield which of the following total interest?

   1) .01X
   2) .04X
   3) .06X
   4) .08X
   5) .16X

3. Find the sum of 18, −6, −8, 2, −10, 4.

   1) 4
   2) 0
   3) −2
   4) −6
   5) −8

4. Last year a car dealer sold 125 cars for approximately $3,000 each. How much did the car dealer take in on the sale of these cars?

   1) $100,000
   2) $125,000
   3) $300,000
   4) $375,000
   5) $475,000

5. What is the next number in the following series?

   .25   1.50   2.75

   1) 0
   2) 1
   3) 2
   4) 3
   5) 4

6. Line AB is parallel to line CD, E, F, G, H and I are vertices of different triangles. CD is divided into 5 equal segments as shown. Which triangle has the greatest area?

   1) E   2) F   3) G   4) H   5) I

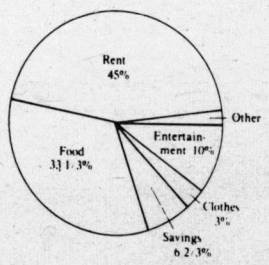

7. The above figure represents how a man spends his weekly salary. What percentage is for other expenses?

   1) 1%   2) 2%   3) 3%   4) 4%   5) 5%

203

Questions 8-10 are based on the bar graph below.

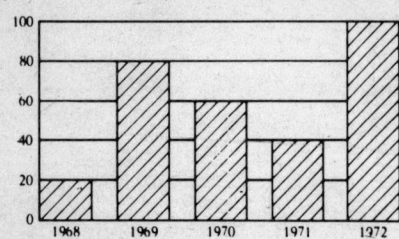

The bar graph represents the percentage of students passing the GED test between 1968 and 1972.

8. The ratio of the percent passing in 1972 to the percent passing in 1968 is

   1) 1:5.
   2) 1:4.
   3) 2:3.
   4) 4:1
   5) 5:1.

9. 60,000 students took the test in 1970. How many students failed the test?

   1) 12,000
   2) 24,000
   3) 36,000
   4) 48,000
   5) 60,000

10. Between what two years was the ratio of passing students 1:3?

    1) 1968:1970
    2) 1969:1971
    3) 1970:1972
    4) 1968:1971
    5) 1970:1971

Questions 11-12 are based on the graph below.

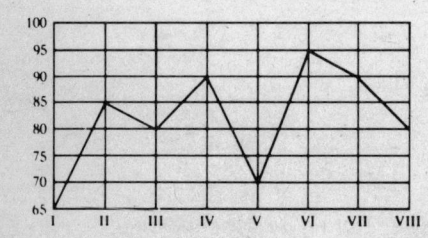

The graph shows the mark for a student's math tests.

11. What was the average for the eight tests?

    1) 80
    2) 81.2
    3) 81.5
    4) 81.7
    5) 81.8

12. Which 3 tests would yield the lowest average?

    1) I II III
    2) II III IV
    3) III IV V
    4) IV V VI
    5) V VI VII

13. Two-thirds of a class are girls. If there are 9 boys in the class, how many girls are there?

    1) 3
    3) 6
    3) 18
    4) 27
    5) 54

14. Which of the following percentages is equivalent to 7/3?

    1) 233 1/3%
    2) 100 2/3%
    3) 90%
    4) 70%
    5) 30%

15. Simplify the expression $x - [2-(x+3)+1]$.

    1) X
    2) 2X
    3) X−1
    4) 2X−1
    5) 2X+3

16. The dimensions of a rectangular solid are 2, 3 and 4 inches. If the dimensions are doubled, the ratio between the original solid and the new solid is

    1) 1:2.
    2) 2:1.
    3) 1:8.
    4) 2:5.
    5) 3:4.

17. If x = .2 and y = (1−x), what is the value of 2xy?

   1) .32
   2) 3.2
   3) 1.6
   4) 32
   5) none of these

18. A salesman receives 33-1/3% commission on all sales. If his commission is $90.00, what were his sales?

   1) $90
   2) $180
   3) $200
   4) $270
   5) $360

19. Find the square root of .81.

   1) .0009
   2) .009
   3) .09
   4) .9
   5) none of these

20. During a 10-day museum exhibit the number of spectators doubled each day. If the exhibit opened on Tuesday and the attendance on Friday of the same week was 800, what was the attendance on opening day?

   1) 800
   2) 400
   3) 200
   4) 100
   5) 50

21. During the past week Mr. White spent the following time studying for the math test:

   Mon: 2 hrs. 15 min.
   Tues: 3 hrs.
   Wed: 45 min.
   Thurs: 1 hr. 40 min.
   Fri: 2 hrs. 20 min.

   What was the average time spent studying math per day?

   1) 2 hrs.
   2) 4 hrs.
   3) 6 hrs.
   4) 8 hrs.
   5) 10 hrs.

22. Which of these fractions is greater than 1/5?

   1) 3/13
   2) 8/26
   3) 12/39
   4) all of these
   5) none of these

23. What is the next number in the series 4, 10, 22, 46?

   1) 80
   2) 94
   3) 100
   4) 104
   5) 110

24. When compared by the square yard, which is a better buy: One yard of carpet A which is 24" wide and sells for $6, or one yard of carpet B which is 36" wide and sells for $9.00?

   1) carpet A is $3 less per sq. yd.
   2) carpet B is $3 less per sq. yd.
   3) carpets A and B are the same price per sq. yard.
   4) carpet B is $1 more per sq. yd.
   5) impossible to determine

25. The number 83.42 contains two significant digits. How should it be written?

   1) 83
   2) 83.0
   3) 83.00
   4) .40
   5) .42

END OF TEST

Go on to do the following Test in this Examination, just as you would be expected to do on the actual exam.

TEST VIII. ARITHMETIC COMPUTATIONS

TIME: 5 Minutes. 10 Questions.

DIRECTIONS: Each question has five suggested answers lettered A, B, C, D, and E. Suggested answer E is NONE OF THESE. Blacken space E only if your answer for a question does not exactly agree with any of the first four suggested answers. When you have finished all the questions, compare your answers with the correct answers at the end of the test.

ANSWERS

1) Add:

   3 ¼
   4 ⅛
 + 4 ½

(A) 11⅝
(B) 11¾
(C) 11⅞
(D) 12
(E) None of these

2) $\dfrac{12.02 \times .0001}{.02} =$

(A) 6.01
(B) .601
(C) .61
(D) 6.1
(E) None of these

3) Subtract:

  58,769
 − 4,028

(A) 54,641
(B) 44,741
(C) 54,741
(D) 53,741
(E) None of these

4) Add:

  5 ft. 4 in.
19 ft. 9 in.
  9 ft. 3 in.
+   10 in.

(A) 44 ft. 4 in.
(B) 35 ft. 2 in.
(C) 33 ft. 2 in.
(D) 30 ft. 26 in.
(E) None of these

5) Multiply:

  48,207
 ×   926

(A) 44,639,682
(B) 45,739,682
(C) 45,638,682
(D) 46,739,682
(E) None of these

ANSWERS

6) Add:

  427
  936
  502
+ 884

(A) 2,836
(B) 2,751
(C) 3,027
(D) 2,749
(E) None of these

7) Subtract:

  8276.91
− 5382.17

(A) 2895.76
(B) 2884.74
(C) 2894.76
(D) 1874.74
(E) None of these

8) Divide:

.7 / 913.5

(A) 130.5
(B) 1305.
(C) 13.05
(D) 1.305
(E) None of these

9) Multiply:

31.18 × 186.7 =

(A) 58213.060
(B) 5836.3060
(C) 5821.3060
(D) 582130.60
(E) None of these

10) Subtract:

8.6 − 2.19 =

(A) 6.41
(B) 5.87
(C) 2.67
(D) 58.7
(E) None of these

END OF TEST

Understanding Charts and Tables

TEST IX. DATA INTERPRETATION

TIME: 35 Minutes. 22 Questions.

DIRECTIONS: *This test consists of data presented in graphic form followed by questions based on the information contained in the graph, chart or table shown. After studying the data given, choose the best answer for each question and blacken the corresponding space on the answer sheet. Answer each group of questions solely on the basis of the information given or implied in the data preceding it.*

Questions 1 to 7

The chart below shows the annual average number of administrative actions completed for the four divisions of a bureau. Assume that the figures remain stable from year to year.

Administrative Actions	DIVISIONS				Totals
	W	X	Y	Z	
Telephone Inquiries Answered	8,000	6,800	7,500	4,800	27,100
Interviews Conducted	I	630	550	500	2,180
Applications Processed	15,000	18,000	14,500	9,500	57,000
Letters Typed	2,500	II	4,350	3,250	14,500
Reports Completed	200	250	100	50	600
Totals	26,200	30,080	27,000	18,100	III

1. What is the value of I?

   (A) 480   (B) 500   (C) 530   (D) 620
   (E) None of these or cannot be calculated from data provided.

2. What is the value of II?

   (A) 4,400   (B) 4,080   (C) 3,400   (D) 3,050
   (E) None of these or cannot be calculated from data provided.

S3509
207

3. What is the value of III?

   (A) 100,350   (B) 100,380   (C) 101,350   (D) 101,380
   (E) None of these or cannot be calculated from data provided.

4. In which division is the number of Applications Processed the greatest percentage of the total Administrative Actions for that division?

   (A) W
   (B) X
   (C) Y
   (D) Z

5. The bureau chief is considering a plan that would consolidate the typing of letters in a separate unit. This unit would be responsible for the typing of letters for all divisions in which the number of letters typed exceeds 15% of the total number of administrative actions. Under this plan which of the following divisions would *continue* to type its own letters?

   (A) W and X
   (B) W and X and Y
   (C) X and Y
   (D) X and Z

6. The setting up of a central information service that would be capable of answering 25% of the whole bureau's telephone inquiries is under consideration. Under such a plan, the divisions would gain for other activities that time previously spent on telephone inquiries. Approximately how much total time would such a service gain for all four divisions if it requires 5 minutes to answer the average telephone inquiry?

   (A) 500 hours
   (B) 515 hours
   (C) 565 hours
   (D) 585 hours

7. Assume that the rate of production shown in the table can be projected as accurate for the coming year and that monthly output is constant for each type of administrative action within a division. Division Y is scheduled to work exclusively on a 4-month long special project during that year. During the period of the project, Division Y's regular workload will be divided evenly among the remaining divisions. Using the figures in the table, what would be, most nearly, the percentage increase in the total Administrative Actions completed by Division Z for the year?

   (A) 8%
   (B) 16%
   (C) 25%
   (D) 50%

Questions 8 to 11

The graph below indicates at 5 year intervals the number of citations issued for various offenses from the year 1950 to the year 1970.

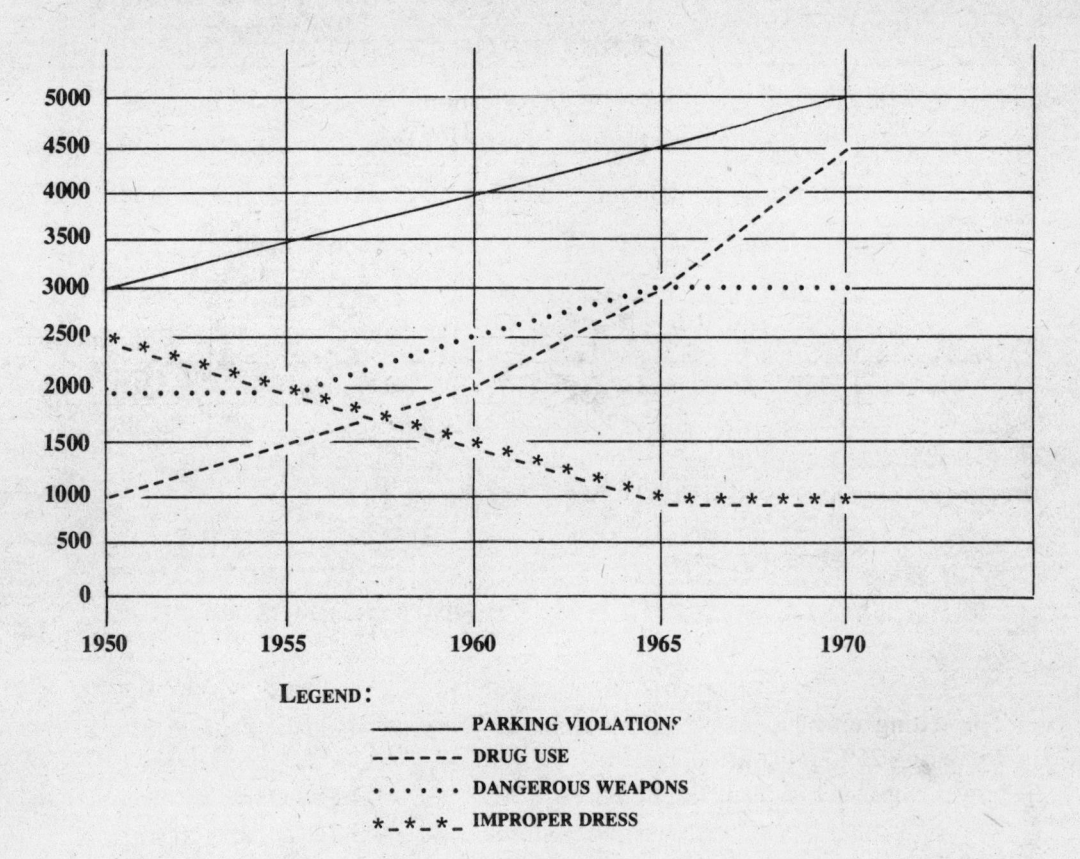

LEGEND:
———— PARKING VIOLATIONS
- - - - - DRUG USE
· · · · · DANGEROUS WEAPONS
--*- IMPROPER DRESS

8. Over the 20-year period, which offense shows an average rate of increase of more than 150 citations per year?
   (A) Parking Violations
   (B) Dangerous Weapons
   (C) Drug Use
   (D) None of the above.

9. Over the 20-year period, which offense shows a constant rate of increase or decrease?
   (A) Parking Violations
   (B) Drug Use
   (C) Dangerous Weapons
   (D) Improper Dress

10. Which offense shows a total increase or decrease of 50% for the full 20-year period?
    (A) Parking Violations
    (B) Drug Use
    (C) Dangerous Weapons
    (D) Improper Dress

11. The percentage increase in total citations issued from 1955 to 1960 is most nearly
    (A) 7%
    (B) 11%
    (C) 21%
    (D) 41%

Questions 12 to 16

The Payroll Summary below represents payroll for a monthly period for a particular agency.

PAYROLL SUMMARY

Employee	Total Earnings	FICA	Withhold. Tax	State Tax	Other	Net Pay
W	450.00	27.00	67.00	18.00	6.00	332.00
X	235.00	14.10	33.00	8.00	2.00	177.90
Y	341.00	20.46	52.00	14.00	5.00	249.54
Z	275.00	[I]	30.00	6.00	2.40	220.10
Totals	1301.00	[II]	182.00	46.00	15.40	[III]

12. What is the Value of I?

    (A) $16.00   (B) $16.50   (C) $17.50   (D) $18.00

13. What is the Value of II?

    (A) $78.06   (B) $78.56   (C) $78.60   (D) $79.56

14. Based on the data given above, the amount of cash that would have to be available to pay the employees on payday is

    (A) $1301.00   (B) $979.54   (C) $905.60
    (D) Cannot be calculated from data given.

15. Based on the data given above, the amount required to be deposited with a governmental depository is

    (A) $243.40   (B) $182.00   (C) $306.06   (D) $321.46

16. Based on the data given above, what would be the amount of cash deducted for FICA from the salary of an employee who earns $300 per month?

    (A) $16.50   (B) $17.00   (C) $18.00
    (D) Cannot be calculated from data given

Questions 17 to 19

The management study of employee absence due to sickness is an effective tool in planning. Answer questions 17 to 19 solely on the data given below.

NUMBER OF DAYS ABSENT PER WORKER (SICKNESS)	1	2	3	4	5	6	7	8 or Over
NUMBER OF WORKERS	76	23	6	3	1	0	1	0

TOTAL NUMBER OF WORKERS: 400   PERIOD COVERED: Jan. 1, 1971—Dec. 31, 1971

17. The total number of man days lost due to illness in 1971 was

    (A) 110 (B) 137
    (C) 144 (D) 164

18. What percent of the workers had 4 or more days absence due to sickness during 1971?

    (A) .25%   (B) 2.5%
    (C) 1.25% (D) 12.5%

19. Of the 400 workers studied, the number who lost no days due to sickness in 1971 was

    (A) 190 (B) 236
    (C) 290 (D) 346

Questions 20 to 22

The following chart shows the differences between the rates of production of employees in Department D in 1961 and 1971. Answer questions 20 to 22 solely on the basis of the information given in the chart.

NUMBER OF EMPLOYEES PRODUCING WORK-UNITS WITHIN RANGE IN 1961	NUMBER OF WORK-UNITS PRODUCED	NUMBER OF EMPLOYEES PRODUCING WORK-UNITS WITHIN RANGE IN 1971
7	500 – 1000	4
14	1001 – 1500	11
26	1501 – 2000	28
22	2001 – 2500	36
17	2501 – 3000	39
10	3001 – 3500	23
4	3501 – 4000	9

20. Assuming that within each range of work-units produced, the average production was at the mid-point of that range (e.g., category 500 – 1000 = 750), then the average number of work-units produced per employee in 1961 fell into the range

    (A) 1001 – 1500 (B) 1501 – 2000
    (C) 2001 – 2500 (D) 2501 – 3000

21. The ratio of the number of employees producing more than 2000 work-units in 1961 to the number of employees producing more than 2000 work-units in 1971 is most nearly

   (A) 1:2   (B) 2:3   (C) 3:4   (D) 4:5

22. In Department D, which of the following were greater in 1971 than in 1961?

   1. Total number of employees
   2. Total number of work-units produced
   3. Number of employees producing 2000 or fewer work-units

   (A) 1, 2 and 3
   (B) 1 and 2, but not 3
   (C) 1 and 3, but not 2
   (D) 2 and 3, but not 1

END OF TEST

Go on to do the following Test in this Examination, just as you would be expected to do on the actual exam.

Deriving Conclusions from Given Data

TEST X. APPLYING GENERAL KNOWLEDGE

TIME: 30 Minutes. 25 Questions.

DIRECTIONS: For each question in this test, read carefully the stem and the five lettered choices that follow. Choose the answer which you consider correct or most nearly correct. Mark the answer sheet for the letter you have chosen: A, B, C, D, or E.

1. Electricity is used as the chief agent in flashing messages from place to place mainly because (A) it is less costly in the long run (B) aerial wiring is eliminated (C) maximum speed is obtainable (D) it is applicable to telegrams (E) the element of space is reduced.

2. The chief reason why water when heated within a presure cooker becomes hotter than water heated within a teakettle is that (A) pressure is reduced (B) water will boil more quickly at a partial vacuum in a teakettle (D) no steam can escape in the cooker (E) the heat is more intense.

3. The chief reason for the post-office's requesting that addresses be written in ink or on the typewriter is (A) pen and ink are supplied by the post-office for the use of its patrons (B) a typewritten address or one written in ink looks neater (C) an address written in pencil may be easily erased by the sender (D) pencil addresses may smudge and become illegible (E) business men seldom have their mail addressed in pencil.

4. The principle reason why electric current, when it is transmitted from a considerable distance to a city, is sent at very high voltage is that (A) at a lower voltage much electricity would be wasted (B) the higher the voltage, the greater the speed (C) high-voltage wires must be strung at a considerable distance from the ground as a measure of precaution (D) the voltage used depends upon the distance the current must be sent (E) the generators are sometimes located a considerable distance from the city where it is to be used.

5. The sound which issues from a violin when a bow is drawn across one of the strings is due chiefly to (A) air waves set in motion by the bow (B) ether waves set in motion by the bow (C) a partial vacuum in the vicinity of the sound chamber which is caused by the vibrating motion of the bow (D) vibration of the string (E) the tenseness of the string.

6. A clay pitcher of water will crack if the water freezes chiefly because (A) during the process of freezing the water expands (B) during the process of freezing the water contracts (C) the crystallization process of ice formation causes the ice to solidify (D) the tension strength of clay decreases as the temperature decreases (E) the rate of expansion of water has the same ratio as that of contraction of the pitcher.

7. Earthquakes are recorded by an instrument known as a (A) galvanoscope (B) seismograph (C) spectroscope (D) stereopticon (E) electromagnet.

8. Radium is more expensive than gold chiefly because (A) it is of value in medicine in healing disease (B) it has extensive use commercially (C) the mining of radium is controlled by a trust (D) compared to gold, the discovery of radium ocurred only recently (E) the refining process of radium is more costly and complicated than that of gold.

9. Helium is preferred to hydrogen for use in dirigibles chiefly because helium (A) is lighter in molecular weight than air (B) is non-inflamable (C) has a greater gaseous content (D) is cheaper and more readily obtainable than hydrogen (E) is a neutral element.

10. Ground glass is sometimes used instead of clear glass in electric light bulbs chiefly because (A) glare is eliminated (B) ground glass is translucent (C) the amount of light is increased (D) the amount of light is decreased (E) ground glass is not opaque.

11. The sun's rays are hotter in summer than in winter because in summer (A) they fall more slantingly (B) there is a lesser density in the earth's atmosphere (C) the earth is closer to the sun (D) they strike the earth's surface more perpendicularly than in winter (E) the angle of declivity is increased.

12. When the inflated inner tube of an automobile tire is punctured, a "blow out" usually occurs because (A) the rubber wears out (B) the internal air pressure is less than the external air pressure (C) the internal air pressure is greater than the external air pressure (D) the internal and external air pressures are the same (E) the size of the puncture is too small to permit gas to escape slowly.

13. Silver is used for mirrors chiefly because (A) it is expensive (B) it provides a good reflecting surface (C) it does not turn yellow from exposure to sunlight (D) very little silver is necessary (E) silver does not corrode.

14. The weight an object possesses is due to the physical phenomenon known as (A) molecular attraction (B) mass (C) solar attraction (D) density (E) gravitation.

15. A lunar eclipse occurs when (A) the sun passes into the shadow of the moon (B) the acceleration of the earth's axis is increased (C) the moon assumes the shape of a crescent (D) the moon passes into the shadow of the earth (E) the moon reaches the equinox.

16. An insulating process is currently being used in modern house construction chiefly because (A) it makes houses sound-proof (B) it makes houses less costly to construct (C) insulation makes a house waterproof (D) the insulation tends to reduce house fueling costs (E) it saves time in construction.

17. Duraluminum alloys are used in aeroplanes chiefly because (A) they are composed of metals (B) they are inexpensive (C) they do not rust (D) they are light in weight (E) they are extremely malleable.

18. It becomes profitable to import a commodity chiefly whenever labor and capital engaged in its domestic production yield (A) a profit which is less than the same agents would yield in other fields (B) a lesser number of products than would be normally expected (C) a profit similar to that which they would yield in other fields (E) a very small profit.

19. The apparent motion of the sun across the sky is caused by (A) the earth's speed (B) the rotation of the earth on its axis (C) the earth's centrifugal force (D) the relative variation in so-called "sun-spots" (E) a spectrum phenomenon.

20. Water tanks are maintained on the top of tall buildings chiefly in order to (A) maintain a reserve supply of water if the normal water supply should fail (B) prevent lightning from striking the building by acting as an arrester (C) have water available in the event of a fire (D) supply the upper floors with water by a process of first pumping it into the tanks (E) convert the water into electric power by a turbine process.

21. The fact that the sun seems to rise in the east and set in the west is proof that (A) only the sun is in motion (B) only the earth is in motion (C) either the sun or the earth is in motion (D) the east and the west are merely abstract concepts (E) there are 12 hours in the average day.

22. One of the chief advantages of transmitting money by postal money order is that (A) a money order cannot be lost (B) if a money order is lost, it can be duplicated from the record of its issue (C) it can be used as currency (D) there is no charge for issuing a postal money order (E) a money order does not have to be indorsed by the payee.

23. The human blood gets its reddish color from a substance in it known as (A) chlorophyll (B) cochineal (C) haemoglobin (D) red plasma red corpuscles.

24. Leather is considered the best material for shoes chiefly because (A) it is waterproof (B) it is durable (C) it is easily procurable (D) it is flexible and durable (E) it can be easily manufactured in various styles.

25. Water will boil at a lower temperature at high altitudes than at sea level primarily because (A) the atmospheric density is reduced (B) the amount of air dissolved in the water is decreased (C) the thermodynamic property of water is decreased (D) energy from the sun aids in the boiling process at high altitudes (E) the solubility of air in the water is increased.

END OF EXAMINATION

Now that you have completed the last Test in this Examination, use your available time to make sure that you have written in your answers correctly on the Answer Sheet. Then, after your time is up, check your answers with the Correct Answers we have provided for you. Derive your scores for each Test Category and determine where you are weak so as to plan your study accordingly.

CORRECT ANSWERS FOR SAMPLE EXAMINATION II.

TEST I. READ AND DEDUCE

1.A	3.D	5.E	7.E	9.E	11.B	13.A	15.C
2.E	4.B	6.C	8.D	10.C	12.D	14.E	

TEST II. SYNONYMS

1.A	6.A	11.B	16.D	21.C	26.C
2.D	7.D	12.B	17.A	22.B	27.C
3.A	8.B	13.A	18.C	23.C	28.A
4.B	9.C	14.A	19.D	24.C	29.D
5.C	10.A	15.D	20.B	25.C	30.B

TEST III. LETTER SERIES

1.B	5.D	9.D	13.C	17.B
2.B	6.B	10.D	14.A	18.B
3.C	7.C	11.B	15.D	19.D
4.A	8.B	12.A	16.C	20.C

TEST IV. ABSTRACT REASONING

1.A	3.B	5.B	7.A	9.C	11.C	13.A	15.C
2.C	4.E	6.D	8.B	10.B	12.B	14.A	16.A

TEST V. READ AND INFER

1.D	3.B	5.C	7.C	9.D	11.D	13.A	15.C
2.D	4.B	6.D	8.B	10.D	12.E	14.B	16.C

TEST VI. LOGICAL SEQUENCE

1.D	4.C	7.A	10.E	13.B
2.A	5.B	8.B	11.D	14.C
3.E	6.E	9.C	12.A	15.D

TEST VII. MATHEMATICS

1.3	5.5	8.5	11.5	14.1	17.1	20.4	23.2
2.4	6.4	9.2	12.1	15.2	18.4	21.1	24.3
3.2	7.2	10.1	13.3	16.3	19.4	22.4	25.1
4.4							

TEST VIII. ARITHMETIC COMPUTATIONS

1. C	3. C	5. A	7. E	9. C
2. B	4. B	6. D	8. B	10. A

TEST IX. DATA INTERPRETATION

1. B	4. B	7. B	10. C	13. A	16. C	19. C	22. B
2. A	5. A	8. C	11. B	14. B	17. D	20. C	
3. D	6. C	9. A	12. B	15. C	18. C	21. A	

TEST IX. EXPLANATORY ANSWERS

1. **(B)** To find the value of I using the lowest possible figures, add the number of Interviews Conducted by Divisions X, Y, and Z. Then subtract this figure from the Total Interviews conducted.

   Thus: 630 + 550 + 500 = 1680
   2180 − 1680 = 500

2. **(A)** To find the value of II using the lowest figures (which allow for the fewest mistakes), add the number of letters typed by Divisions W, Y, and Z. Then subtract from the Total Letters Typed.

   Thus: 2500 + 4350 + 3250 = 10100
   14500 − 10100 = 4400

3. **(D)** To find the value of III, add all the Totals of all Administrative Actions
   27100 + 2180 + 57000 + 14500 + 600 = 101380

4. **(B)** There are three steps necessary to the solution of this problem:
   1) Establish a ratio of Applications Processed: Total Administrative Actions for Each Division.

      Div. W   15000:26200
      Div. X   18000:30080
      Div. Y   14500:27000
      Div. Z   9500:18100

   2) Simplify each ratio by dividing the first term by the second term and
   3) convert this figure to a percentage by multiplying by 100.

      Div. W 15000 ÷ 26200 = .572 × 100 = 57.2%
      Div. X 18000 ÷ 30080 = .598 × 100 = 59.8%
      Div. Y 14500 ÷ 27000 = .537 × 100 = 53.7%
      Div. Z 9500 ÷ 18100 = .524 × 100 = 52.4%

   The division in which the number of applications processed is the greatest percentage of total Administrative Actions is Division X.

218 / *P.A.C.E. Professional-Administrative Career Exam*

5. **(A)** The easiest way to solve this type of problem is to take 15% of the total Administrative Actions for each Division and then determine by inspecting the chart whether or not the number of letters typed exceeds this figure.

   Div. W   26200 × .15 = 3930 which is greater than 2500 (number of letters typed)

   Div. X   30080 × .15 = 4521 which is greater than 4400 (number of letters typed)

   Div. Y   27000 × .15 = 4050 which is less than 4350 (number of letters typed)

   Div. Z   18100 × .15 = 2715 which is less than 3250 (number of letters typed)

   Therefore under the new plan only Division W and X would continue to do their own typing since the number of letters typed in these two divisions does not exceed 15% of the total Administrative Actions of each division.

6. **(C)**   27100 Total Telephone Inquiries Answered by all Divisions
   ×.25 Calls that could be answered by a Central Information Service
   6775 Number of Telephone Inquiries that could be answered by a Central Information Service

   At 5 minutes per call that means 6775 × 5 or 33875 minutes could be saved by having a Central Information Service.

   Since there are 60 minutes in an hour, 33875 ÷ 60 = 564.5 Hours could be gained by all four divisions if such a service were instituted.

7. **(B)**   Division Y is responsible for 27,000 Administrative Actions per year

   Therefore in 4 months which is 4/12 or 1/3 year, Division Y would be responsible for 27000 × 1/3 or 9,000 Administrative Actions.

   9,000 Administrative Actions divided evenly among Divisions W, X and Z = 9000 ÷ 3 or 3000 Administrative Actions to be added to each division's work load for the coming year.

   An increase of 3000 Actions over the 18100 actions completed by Division Z for the current year is equal to 3000 ÷ 18100 = .16 or 16%.

8. **(C)**   An average rate of increase of 150 citations per year over a 20 year period = 150 × 20 or an increase of 3000 citations in 20 years. Reading from the graph:

   Parking Violations increased from 3000 in 1950 to 5000 in 1970. This is an increase of 2000 citations in 20 years.

   Drug Use increased from 1000 in 1950 to 4500 in 1970. This is an increase of 3500 in 20 years.

Dangerous Weapons increased from 2000 in 1950 to 3000 in 1970. This is an increase of 1000 in 20 years.

Improper Dress obviously *decreased* over the 20 year period shown and so is not to be considered in this question.

The only offense which shows an increase of 3000 (or more) over the 20 year period is Drug Use.

9. **(A)** A constant rate of increase or decrease is indicated on a graph by a straight line. Inspection of this graph shows that only citations for Parking Violations progress in a straight line from 1950 to 1970, increasing by 500 citations for each 5 year period.

10. **(C)** Over the full 20 year period citations for Parking Violations increased from 3000 to 5000.

% of Increase = $\frac{\text{Amount of Increase}}{\text{Original Amount}} \times 100$

% of Increase (Parking Violations) = $\frac{2000}{3000} \times 100 = .66 \times 100 = 66\%$

% of Increase (Drug Use) = $\frac{3500}{1000} \times 100 = 3.5 \times 100 = 350\%$

% of Increase (Dangerous Weapons) = $\frac{1000}{2000} \times 100 = .5 \times 100 = 50\%$

% of Decrease (Improper Dress) = $\frac{1500}{2500} \times 100 = .6 \times 100 = 60\%$

The only offense which shows a total increase or decrease of 50% is Dangerous Weapons.

11. **(B)** To find the percentage increase in total citations issued from 1955 to 1960, you must first find the number of citations issued in 1955 and 1960.

Citations issued in 1955 =
  3500 (Parking Violations)
  2000 (Improper Dress)
  2000 (Dangerous Weapons)
  1500 (Drug Use)
  9000 Total Citations Issued

Citations issued in 1960 =
  4000 (Parking Violations)
  2500 (Dangerous Weapons)
  2000 (Drug Use)
  1500 (Improper Dress)
  10000 Total Citations Issued

10000 − 9000 = 1000 Increase

% Increase = $\frac{1000}{9000} \times 100 = .11 \times 100 = 11\%$

12. **(B)** "I" is FICA or one of the Deductions made from the Total Earnings of Employee Z. To find the value of "I", first find the Total Deductions for Employee Z:

Total Deductions = Total Earnings − Net Pay = 275.00 − 220.10 = $54.90.

Next, find the total known deductions for Employee Z:
30.00 + 6.00 + 2.40 = 38.40

FICA ("I") = Total Deductions − Known Deductions = 5490 − 38.40 = 16.50

13. **(A)** Using the information you have just gained from the previous question, substitute $16.50 for "I" in the table and then add all the figures in the FICA column to arrive at the Total.

$27.00 + 14.10 + 20.46 + 16.50 = $78.06

14. **(B)** The amount of cash necessary to pay the employees is the total of Net Pay. This figure is represented on the chart as "III". However, its value can be calculated by adding all the figures in the Net Pay column.

$332.00 + 177.90 + 249.54 + 220.10 = $979.54

Alternative (A) is incorrect because it represents Total Earnings which includes taxes and other deductions which are not paid to the employees.

15. **(C)** The amount which must be deposited with a governmental depository is the total of FICA + Withholding Tax + State Tax or

$78.06 + 182.00 + 46.00 = $306.06

The $15.40 (Total of the "Other" column) covers such employee benefits as health and life insurance and does not have to be paid to a governmental depository.

16. **(C)** To answer this question, it is necessary to determine the percentage of each employee's Total Earnings which his FICA deduction represents.

Employee W: $\frac{27.00}{450.00}$ = .06 or 6%   Employee Y: $\frac{20.46}{341.00}$ = .06 or 6%

Employee X: $\frac{14.10}{235.00}$ = .06 or 6%   Employee Z: $\frac{16.50}{275.00}$ = .06 or 6%

Since FICA represents 6% of the Total Earnings of each employee appearing on the Payroll Summary, it will also represent 6% of the Total Earnings of any other employee. Thus, $300 × .06 = $18.00 (FICA deduction for an employee earning $300 per month)

17. **(D)**
    76 workers absent 1 day each = 76 × 1 = 76 days missed
    23 workers absent 2 days each = 23 × 2 = 46 days missed
    6 workers absent 3 days each = 6 × 3 = 18 days missed
    3 workers absent 4 days each = 3 × 4 = 12 days missed
    1 worker absent 5 days = 1 × 5 = 5 days missed
    1 worker absent 7 days = 1 × 7 = 7 days missed

    76 + 46 + 18 + 12 + 5 + 7 = 164 Total days lost to illness in 1971.

18. **(C)**
    No. of workers out 4 days = 3
    No. of workers out 5 days = 1
    No. of workers out 6 days = 0
    No. of workers out 7 days = 1
    No. of workers out 8 days = 0

    3 + 1 + 0 + 1 + 0 = 5 workers out 4 or more days in 1971
    Total number of workers = 400

    % of Workers out 4 or more days = $\frac{5}{400}$ × 100 = .0125 × 100 = 1.25%

19. **(C)**
    Total number of workers who have been out sick = 76 + 23 + 6 + 3 + 1 + 0 + 1 + 0 = 110

    400 Total Number of Workers
    −110 Total Number of Workers who have been out sick
    290 Number of workers who have lost no days due to sickness

20. **(C)**
    First find the number of employees in 1961:
    7 + 14 + 26 + 22 + 17 + 10 + 4 = 100 employees

    Then find total number of work-units produced using mid-point of each range:

    7 × 750 = 5250
    14 × 1250 = 17500
    26 × 1750 = 45500
    22 × 2250 = 49500
    17 × 2750 = 46750
    10 × 3250 = 32500
    4 × 3750 = 15000
    212000 Total Work-Units Produced

    Divide number of work-units produced by number of workers to get average number of work-units per employee:
    212000 ÷ 100 = 2120 Work-units per Employee

    This falls in the range of 2001 − 2500.

21. **(A)**

Number of employees producing more than 2000 work-units in 1961 = 22 + 17 + 10 + 4 = 53

Number of employees producing more than 2000 work-units in 1971 = 36 + 39 + 23 + 9 = 107

Ratio of employees producing more than 2000 work-units in 1961 to those producing more than 2000 work-units in 1971 = **53 : 107 which is most nearly 1 : 2.**

22. **(B)**

1.) Number of employees in 1961 = 100 (See question 20)
Number of employees in 1971 = 150
(4 + 11 + 28 + 36 + 39 + 23 + 9 = 150)

2.) Work units produced in 1961 = 212000 (See question 20)
Work units produced in 1971 = 362500

```
 4 ×  750 =   3000
11 × 1250 =  13750
28 × 1750 =  49000
36 × 2250 =  81000
39 × 2750 = 107250
23 × 3250 =  74750
 9 × 3750 =  33750
           362500  Total Work-units produced in 1971.
```

3.) Employees producing 2000 or fewer work-units in 1961 =
7 + 14 + 26 = 47

Employees producing 2000 or fewer work-units in 1971 =
4 + 11 + 28 = 43

Therefore, 1 (Total number of employees) and 2 (Total number of work-units produced) were greater in 1971 than in 1961.

TEST X. APPLYING GENERAL KNOWLEDGE

1.C	5.D	8.E	11.D	14.E	17.D	20.D	23.C
2.D	6.A	9.B	12.C	15.D	18.A	21.C	24.D
3.D	7.B	10.A	13.B	16.D	19.B	22.B	25.A
4.A							

Professional & Administrative Career Exam

ARCO BOOKS FOR MORE HELP

Now what? You've read and studied the whole book, and there's still time before you take the test. You're probably better prepared than most of your competitors, but you may feel insecure about one or more of the probable test subjects. If so, you can still do something about it. Glance over this comprehensive list of books written with a view to solving your problems. One of them may be just what you need at this time ... for the extra help that will assure your success.

CIVIL SERVICE AND TEST PREPARATION—GENERAL

Title	Code	Price
Able Seaman, Deckhand, Scowman	01376-1	5.00
Accountant—Auditor	00001-5	8.00
Addiction Specialist, Senior, Supervising, Principal, Turner	03351-7	8.00
Administrative Assistant	00148-8	8.00
Air Traffic Controller, Turner	02088-1	8.00
American Foreign Service Officer	04219-2	8.00
Apprentice, Mechanical Trades	00571-8	6.00
Assistant Accountant	00056-2	8.00
Assistant Station Supervisor, Turner	03736-9	6.00
Associate and Administrative Accountant	03863-2	8.00
Attorney, Assistant—Trainee	01084-3	8.00
Auto Machinist	04379-2	8.00
Auto Mechanic, Autoserviceman	00514-9	6.00
Bank Examiner—Trainee and Assistant	01642-6	5.00
Battalion and Deputy Chief, F.D.	00515-7	6.00
Beginning Office Worker	00173-9	6.00
Beverage Control Investigator	00150-X	4.00
Bookkeeper—Account Clerk, Turner	00035-X	6.00
Bridge and Tunnel Officer—Special Officer	00780-X	5.00
Building Custodian	00013-9	8.00
Bus Maintainer—Bus Mechanic	00111-9	5.00
Bus Operator	01553-5	5.00
Buyer, Assistant Buyer, Purchase Inspector	01366-4	6.00
Captain, Fire Department	00121-6	10.00
Captain, Police Department	00184-4	10.00
Carpenter	00135-6	6.00
Case Worker, Turner	01528-4	8.00
Cashier, Housing Teller	00703-6	6.00
Cement Mason—Mason's Helper, Turner	03745-8	6.00
Chemist—Assistant Chemist	00116-X	5.00
City Planner	01364-8	6.00
Civil Engineer, Senior, Associate, & Administrative, Turner	00146-1	8.00
Civil Service Arithmetic and Vocabulary	00003-1	5.00
Civil Service Course, Gitlin	00702-8	5.00
Teacher's Manual for Civil Service Course, Gitlin	03838-1	2.00
Civil Service Handbook	00040-6	3.00
Claim Examiner—Law Investigator	00149-6	5.00
Clerk New York City	00045-7	4.00
Clerk—Steno Transcriber	00838-5	6.00
College Office Assistant	00181-X	5.00
Complete Guide to U.S. Civil Service Jobs	00537-8	3.00
Construction Foreman and Supervisor—Inspector	01085-1	8.00
Consumer Affairs Inspector	01356-7	6.00
Correction Captain—Deputy Warden	01358-3	8.00
Correction Officer	00186-0	6.00
Court Officer	00519-X	8.00
Criminal Law Quizzer, Salottolo	02399-6	8.00
Criminal Science Handbook, Salottolo	02407-0	5.00
Detective Investigator, Turner	03738-5	6.00
Dietitian	00083-X	6.00
Draftsman, Civil and Mechanical Engineering (All Grades)	01225-0	6.00
Electrical Engineer	00137-2	10.00
Electrical Inspector	03350-9	8.00
Electrician	00084-8	8.00
Electronic Equipment Maintainer, Turner	01836-4	8.00
Elevator Operator	00051-1	3.00
Employment Interviewer	00008-2	8.00
Employment Security Clerk	00700-1	6.00
Engineering Technician (All Grades), Turner	01226-9	8.00
Exterminator Foreman—Foreman of Housing Exterminators	03740-7	6.00
File Clerk	04377-6	5.00
Firefighting Hydraulics, Bonadio	00572-6	7.50
Fireman, F.D.	00010-4	6.00
Food Service Supervisor—School Lunch Manager	01378-8	6.00
Foreman	00191-7	5.00
Foreman of Auto Mechanics	01360-5	6.00
Gardener, Assistant Gardener	01340-0	6.00
General Entrance Series, Arco Editorial Board	01961-1	4.00
General Test Practice for 101 U.S. Jobs	04421-7	6.00
Guard—Patrolman	00122-4	5.00
Heavy Equipment Operator (Portable Engineer)	01372-9	5.00
Homestudy Course for Civil Service Jobs, Turner	01587-X	6.00
Hospital Attendant	00012-0	4.00
Hospital Care Investigator Trainee (Social Case Worker I)	01674-4	5.00
Hospital Clerk	01718-X	3.00
Hospital Security Officer	03866-7	6.00
Housing Assistant	00054-6	5.00
Housing Caretaker	00504-1	4.00
Housing Inspector	00055-4	5.00
Housing Manager—Assistant Housing Manager	00813-X	5.00
Housing Patrolman	00192-5	5.00
How to Pass Employment Tests, Liebers	00715-X	5.00

S3693

224 / P.A.C.E. Professional-Administrative Career Exam

Title	Number	Price
Internal Revenue Agent	00093-7	5.00
Investigator—Inspector	01670-1	5.00
Junior Administrator Development Examination (JADE)	01643-4	5.00
Junior and Assistant Civil Engineer	01228-5	5.00
Junior Federal Assistant	01729-5	6.00
Laboratory Aide	01121-1	5.00
Laborer—Federal, State and City Jobs	00566-1	4.00
Landscape Architect	01368-0	5.00
Laundry Worker	01834-8	4.00
Law and Court Stenographer	00783-4	6.00
Law Enforcement Positions	00500-9	6.00
Librarian	00060-0	10.00
Lieutenant, F.D.	00123-2	8.00
Lieutenant, P.D.	00190-9	8.00
Machinist—Machinist's Helper	01123-8	6.00
Mail Handler—U.S. Postal Service	00126-7	6.00
Maintainer's Helper, Group A and C—Transit Electrical Helper	00175-5	6.00
Maintenance Man	04349-0	6.00
Management and Administration Quizzer	LR 01727-9	8.50
Management Analyst, Assistant-Associate	03864-0	8.00
Mathematics, Simplified and Self-Taught	00567-X	4.00
Mechanical Apprentice (Maintainer's Helper B)	00176-3	5.00
Mechanical Aptitude and Spatial Relations Tests	00539-4	6.00
Mechanical Engineer—Junior, Assistant & Senior Grades	03314-2	8.00
Messenger	00017-1	3.00
Mortuary Caretaker	01354-0	6.00
Motor Vehicle License Examiner	00018-X	5.00
Motor Vehicle Operator	00576-9	4.00
Motorman (Subways)	00061-9	6.00
Nurse	00143-7	6.00
Office Assistant GS 2-4	04275-3	8.00
Office Machines Operator	00728-1	4.00
1540 Questions and Answers for Electricians	00754-0	5.00
1340 Questions and Answers for Firefighters, McGannon	00857-1	6.00
Painter	01772-4	5.00
Parking Enforcement Agent	00701-X	4.00
Patrol Inspector	04301-6	8.00
Peace Corps Placement Exams	01641-8	4.00
Personnel Examiner, Junior Personnel Examiner	00648-X	6.00
Plumber—Plumber's Helper	00517-3	6.00
Police Administration and Criminal Investigation	00565-3	6.00
Police Administrative Aide, Turner	02345-7	5.00
Police Officer—Patrolman P.D. Murray	00019-8	6.00
Police Science Advancement—Police Promotion Course	02636-7	10.00
Policewoman	00062-7	6.00
Post Office Clerk-Carrier	00021-X	6.00
Postal Inspector	00194-1	5.00
Postal Promotion Foreman—Supervisor	00538-6	6.00
Postal Service Officer	01658-2	5.00
Postmaster	01522-5	5.00
Practice for Civil Service Promotion	00023-6	6.00
Practice for Clerical, Typing and Stenographic Tests	04297-4	6.00
Principal Clerk—Stenographer	01523-3	5.00
Probation and Parole Officer	04203-6	8.00
Professional and Administrative Career Examination (PACE)	03653-2	6.00
Professional Careers Test	01543-8	6.00
Professional Trainee—Administrative Aide	01183-1	5.00
Public Health Sanitarian, Coyne	00985-3	8.00
Railroad Clerk	00067-8	4.00
Railroad Porter	00128-3	4.00
Real Estate Assessor—Appraiser—Manager	00563-7	8.00
Resident Building Superintendent	00068-6	5.00
Road Car Inspector (T.A.), Turner	03743-1	8.00
Sanitation Foreman (Foreman & Asst. Foreman)	01958-1	6.00
Sanitation Man	00025-2	4.00
School Crossing Guard	00611-0	4.00
Securing and Protecting Your Rights in Civil Service, Resnicoff	02714-2	4.95
Senior Clerical Series	01173-4	5.00
Senior Clerk—Stenographer	01797-X	8.00
Senior File Clerk, Turner	00124-0	8.00

START YOUR CAREER BY MAILING THIS COUPON TODAY.

ORDER NOW from your bookseller or direct from:

ARCO PUBLISHING COMPANY, INC. 219 Park Avenue South, New York, N.Y. 10003

Please Rush The Following Arco Books
(Order by Number or Title)

☐ I enclose check, cash or money order for $_____ (price of books, plus $1.00 for first book and 25¢ for each additional book, packing and mailing charge) No C.O.D.'s accepted.

Residents of N.Y. and Calif. add appropriate sales tax.

☐ Please tell me if you have an ARCO COURSE for the position of ....

☐ Please send me your free COMPLETE CATALOG.

NAME_____

STREET_____

CITY_____ STATE_____ ZIP #_____

Every Arco Book is guaranteed. Return it for full refund within ten days if not completely satisfied.

S3693